CLAIMING
OTHERS

CLAIMING OTHERS

Transracial Adoption and National Belonging

Mark C. Jerng

 University of Minnesota Press
Minneapolis
London

Portions of chapter 3 were previously published as "The Character of Race: Adoption and Individuation in William Faulkner's *Light in August* and Charles Chesnutt's *The Quarry*," *Arizona Quarterly* 64, no. 4 (2008); reprinted by permission of the Regents of the University of Arizona. Portions of chapter 5 were previously published as "Recognizing the Transracial Adoptee: Adoption Life Stories and Change-rae Lee's *A Gesture Life*," *MELUS: Journal of the Society for the Study of Multi-Ethnic Literature of the United States* 31, no. 2 (Summer 2006): 41–67; reprinted by permission of *MELUS*.

Published by the University of Minnesota Press
111 Third Avenue South, Suite 290
Minneapolis, MN 55401-2520
http://www.upress.umn.edu

Library of Congress Cataloging-in-Publication Data
Jerng, Mark C.
    Claiming others : transracial adoption and national belonging /
Mark C. Jerng.
        p. cm.
    Includes bibliographical references and index.
    ISBN 978-0-8166-6958-5 (hc : alk. paper) –
    ISBN 978-0-8166-6959-2 (pb : alk. paper)
    1. American literature – 20th century – History and criticism.
    2. Interracial adoption in literature. 3. Adoption in literature.
    4. Race in literature. 5. Interracial adoption. I. Title.
    PS228.I69J47 2010
    810.9′35254 – dc22   2010031953

Printed in the United States of America on acid-free paper

The University of Minnesota is an equal-opportunity educator and employer.

16 15 14 13 12 11   10 9 8 7 6 5 4 3 2

Contents

Introduction

Transracial Adoption and the Reproduction of Personhood

Adoption as an act that severs all legal ties between a child and its biological parents is a fairly recent legal concept. The 1851 Massachusetts statute that formed the precedent and basis for our modern understanding of adoption specifically broke from English jurisprudence, which held the child–biological parent bond inalienable "by any act of the parents themselves"[1] and "prohibited the absolute, permanent, and voluntary transfer of parental power to third persons."[2] While this legal statute was passed with surprisingly little comment at the time, its effects have been far-reaching. Legally, this construction of adoption would gain legitimacy through the nineteenth and twentieth centuries, becoming an international phenomenon today. Socially, the development of adoption has raised issues around our political frameworks of family, nationality, and race and has sparked off controversial debates over privacy and secrecy, state welfare, children's rights, and international human rights. But perhaps most important, this formalization of adoption displaces the centrality of birth for our understandings of who we are in ways that we have yet to fully understand. Persons adopted within this modern conception challenge fundamental expectations and assumptions about personhood because they highlight the ways that birth situates the origins, continuities, genealogies, and histories that provide the conditions for legibility within political society. Adoption in this sense assumes that adopted persons will change identity — they will take on a new name, become part of a new family and sometimes a new country. And yet the precise parameters of this shift in the social standings of adopted persons have been unclear, contested, and negotiated in ways that reveal the interrelated construction of the categories of family, nation, and race.

In his short play *Trying to Find Chinatown*, David Henry Hwang comically dramatizes precisely this question of whether adoptees can change social identities. The play depicts a white man, Benjamin, who is adopted by Chinese American parents from the Midwest. Having fully assumed the cultural and racial identity of his adopted family, Benjamin is searching for his "roots" in Chinatown. He asks a Chinese American street musician, Ronnie, where he could find Chinatown. A series of comic misunderstandings ensues built around the inability of each person to fulfill the other's expectations. Ronnie takes Benjamin as a racist white man who is exoticizing and objectifying him as a Chinatown tour guide (RONNIE: "So why is it that you picked *me*, of all the street musicians in the City, to point you in the direction of Chinatown?").[3] Benjamin then confuses Ronnie by answering back with his vocabulary of antiorientalism and his knowledge of Asian American studies. Benjamin talks about taking "pride in my ancestors who built the railroads" and exploring the "history of oppression which is my legacy," throwing Ronnie into a fit (12). Then Benjamin states that he understands Ronnie's confusion and explains by saying that he was adopted:

> RONNIE. I don't know what kind of bullshit ethnic studies program they're running over in Wuss-consin, but did they bother to teach you that in order to find your Asian "roots," it's a good idea to first be Asian?
>
> (*Pause*)
>
> BENJAMIN. Are you speaking metaphorically?

RONNIE. No! Literally! Look at your skin!

. . .

BENJAMIN. You see, I was adopted by Chinese American parents at birth. So, clearly, I'm an Asian American —

RONNIE. Even though you're blond and blue-eyed.

BENJAMIN. Well, you can't judge my race by my genetic heritage alone.

RONNIE. If genes don't determine race, what does?

BENJAMIN. Perhaps you'd prefer that I continue in denial, masquerading as a white man? (12–13)

Benjamin then talks about gaining a real sense of Asian American community steeped in the traditions of Chinese myth and spirituality and accuses Ronnie of being one of those "self-hating *assimilated* Chinese Americans" (14). The play ends with Ronnie's resistance to this cultural nationalist version of Chinese American identity and Benjamin immersing himself into the spiritual lineage of his adopted forefathers. Both Benjamin and Ronnie claim distinct versions of Chinese American identity in relation to the question of "birth." Though Benjamin's skin is white, he believes he is Asian American by virtue of adoption and is seeking to gain the cultural, political, and geographical trappings of that identity. Ronnie has a strictly geneticist view of racial identity and yet does not have a cultural nationalist view of Asian American identity, seeking to expand conceptions of Chinese American culture by drawing from a broad swath of cultural resources and references (Hendrix, Armstrong, Urbaniak). This play shows the way in which "birth" acts as a pivot around which personal, national, racial, and familial identities revolve.

Hwang's play is a comic send-up of our assumptions about what birth into a specific family, culture, or race entails.

Though Benjamin disrupts biological determinisms of race around birth through his adoption, he reasserts cultural determinisms of racial heritage. And while Ronnie reasserts biological determinisms of race around birth, he disrupts cultural determinisms of racial heritage. Neither character finds common cause or community in the other. Each remains politically and socially illegible to the other because of the ways in which they choose genealogies. Birth often acts as the implicit norm behind the consolidation of categories like nation, family, and race. A review of modern and contemporary citizenship rules reveals the prominent role played by birth and lineage as constitutive criteria for belonging and membership.[4] Birth has just as prominent a place in political philosophies of identity and citizenship. The primacy of birth is used to guarantee everything from civic recognition and identity to a sense of continuity, self-possession, and entry into a specific history that is one's own.[5] For adoptees, these social and political modes of being accessed through birth cannot be taken for granted. As Hwang's play shows, the displacement of birth creates a heady confusion regarding how to map these different forms of collectivity onto socially legible constructions of personhood. To be adopted in the modern formulation is specifically to be at the crossroads of multiple histories, the possession of which is never certain. Adoptees engage the world with neither a sense of continuity nor entry into a specific history that is one's own, bearing uncertainly the projections of national and societal forms of birthright.

To what extent adoptees change cultures, civic and social identities, and even races has been the object of legal scrutiny, social discourse, and literary representations in ways that have crucial implications for the historical constructions of U.S. personhood, national membership, and race. *Claiming Others* argues that transracial adoption reveals specific crises in the reproduction and naturalization of norms of personhood at the conjunction of familial, national, and racial logics. These interlocking logics can be perceived at two levels. There is a metaphoric/symbolic level in which rhetoric and discourse continually associate nation and race with family. One need only think of Abraham Lincoln's description of the United States on the eve of civil war as a "house divided," or the Million Man March, or the contemporary idea that transracial adoption represents the construction of social relations based on choice over and against the biological forms of ethnic and racial construction, to see manifestations of these associations.[6] Throughout the book, I argue that transracial adoption invokes and contests these metaphoric ways of thinking about the relationships among family, race, and nation and the ways that they consolidate certain versions of personhood and legitimize specific kinds of attachments over others.

But there is also an institutional and structural level whereby the state regulates and administers practices of filiation and affiliation that legitimize and produce racial categories in conjunction with family forms and reproductive practices. These regulations involve miscegenation laws, immigration and citizenship laws as they bear on the construction of familial ties, adoption practices, child custody, as well as a host of biopolitical measures and norms regarding population, health care, and housing.[7] Through analyzing this level of interaction, we see the naturalization of norms of individuation against and within which transracial adoption appears. *Claiming Others* addresses both these symbolic and structural levels by which the interlocking rules and norms of kinship/citizenship/race manage political membership, belonging, and the status of persons. Recent work in anthropology and social theory has analyzed the fluidity, flexibility, and constructed nature of kinship as it has been used to conceptualize both the "fixing and crossing of boundaries" among categories of nation, race, and family.[8] This study builds on such work by analyzing how transracial adoption reveals these categories as constituting an overlapping and interwoven set of practices that transform, normalize, and ultimately reproduce specific forms of personhood.

I use the terms "transracial" and "transnational" adoption, then, not just to denote a movement from one race to another, or from one nation to another. Rather, I employ these terms as shorthand and sometimes interchangeably for a broader conception that attends to the mutually imbricated relationships among kinship, national belonging, citizenship, race, and religion and not just to questions of race or nationality, respectively. Historically, various rationales and logics were used to shape the transfer of children across peoples, and they often invoked partial understandings of race, nationality, and kinship as they emerged in relation to one another. I suggest that transracial and transnational adoption in this sense highlights specific articulations of a familial nation-form throughout U.S. history as it is transformed through a set of historical crises around race relations. Transracial adoption appears most prominently in literature, public discourse, and social practices during precisely some of these large-scale national traumas focused on the formation of its citizenry and the question of national and racial belonging: Native American removal; slavery and emancipation; the height of Jim Crow/segregation; and the Korean and Vietnam wars. That representations and practices of transracial adoption constellate around these areas is not surprising. On one surface reading, these representational and social practices could be interpreted as a symbolic solution, as a way to mask the exclusionary and appropriative mechanisms of the state as it continues to reproduce an ideology of national homogeneity. It would be easy to subsume these different representations under a larger framework of reproducing racial hierarchies through white American paternalism and the infantilization of minority subjects. Racialized norms of citizenship have certainly been buttressed by the sanctification of white fathers and mothers as benefactors to infantilized racial others throughout history, whether in the discourse of slavery or as a justification for America's various imperial ventures.[9]

Such an examination of racial difference as produced in hierarchical terms is incomplete because it assumes a paradigm of one-way domination. Its narrative of a *consolidation* of an already-legible whiteness does not appreciate the extent to which whiteness, blackness, indigeneity, and Asianness are constituted in relation to each other. As such, it leaves us without an account of the negotiations over attachment, belonging, possession, and dependence within these kinship practices. Like many of the scholars of adoption and race with whom I will be in dialogue in the pages that follow, I am drawn to this subject by the transformative potential of transracial adoption for our notions of kinship and social relationality, while at the same time cautious in my assessments, accounting for the range of ways in which it reproduces structures of inequality.[10] In order to measure *what*, exactly, transracial adoption reproduces, I analyze the contestations over attachment within adoption that do not just reproduce power relations along racial lines, but constitute social bonds that shape modes of personhood and the capacity to legitimize one's place in the world, what the political theorist Judith Shklar calls social "standing."[11] By tracking representations of transracial adoption with attention to their historical particularities, the forms they take, and their mutually constitutive relationship to social and political discourses, I illuminate four different notions of personhood at the heart of the familial nation-form: a legal-territorial framework of personhood built on the securing of borders; a liberal-political framework of personhood produced through the conjunction of freedom and citizenship; a psychological framework of personhood regulated by norms of proper individuation; and a human rights framework of personhood that aspires toward personal and moral recognition. Each of these forms of personhood is codified, contested, transformed, and reproduced in relation to specific national-racial crises in the construction of a people. But the linear structure of this account is not meant to suggest that one form of personhood simply ends when another begins. They constitute, rather, a spectrum of norms with regard to personhood that are in constant negotiation. The discursive practices around transracial adoption reveal how acts of claiming others that organize the parent–child bond reproduce and contest forms of "natural" personhood within the familial nation-form.

Claiming Others follows the chronology of these historical events and sensibilities, tracking the emergence of representations of transracial adoption in relation to contemporaneous legal and social discourse across almost two centuries. In the nineteenth century, adoption is just beginning to be legally codified, and even decades after the first adoption law in Massachusetts in 1851, it had not yet been socially, publicly, or politically legitimized. Thus, it is fiction writers, legal thinkers, and individuals who tease out the implications of adoption without ready-made definitions. Writers tell stories concerning adoptive relationships where the word "adoption" is used without a precise legal or social definition and when the social meanings for adoption are still fluid. As I note in the first two chapters, James Fenimore Cooper seems to blend Native American practices of adoption with ideas of a patrilineal transmission in his use of the word "adopt," while Lydia Maria Child and Frederick Douglass use the word "adopt" more in terms of guardianship with just a slight hint of the notion of family construction that is inherent in modern ideas of adoption. These uses of the word "adopt" and the continuities and discontinuities among them reveal specific engagements with national and racial discourses around the parent–child bond. These writers explore the implications of adoption for personal and social status, as well as for national and racial belonging. I choose texts and authors from this era that explicitly take up how an adoptive relationship or the status of adoption might complicate the interrelations among familial, national, and racial constructions of community.

Moreover, many of these authors are not only important literary figures but also instrumental in crafting some of the discursive frameworks around Native American removal and slavery through the lens of domesticity. Both Catherine Maria Sedgwick and Lydia Maria Child write nonfiction protest tracts on these topics informed by their imaginative engagements with adoption. I argue that these authors provide the terms and narratives through which the language of adoptive relationships gets taken up in law and governmental policy, with particular consequences for the racialization and naturalization of personhood. In the nineteenth century, literature anticipates and provides the understandings through which a still inchoate notion of adoption gets taken up in a political discourse about the family that secures a familial nation-form. These emergent notions of adoption and the nationalization of the parent–child bond appear most concretely in political discourse revolving around Native Americans as "domestic dependents" and in debates about the social status of ex-slaves.

In the twentieth century, adoption becomes a fully modern and state institution and begins to emerge as a mechanism by which families and races get shaped. It becomes legitimized as a social practice that becomes part of how the state manages and produces its "people." Here the relationship between adoption stories and social and legal discourse shifts. No longer teasing out the implications of adoption that have not yet been codified or formed — and thus forming some of the crucial ways through which adoption is thought — now writers are utilizing, adapting, and engaging with the social constructions of adoption by the state, social work, psychology, and sociology. Unlike the ad hoc adoptions represented in the nineteenth century, authors explicitly reference the legal and social institutions regulating and producing adoption. Literature and social discourse resignify adoption practices in ways that complicate the legal and social conditions of adoption and their effects on conceptions of family and personhood. Throughout the century, adoptees increasingly publish self-conscious reflections on the legal, social, and political conditions of adoption, beginning as early as 1920.[12]

In the late twentieth century, adoption narratives written or produced by transracial and transnational adoptees as well as by writers who are not adopted circulate with greater frequency, producing a self-consciousness around adoptee subjectivity and engaging with the conditions and norms of personhood within adoption. These chapters dealing with the modern institutions and imaginings of adoption track forms of personhood built around psychic individuation, social recognition, and the universality of the human rights subject as someone who has a right to a name and nationality. Here I choose texts and authors that not only reflect on the governing legal and social assumptions regarding adoption but also rework some of the narrative parameters through which adopted lives are told.

Reproducing the Familial Nation-Form

Nation, family, and race have intertwined relationships that have served to reinforce each other and their reproduction. Whether it is thinking of the family as a microcosm of the nation, or imagining the nation as a racially homogeneous group, or theorizing families as the basis for states, political discourses and narratives of the nation reiterate the metaphorical and analogical relationships among family, nation, and race. Scholars such as Jay Fliegelman, Russ Castronovo, Karen Sánchez-Eppler, Walter Benn Michaels, and Caroline Levander have analyzed the rhetorical workings of these analogies as they act in the service of American national construction and racial formation, often isolating the particular work done through figurations of the child.[13] Other scholars such as Ann Stoler, Doris Sommer, and David Theo Goldberg, among others, have analyzed the intertwined discourses of bourgeois sexuality and racism as foundational fictions constitutive of the nation-state.[14] Emphasizing colonial and imperial practices, work on liberalism and nationalism has emphasized how racial exclusions sustain universal liberal subjects and how the principles of racial belonging relied on normalizing discourses of sexual morality, parenting, domesticity, and hygiene. As Ann Stoler writes, "Both racial and sexual classifications appear as ordering mechanisms that *shared* their emergence with the bourgeois order of the early nineteenth century."[15]

This work powerfully points to the interrelations among categories of nation, race, and family in national narratives, as well as the normalizing discourses around the body and sexuality through which the (racialized) bourgeois subject is formed. These interrelations emphasize the category of purity as a central engine and anxiety for national reproduction. But specific mechanisms of generational transmission that mediate questions of inheritance, property, attachment, continuity, and belonging as they impinge on notions of national and racial membership remain to be explored.[16] The parent–child bond and the specific regulation of kinship bonds used to guarantee transmission and filiation are crucial sites through which persons are both nationalized and naturalized. Kinship rules are instrumental in producing political society and what a people is. Arguing against the analogical mode of putting family, nation, and race together — a mode of thinking that has motivated and continues to motivate so many of our foundational and symbolic national narratives — Jacqueline Stevens isolates kinship and birth rules for membership as being particularly central in the reproduction of political society: "The nation entails specific political conventions that produce affective, familial-like attachments. Every political society does this, which is to say that every political society exists in tandem with a familial nation."[17] The "people" are not a prepolitical entity; even the substantive forms of habits, customs, and traditions of the "people" are articulated through state practices. And these state practices, as Stevens enumerates, predominantly revolve around the family.[18] Too often read as "natural," prepolitical, or biological, family is political in convention and character: "Political societies develop birth practices so as to provide a connection between the current population and those of the past and future, via laws and related regimens of intergenerationality.... [They] institutionalize the relation between birth, history, and kinship rules in ways that make concrete the attachments of parents and children."[19] The nation regulates and institutes kinship so as to "reproduce the state" and secure personhood as meaningfully lived within the normativity of generational transmission.

Building on work on nationalism that seeks to understand how a "people" is produced as a national community and what kinds of affective ties and attachments to nation are used to form a national community, Étienne Balibar similarly posits familial and racial forms of instituting community as central to the building of the nation-form. He locates the nationalization of family as one of the main engines of national formations: "today *it is the state which draws up and keeps the archive of filiations and alliances*" as seen in the "simultaneous emergence of 'private life,' the 'intimate (small) family circle,' *and* the family policy of the state, which projects into the public sphere the new notion of population and the demographic techniques for measuring it, of the supervision of its health and morals, of its reproduction."[20] Moreover, these institutional practices that administer the genealogical form of the nation provide the terms for the idea of a racial community: "The symbolic kernel of the idea of race (and of its demographic and cultural equivalents) is the schema of genealogy, that is, quite simply the idea that the filiation of individuals transmits from generation to generation a substance both biological and spiritual and thereby inscribes them in a temporal community known as 'kinship.'"[21] Race itself becomes concretized and meaningful for the construction of a "people" through this framework of generational transmission.

Stevens's and Balibar's analyses of political membership provide crucial tools for thinking about the constructions, contestations, and regulations around adoption and how it is in dialogue with the familial nation-form's attempts to construct certain modes of personhood and relationality. As the relational bonds between parent and child become nationalized, adoption becomes a particularly contested site for assumptions around birth, territory, and lineage that are used to shape who counts as a person. The attachments between persons then become objects of political intervention through which personhood is constituted. This framework thus enables an analysis of the mutually imbricated relations among kinship, nationality, and race, how one emerges in relation to another and how together they negotiate the boundaries between persons. This is not just to follow the truisms of intersectional analysis — that race always acts in concert with gender, sexuality, etc. Describing race, kinship, and nation as effects of various social practices and modes of conception rather than as categories, we see how race, for example, is a mode of collective identification that overlaps with and is parasitic on other forms.[22] It draws from other historically specific narratives, practices, and modes of conceptualization for its logics, rhetorical force, and material appearance. As Stoler writes, racial discourse does not constitute a unified field but is "permeated with resurrected subjugated knowledges that may resurface with them."[23] In other words, it makes use of knowledges previously discounted or disqualified in ways that allow them to reemerge. Practices of adoption reveal this sedimented nature of racial discourse — drawing as it does from psychoanalytic knowledges, sometimes outdated religious sensibilities, sentimental strategies, local histories, and national narratives, all at the same time. Race and nationality constitute peculiarly primary and defining modes of group attachment for state- and self-definition purposes because they situate personhood within a "narrative structure that offers an individual a past and future via intergenerational families."[24] I thus analyze legal regulations, social discourse, and literary forms for the ways in which the multiple meanings of race, kinship, and nation overlap to shape processes of identification and modes of being a social subject.

Through this framework, we see that race gets defined and redefined in relation to adoption and vice versa. In the nineteenth century, sentimental, religious, and political languages of kinship framed how social bonds are mediated through race. Sentimental languages of kinship had the effect of privileging the uniqueness and primacy of early parent–child bonds that tended to equate race and (primary) family whereas notions of adoption based on substitution tended to detach racial identity from familial identity. In the late nineteenth century and onward, institutional frameworks of adoption using a variety of discourses taken from evolutionary biology to psychoanalysis read and produce articulations among personhood, race, nationality, and family differently. Whether through a metaphorics of blood, the idea of latent heritable characteristics, or the construction of the psychology of the adopted child, race becomes located within processes of individual development with crucial effects on notions of personhood. In the late twentieth century and early twenty-first century, the language of genetics becomes another lens through which family, race, and nation are defined within and through each other.[25]

Regulating the Parent–Child Bond

I have outlined a framework that delineates the negotiation of personhood across rules of membership within the familial nation-form, kinship practices, and race regulations. These norms and practices form persons by regulating their forms of attachment and relationality — specifically the parent–child bond. Far from a natural, prepolitical relationship untouched by various social conventions, the parent–child bond is ceaselessly constructed along and sometimes against institutional lines. It is weighted with the demands of birth, lineage, transmission, continuity, and history. It is beset by the dynamics of dependence, consent, legitimacy, individuation, and recognition. Transracial adoption highlights these political and social investments in and shaping of the parent–child bond because it names a relation whose norms and conditions are contested and opaque.

Adoption stories constantly worry over the uncertainty of relating to another. Notions of adoption typically privilege the idea of choice: parents choosing children; children being specially chosen; kinship formed through choice rather than consanguinity. I use the word "claiming" to emphasize instead the disjunctive act of being taken up into another history and another set of conditions and relationships. It is to suggest that individuals do not come preformed, nor are they prepolitical entities — they are constructed, legitimized, and regulated through different acts of claiming, attachments, and demands that traverse not just familial boundaries but the various boundaries between persons drawn by the political forms of the state and racial construction. For adoption has throughout its history in the United States raised questions around the grounds for claiming someone else as one's own. Between the 1820s and the present, various social and legal conventions, fictional strategies, and narrative logics emerge to define and narrate the ambiguous relationship of transracial adoption. The emergence of these various narrative logics and social forms index the shifting implications and meanings of a relationship that remains difficult both to define and to justify, difficult not only because it is perceived as violating the norms of familial and racial relationships but also because it challenges our foundational conceptions of personhood. Without the sanction of biological or social norms, how does one relate to another?

It is useful to recall that this problem of conceptualizing parent–child relations lies deep in the philosophical lineage of liberal humanism. John Locke's social contract theory of authority produces the consensual subject by first reenvisioning the parent–child relation against Sir Thomas Filmer's analogizing of parental and state authority. Locke denaturalizes the family: the parent has no "natural" authority over the child as in Filmer's argument for the natural power of kings. Rather, the parent is the parent to his child only to the extent that he provides care, shelter, and a home for the child. This version of the state relies on a particular notion of parent–child relations that makes the child into a model for the potential political subject.[26] Feminist theorists have critiqued the legacy of Lockean thought for ignoring the ways the state regulates and institutes the family as such, thus separating family from politics, the "private" from the "public." This separation and consequent erasure of women have been instrumental in creating the norms for what counts as a liberal subject.[27] Theorists in anthropology, psychology, and sociology have likewise expanded notions of personhood by highlighting the roles of gender and social bonds.[28]

The child, whose invisibility provides the conditions for fashioning the terms of personhood, provides an analogous case to the place of women in liberal political theory. The fact of children's dependence on others and their potentiality places them at the center of Lockean theories of consent, but it is also this dependence that excludes them from consideration as possessing the rights and properties of liberal subjects. Susan Moller Okin puts it well when she writes that liberal theorists "take mature, independent human beings as the subjects of their theories without any mention of how they got there."[29] While these theoretical insights mark the peculiar position of the child, they require a more particularized description of the process of normalizing and legitimizing the parent–child bond. For the child also raises distinct issues around intergenerational transmission, continuity, and individuation. The chapters that follow develop a description of this historical process, with particular attention to the construction of social boundaries between peoples, turning to literature, social and political discourse, and legal forms that narrate transracial adoption across Native American, African American, and Asian American contexts.

The authors and works considered here all address the fundamental problem of what binds particular parents with particular children, and how this problem shapes and is shaped by anxieties around history, genealogy, and determinations of one's place in the world. The multiple and varied ways in which this investment in the parent–child bond takes place suggest a new dimension to our understandings of the relationships between race and liberal humanism, as well as to the ways in which the meanings of race are realized. It is common to think of racial exclusion as a powerful means of constituting and consolidating liberal subjects. This process, moreover, is customarily interpreted at the level of the individual citizen or collective group. To see how the regulation of the parent–child bond is a crucial form for the production of a people, however, is to analyze the workings of race at the level of relationships and attachments, and how they encode certain forms of personhood.[30] Race and nation themselves thus take on added meanings apart from their constructions as sociological or legal categories. These works grapple with the tensions between the social norms that regulate the parent–child relation and the psychic needs and desires expressed through it. As such, they treat race and nation both in relation to a flexible and fluid set of norms and as objects of various psychic and affective investments.

As mentioned above, processes of literary representation sometimes anticipate and sometimes transform and contest legal, political, and social articulations of personhood at the juncture of the familial nation-form. Each chapter thus places various legal and political discourses in relation to stories and narratives in order to perceive the reciprocal relationships whereby a construction of the parent–child bond in one domain responds to or shapes understandings in another domain. To register the particular shaping force of narratives and stories on the formation of parent–child bonds is not only to highlight literature's specific function in this project, but also to acknowledge the dependence of social norms of personhood and national belonging on what Stevens earlier called a "narrative structure that offers an individual a past and future via intergenerational families." These interrelations bring to light this book's methodological commitments to literary form and psychoanalysis that depart from other analyses that are more reliant on ethnographic or sociological analyses of social records, public pronouncements, and the private reflections of those involved in adoption.[31] Both of these emphases, on literary form and psychoanalysis, though often accused of being ahistorical and universalizing, represent not a turn away from the social and historical implications of adoption but rather my attempt to get at the specific set of issues around personhood that adoption raises: the interface between social norms and psychic investments in determining the parent–child bond; the negotiation of one's place in the world within the dictates of an intergenerational form; the reinterpretation of race and nationality as objects of psychic processes.

This book takes up fictional narrative in particular because the form of stories plays a powerful role in constituting our notions of personhood. This relationship has not gone unnoticed. The novel is famous for its description and elaboration of the liberal individual subject in Lockean terms. In *How Novels Think,* Nancy Armstrong makes the argument that the history of the novel and the history of the modern subject — the self-governing, self-determining, autonomous and independent individual — are synonymous. She suggests that the British novel in particular elaborates the Lockean hypothesis of the contractual individual and fends off troubling alternatives to this mode of individuality.[32] This model helps us read the prominent place of the orphan within American literary history as a figure through which fiction both elaborates a certain Lockean notion of the individual and connects this mode of individualism to a larger national narrative.[33] The orphan is marked by its separation from the bonds of family, tradition, and authority; he is the free, independent, liberated individual.

Adoption, on the other hand, has often been recognized for its prominence in myth and the quest for origins plot typical of the structure of romance. Indeed, the uncertain birth of the adopted character has long been seen as typical of a whole set of myths and stories throughout history—Moses and Oedipus being the most prominent examples.[34] But despite its frequent occurrence, adoption in its social particularity within literature—as responding to or in relation to a set of social facts and meanings around adoption—has been less analyzed.[35] I focus not on adoption as a mythopoetic device but on those literary texts that are specifically describing, commenting, or reflecting on the social status and condition of adoptees and/or the process of adoption. Part of how I tracked this was simply through the use of the word "adoption" or "adopt" itself, what meanings accrued to it, and how it served to reorganize conventions of narrative form and character construction.

If specific narrative forms have been most successful in developing the integrity and interiority of the freestanding individual, they construct versions of personhood that are especially difficult to claim in the case of adoption because the adoptee is defined only in relation to another character, only as part of a relationship and structure from which his or her status as adoptee derives.[36] At the same time that the adoptee is a person whose inclusion within given social structures is always in question, he or she is defined only as a part of someone else. The literature of transracial adoption articulates the negotiations among different attempts (on the part of the state, parents, social workers, and adoptees) to appropriate and provide the conditions for the living of a life. Attention to form—broadly, how the stories are told and what descriptive and narrative techniques are utilized—is so crucial because it materializes the conditions of representability through which transracial adoptees are made to appear. The forms of adoption literature provide the terms in which transracial adoptees become knowable and relatable. Form in this sense provides a means for constructing that which is not yet given a concept or definition, as is the case in the matter of adoption.

Indeed, while some ways of narrating transracial adoption are privileged, others are foreclosed.

Narrating Adoptive Bonds

The dominant form that has made transracial and transnational adoptees presentable as subjects in the contemporary moment — search and reunion narratives in which adopted children find and meet their birth parents — provides a case in point. This narrative form has certain political and social implications for how their personhood is recognized, for they structure models of personhood built on continuity and an unmediated relationship to home or some original culture. But adoptees often do not find the key to their lives as these narrative trajectories often suggest. Their reunion with their parents is often met with ambivalence, frustration, and misunderstanding, because of the way in which their idealizations run against and within this narrative of return. In this way, there exists a dynamic, reciprocal relationship between the forms and conventions of narration and processes of imagining and constituting adoptive personhood.

Narratives attempt to put into some kind of meaningful shape the experience of adoption and seek to imagine the adoptee.[37] At the same time, literary models of representation produce forms of identification for adoptees. Emily Hipchen writes at the beginning of her adoption memoir, encapsulating this process of identification and attachment internal to adoption writing:

> I am reading memoirs these days, swallowing them up...as if they are the only sustenance I have. I want to know other people's lives. Why they write them. What they write about. How they write about them. I find they are not so different from mine, really, only the details vary. One woman describes

> how she found out that her family is Jewish, another discov-
> ers her real face.... Every day like a criminal whose weapon is
> scissors I secret from the newspaper stories of my life.[38]

Eschewing the "I was born" beginning of memoir and life
writing, Hipchen begins with the process of finding her life
in the stories around her and variously incorporating them,
identifying with them, and projecting herself onto them. This
is similar to what Nancy Miller argues as the model of relation embodied in memoir: "The bonds and desires that attract
readers to the contemporary memoir have everything to do
with attachment. What seems to connect memoir writers and
their readers is a bond created through identifications and —
just as importantly — disidentifications."[39] While this process
occurs in reading in general, it gets explicitly thematized within
adoption narrative and fiction around the terms and conditions of personhood. Precisely because genealogical forms and
biologically grounded notions of personhood are so dominant — are, in fact, identified with being an individual as a
developmental and historical unity — narratives become crucial sites for negotiating these processes of attachment and
dependence through which the self's capacity to relate is
formed. I thus read the emergence of the adoptee as both a
thematic appearing in various permutations throughout literary and cultural history and as a problem of narrative form
in which the capacity of narrative to "take in" the adoptee
opens up issues central to the political and social conditions of
personhood.

This emphasis on formal dimensions of narrative is meant
to nuance analyses that would solely place the representation of
adoption within a wider ideological debate between "biology"
and "choice." Within this context, adoption stories are often
treated as either reinforcing or questioning prevailing political
and moral evaluations of adoption at the time. But my readings

of these works seek to excavate not only a wide set of engagements with the implications of adoption for intergenerational structures of race, nation, and kinship, but also an account of the various psychic processes embedded in these fictions and narratives of personhood. Freud's "Family Romances" is a good starting point for this inquiry, precisely because it uses the fantasy of adoption as a crucial way to consolidate a certain fiction of personhood built around a single set of parents. It is often cited in discussions of adoption because it renders adoption into a universal feeling: Freud suggests that all children feel like they are adopted at some point in their lives. Read against the grain of its own intergenerational narrative for the production of the liberal humanist subject, Freud's "Family Romances" provides an apt illustration of the relationship between the regulation of the parent–child bond and the naturalization of a specific norm of personhood that I have been discussing up until now primarily within the tradition of political theory. As such, it highlights, but does not fully develop, some of the intersubjective processes such as identification, transference, and projection that appear so prominently in adoption literature as a means of negotiating conditions of dislocation.

Freud famously begins this essay with the reassertion of the parent–child dynamic as the normative structure for personhood:

> The liberation of an individual, as he grows up, from the authority of his parents is one of the most necessary though one of the most painful results brought about by the course of his development. It is quite essential that that liberation should occur and it may be presumed that it has been to some extent achieved by everyone who has reached a normal state. Indeed, the whole progress of society rests upon the opposition between successive generations.[40]

In Freud's narrative, separation from the parents and "opposition between successive generations" become key markers for the norms of personhood. At the same time, the essay alerts us to how the process of separation is attended by the problems of attachment and how one relates to another. Freud suggests that all children fantasize that their parents are not their own as a way of negotiating their ambivalent relationship to their parents' authority. This fantasy is the result of the extrafamilial forces that traverse the space of the family. Freud details the method of comparison and social categorization that attends this process: "As the child develops intellectually he cannot help gradually getting to know the category his parents belong to. He becomes acquainted with other parents, compares them with his own, and so becomes entitled to doubt the incomparable and unique status he once attributed to them."[41]

This narrative of generational construction gets preoccupied with the comparisons and a rethinking of the "category" to which his parents belong — immediately bringing the question of the social markers of class, race, and nationality right into the heart of the psychic. What kinds of attachments are possible is not only a psychic formation but a social formation. Idealization of the parents is immediately complicated by other intersubjective processes such as projective identification and transference in which others may assume or act out the psychic relations of familial form. And yet at the end of this short essay, Freud comforts parents with the thought that the child's adoption fantasy simply refers to a nostalgic return to his originary ideals of the parents: "For if one takes a close look at the commonest of these romances — the replacement of both parents or just the father by grander personages — one discovers that these new, distinguished parents are provided with features that derive from the child's actual memories of his real, more humble parents: the child does not really eliminate his father, but exalts him."[42] Idealization wins out as it preserves the oneness of the parent and the true, legitimate parent–child bond. Freud preserves the prerogative of the singular family and thereby ensures that the adoption fantasy is merely a vehicle for the transformation of the child into the liberal individual.

In fact, this is very much the legacy of Freudian theory for the institutional development of adoption. It is taken up both to justify adoptive practices and the possibility of maintaining a "psychological" parent apart from the biological parent, at the same time that it continually reasserts this "proper" and "normal" developmental sequence for the child in order to become an individual. But what if we were to take up the implicit suggestion in the essay of the family as traversed by various social fantasies? This would be to reread the family romance not in service of the necessary "separation" that turns us into modern individuals, but in service of a narrative of attachment and dependence that subverts this particular form of personhood, complicated as it is by the possibility of two families, two sets of parents, and possibly two races or nations. The fantasy of adoption suggests that the places of the parents are always multiply filled in ways that express the ambivalence of the child's identity in relation to himself or herself and others. In other words, it speaks to the fact that the relationship between "who you are" and "where you come from" cannot be easily resolved into a single identification.[43]

The vision of the individual "liberated" from his parents in "Family Romances" is complicated by work within object-relations and relational psychoanalysis. While psychoanalysis largely comes up with theories of psychic trajectory that arrive at the independent, autonomous subject of Enlightenment theory, the object-relations tradition including the work of Melanie Klein and Donald Winnicott partially turn away from ego-centered models of analysis toward the theorization of intersubjective bonds and the boundaries between subject and object. Klein's emphasis on internal objects and Winnicott's theorization of the transitional moments of subject–object interaction both bring to light processes where subject and object are not differentiated or separable, when the ego's boundaries are not secure, and in which an object is formed in part *through* the psychic reality of another.[44] They theorize mechanisms such as projection, idealization, identification, transference, and recognition that emphasize subjectivity as it is impinged on by the object. They register the ways that children and adults live *through* each other's projections and idealizations, not apart from them or simply against them in some neutral, ego-centered position of freedom and choice.[45] These theoretical insights are crucial for staying attuned to the processes of transracial and transnational adoption, which are, as several scholars have noted, marked by projection and idealization.[46] As we will see, the literature on transracial adoption highlights this mode of living through projections in ways that challenge notions of personhood that rely on the freedom of the free-standing individual. Race here becomes a primary psychic investment in various adoption stories for the negotiation of the boundaries of personhood.

Analyses of race and psychoanalytic methodologies have not always coexisted easily because of the fear that race will thereby lose its objective, social, and historical force. But the most compelling work in race and psychoanalysis is attentive to the historical contingencies of psychic processes and adds layers to the meanings that race attains by recognizing that race is not a unified phenomenon, that it traverses both psychic and social domains.[47] Failure to appreciate the mixture of knowledges that comprise race leads toward rather static conceptions that would solely analyze it in relation to familiar political vocabularies of equality or social ideals of racial integration. This is precisely the case with current historicizations of transracial adoption, to which I now turn. *Claiming Others,* then, is finally also a way of reimagining the vocabularies of race and belonging that assume too quickly ready-made legal and social categories of race without considering the affective bonds that mark its presence.

Transracial Adoption and Racial Histories

Situating this project within work on race and reproduction and the longstanding associations among family, race, and nation so crucial for the familial nation-form is already to rewrite the history of transracial adoption, which organizes these terms quite differently. The typical historicization of transracial adoption assumes that the issue of race is exterior to the question of adoption, facilitating a grand narrative of racial integration and the telos of racial equality. Thus the beginnings of adoption in the United States are narrated without any relation to racial concerns. Social and legal historians of adoption like E. Wayne Carp, Julie Berebitsky, and Jamil Zainaldin emphasize the emergence of practices of adoption in relation to English practices and law.[48] Zainaldin's legal history goes on to center the origin of adoption around its legal formalization in the 1851 Massachusetts statute, which severed all legal ties between a child and its biological parents, created similar rights and duties between a child and its adoptive parents, and clarified the child's right to inherit from its adoptive parents.[49] After a period from 1851 until the turn of the century in which religious organizations were the main sites for adoption, it is in the early twentieth century that adoption becomes institutionalized under the aegis of the state. Here a tacit policy of race-matching reigns in which social workers match prospective parents and adoptees based on a host of physical, emotional, and intellectual traits, fueled by concerns around heredity and blood. Fighting against the stigma of adoption and the privileging of biological families as "natural," the institutions of adoption put into practice policies of secrecy in which adoptees were not told of their birth records, and in which adoptive families passed as "natural" families.[50]

According to these dominant histories of adoption in the United States, then, transracial and transnational adoption come later, emerging only after World War II. As this story goes, the end of World War II left thousands of homeless children in many parts of the world. The demographic changes in the population of homeless children, shifts in reproductive practices that reduced the number of white children available for adoption, as well as changes in social attitudes, gave rise to transracial adoption. Transracial adoption is conceived as supplementary to the history of adoption: the tacit, unwritten rule of the "sameness" of adoption (children should look and "be" like their parents; adoptive families should "look" like "natural" families) gives way to a vision of adoption accommodating racial difference out of necessity.[51] This history of transracial adoption as one of accommodating difference fits neatly with and parallels movements toward racial integration in the United States.

As such, transracial adoption is often seen as an effect of the gains of the Civil Rights movement, placing it into a national narrative of increasing racial integration, racial equality, and cultural pluralism.[52] As Barbara Melosh writes, "Adoption has been accepted more readily and practiced more widely in the United States than in any other comparable industrialized nation — an acceptance that observers have attributed to the relative openness of American society, its fluid class and social structure, its racial and ethnic diversity."[53] The most influential and dominant histories and narratives for adoption have all been nation based, inextricably tying the history of adoption to particular national imperatives. Both Melosh's *Strangers and Kin* and Adam Pertman's *Adoption Nation* locate adoption as a particularly and peculiarly American phenomenon, one that is read solely in relation to certain national ideals and narratives.[54] The historicization of transracial and transnational adoption implicitly constructs a narrative of racial and national integration, measuring adoption in terms of ideals of racial equality and national integrity. What these histories assume is that family is a subset of the nation. In other words, they assume the adage that the family is a microcosm of the nation and draw an analogy between the two. In doing so, they neglect the particular practices by which family, nation, and race overlap and disjoin. Their analyses thereby reduce the multiple ways in which race gets negotiated apart from this grand narrative of integration.

It is instructive, then, to overlay the history of racialization with the history of adoption in ways that do not assume a narrative of racial integration and incorporation at the national level (the idea that the nation is becoming progressively more tolerant and integrated), but which put into question the very forms of nationalization and inclusion. I juxtapose Native American, African American, and Asian American cases of adoption in order to analyze the conjunction of racial, familial, and national logics that play out the relationships between competing norms of personhood. Each of the historical, legal, and literary clusters that I focus on marks a crisis in nationalization and naturalization. This narrative need not retrench the identification of whiteness with the dominant ideals of citizenship and racialized others with the abjection of dependence. As such, we can begin to reorient race relations in America not just as a history of the struggle between white Americans and racialized others, but rather as a struggle over the legal and affective terms of citizenship, relationality, and personhood.

Reframing Transracial Adoption
in the Contemporary Moment

Claiming Others resituates transracial adoption from a mid-to-late twentieth-century story to a historical phenomenon with roots deep in the formation of national and racial identifications. But I do so not to ignore contemporary political debates in favor of more historical concerns. On the contrary, I do so in order to reveal both continuities and discontinuities in the imagination of transracial adoption and in order to argue for a more nuanced attention to the interrelations between the formations of racial boundaries and personhood that some of the contemporary frameworks lack. Contemporary public discourse typically concentrates on the increased visibility of transracial and transnational adoptions in the late twentieth and early twenty-first centuries.[55] The visibility and pervasiveness of this phenomenon have prompted many to view adoption as subverting our common-sense assumptions about kinship, community, nationality, and identity. As Adam Pertman writes with a sense of awe and exhilaration, "Before our eyes, in our homes and schools and media and workplaces, America is forever changing adoption even as adoption is forever changing America. This is nothing less than a revolution."[56] Pertman's enthusiasm is shared by many who hold up transracial and transnational adoption as subversive of the ideology of consanguinity and the essentialisms of biology and race, and as the promise of a new social order, one that is multiracial, integrated, and based on affiliation.[57]

Memoirs, documentaries, fiction, and movies increasingly depict adoption from various perspectives, often centering especially on the dramatic reunion with the "lost" biological parents. Their exploration of the contradictions and paradoxes that they encounter when faced with the incoherence of racial and familial categories constitutes another crucial thread in the interest in adoption. These stories typically unfold the complex trajectories of the life stories of adoptees as they negotiate family ties across racial, national, and cultural divides and often seek to fill in the gaps in their lives. In a November 13, 2007, piece from the popular *New York Times* blog "Relative Choices: Adoption and the American Family," Hollee McGinnis tells a story about her growth as an adoptee. Hollee, a Korean adoptee raised in an Irish American household in the suburbs of New York City, recounts her life as one that moved from a happy childhood oblivious to the meaning of adoption to a growing consciousness of her difference from Americans and her inability to meet people's expectations about who she is. She ultimately reconciles the two parts of her identity — Korean and American, birth country and adoptive country:

> Ultimately I realized this conflict about my identity arose because I felt I had only two choices: Korean or American. The reality was that I was both. I felt to identify simply as being Asian would be to deny the love and nurture of my adoptive parents; and to identify solely as American, I would be denying my Korean ancestry and heritage. When I began to embrace both identities rather than trying to "fit in" I realized the gains in my life that came from this duality.[58]

This familiar narrative formula of negotiating cultural identity emphasizes the struggle to reconcile two or more cultures, nationalities, or races; it foregrounds the dynamics of cultural belonging and national identification as occurring between two discrete categories of identity.[59] It emphasizes the inability to locate oneself within a specific national or racial framework even as it valorizes the necessity to reconcile these differences and to "embrace both." If many of the 133 responses generated by this story can be taken as any indication, Hollee's description of her identity crisis remains a persistent form of thinking through cultural and national belonging for adoptees and nonadoptees alike.[60] Persons of disparate backgrounds and circumstances attach themselves to Hollee's story because it is such a powerful and legible discourse for thinking about identities that are not reducible to a single identification.

Indeed, stories such as Hollee's shape public understandings of identity formation within adoption as a profoundly personal struggle to reconcile extreme differences. They identify biological origins with some "real" sense of identity and belonging. While they sometimes point to discriminatory practices on the part of adoptive parents, social workers, and state regulators, these instances are rendered as the actions of individuals and not read in terms of larger systemic or structural issues. While economic issues are often raised, decrying financial abuses in the selling of children or joking about the commodification of cultural difference on the part of Hollywood celebrities, these stories do not widen their view to include national and statist practices in the regulation of social reproduction. Using frameworks for social and personal actions ensconced in the assumptions of liberal political theory, private actions are pitted against state decisions, "choice" against biological necessity, and tolerance against racism. Additionally, stories and public discourse reiterate narratives of black, Asian, and Latin American children in need, reproducing power inequalities along racial-ethnic lines.

Different stories have emerged with the recent work on transracial and transnational adoption, straining against these popular assumptions and framings. Sandra Patton analyzes domestic transracial adoptions in relation to the racialized regulation of women and the negotiation of power among state agencies, social workers, adoptive parents, and adopted children.[61] Christina Klein and Laura Briggs place transnational adoption in relation to discourses concerning larger global movements of humanitarianism and Cold War ideology.[62] Eleana Kim contextualizes the construction of transnational adult adoptees within the nationalizing practices of Korea.[63] Sara Dorow, Toby Volkman, Ann Anagnost, and Barbara Yngvesson all view transnational adoption in terms of a "cultural economy of circulating relationships of power and exchange," analyzing roots trips, adoptive parents, and adult adoptees for their myriad negotiations with the meanings of race, culture, and kinship.[64] David Eng analyzes the multiple histories and economic processes of transnational adoption within the purview of mourning, drawing out the labor performed by adoptees in producing the heterosexual family.[65] Margaret Homans draws on trauma theory in order to think about the processes of fiction-making embedded in adoption stories.[66] The collection *Outsiders Within: Writing on Transracial Adoption* makes connections across various local and global processes, from Christian missions to state practices to the racialization of poverty.[67]

Like these works, *Claiming Others* seeks a larger historical purview, engaging an analysis of how multiple histories and processes come to inscribe and shape transracial and transnational adoption. The ensuing chapters reveal how concerns about intergenerational form shape the terms of personhood in a set of specific historical periods. In chapter 1, I argue that the beginning of our contemporary bourgeois notion of adoption lies not (as current historical accounts would have it) as principally a break with English common law and colonial practices of adoption but as a practice that is formed in relation to Native American practices of adoption. In fact, I argue that the former achieves its status only by negating the latter. Native American adoption practices based on substitution (the adoptee substitutes for the death of a loved one) differ from the emerging notion of adoption that treats adoptees "as if" they were kin. In particular, the former implies a certain version of personhood that becomes a primary site for white settlers' anxieties about their own cultural and national identity. The chapter thus provides a different understanding of the emergence of adoption in the United States by theorizing race not as something added on to an already established concept of adoption, but rather as something inherent to the formulation of adoption itself. It sets the stage not only for reconceptualizing the history of adoption, but also for rethinking nationality as a function of competing definitions of personhood and contested forms of attachment. I read the narratives of unredeemed captives, who are positioned both outside and inside the nation by virtue of their adoption by Native Americans, alongside frontier romances that are located along the borders of unconquered territories and a nascent national space. These narratives are thematizing adoption just as the nation is debating policies of removal and the Marshall court codifies the official legal status of Native Americans. Together they explore how these competing definitions of adoption reflect the unstable political and legal transformation of Native Americans into "domestic dependents."

Abolitionist writers and slave narratives tease out the implications of adoption during a time when developing notions of citizenship and emancipation cannot be separated from the rules and grammar of kinship. If the project of consolidating a certain form of national, territorial personhood had to get rid of anxieties regarding familial substitution, the problems of dependence raised by adoption encapsulate difficulties in codifying personhood as free, independent, and emancipated. Chapter 2 focuses on abolitionists' portrayals of the adoption of slaves as part of their political visions of emancipation. I show how Lydia Maria Child, Frederick Douglass, and Harriet Beecher Stowe, as well as the Senators framing the Thirteenth Amendment, all run into the entanglements of kinship, slavery, and dependence when trying to codify the rights, realities, and feelings of emancipated subjects. The figure of the adoptee embodies a powerful rhetorical strategy of the abolitionists in demonstrating their protection of and responsibility toward the rights of the enslaved. But this trope of adoption runs aground their attempts to narrate the process of emancipation, exhibiting the strictures within conceptions of kinship that are formative of, and not ancillary to, constructions of citizenship. In fact, Lydia Maria Child turns to a *transnational* family romance precisely in order to narrate the adoption of slaves by white Northerners.

In chapter 3, I track how social practices of adoption begin to develop narrative logics of constituting race. The institutionalization of adoption at the level of the state begins in the early twentieth century, and here we see the development of the idea of matching children for adoption with parents based on similar "traits" such as race, religion, intelligence, and temperament. I show how practices of matching in adoption and the depiction of adopted characters by William Faulkner and Charles Chesnutt deploy anxieties over the child's background in ways that reconstruct race as something "inside" one's body. Analyzing social workers' manuals and statements on adoption as well as these literary texts' contorted efforts to create an adopted character whose race is questionable, I show how race is *enacted by* adoption. As such, race, I argue, is most productively read not as a property of distinct, separate individuals, but rather as an effect of anxieties about relating to another. This chapter thus uses the early institutionalization of adoption to rethink the theoretical terms with which we think race.

Chapters 4, 5, and 6 move to the contemporary moment, a distinctive one in the history of transracial adoption because of the increased public visibility of adoptees and the proliferation of public debates on the rights and needs of transracial and transnational adoptees. Chapter 4 analyzes the "right to identity" demanded within adoptee rights movements in relation to the codification of children's rights, the application of psychoanalysis to adoption, and debates over transnational adoption.

The legal struggle to open records has provided the language to legally and socially recognize transnational adoptees as "real," autonomous, and agential subjects. But the terms of this legibility rely on psychological and standards that normalize the spatiotemporal boundaries of the adoptee within racial, familial, and national logics. I show how the writings of transnational adoption rely on these notions of personhood codified through the "right to identity" even as they enact modes of projection and identification that contest these norms. In this way, the articulation of transracial adoptees' claims needs to be understood as a radical intervention in the conditions of personhood and the nature of rights.

Chapter 5 analyzes how the demands for recognition voiced by adoptees ask us to rethink the aspiration for social recognition as the grounds for rendering personhood legible. I juxtapose two anthologies, two documentaries, and Chang-rae Lee's novel *A Gesture Life* in order to read how different genres and narrative strategies are used to demand and enact recognition. Instead of a model whereby one person confers recognition on another — the dominant and prevailing model of political representation — I theorize a model in which those conferring recognition must be understood as having their own anxieties of recognition. In particular, I read the temporal structures of Chang-rae Lee's *A Gesture Life* as powerfully enacting the conditions of adoptive personhood in ways that revise the terms of social recognition.

While contemporary adoption discourse proclaims an "adoption revolution" that challenges biological norms of personhood, there is a simultaneous move to "readmit biology, genealogy, and genetics into the adoption picture." [68] My Conclusion analyzes this paradox and suggests that the return to biological normativity signals not so much the ideological hold of biological conceptions but rather its centrality for common representations of personhood. This normative representation of personhood is strengthened and codified by two separate narrative frames: a psychic itinerary of identification predicated on biological resemblance and the use of family as a metaphor for larger forms of collectivity, including race and nation. I analyze psychological and philosophical discourse about adoption as well as contemporary transnational adoption memoir and fiction in order to suggest how adoption stories struggle against and within these prevailing frames. By transforming some of the conventional ways in which narrative is used to render family, these stories do not so much disrupt ideologies of consanguinity as they enact crises of unity that rethink our capacity to know what a family is.

Focusing on the intergenerational bond as a crucial form through which the nation organizes its people, I argue that the literary and cultural formations of transracial adoption help us theorize the historically shifting relationship between the regulation of interracial relations and the naturalization of individual personhood. Forms of personhood, I contend, emerge in relation to specific arrangements of family, nation, and race relations, rendering certain subjects legible and others socially or politically illegible. By shifting the ground of the question from racial and cultural identity to the conditions of personhood, we can see how the entangled forms of nation, race, and kinship regulate not just social hierarchies but also the construction and destruction of the attachments between persons.

I

ON THE BORDERS
OF KINSHIP

1

COMPETING LOGICS
OF POSSESSION

Unredeemed Captives in the 1820s

In a chapter entitled "Distresses of a Frontier Man," J. Hector St. John De Crevecoeur alternates between romanticizing the nature and simplicity of life with the Indians and fearing the dangers of being incorporated into Indian life. Fascinated by the figure of the settler who is captured by Indians and refuses to return to colonial or frontier society, Crevecoeur pronounces with astonishment:

> By what power does it come to pass that children who have been adopted when young among these people can never be prevailed on to readopt European manners? Many an anxious parent have I seen last war who at the return of the peace went to the Indian villages where they knew their children had been carried in captivity, when to their inexpressible sorrow they found them so perfectly Indianized that many knew them no longer, and those whose more advanced ages permitted them to recollect their fathers and mothers absolutely refused to follow them and ran to their adoptive parents for protection against the effusions of love their unhappy real parents lavished on them! Incredible as this may appear, I have heard it asserted in a thousand instances, among persons of credit.[1]

After recounting the history of two "Indianized" settlers, Crevecoeur concludes with a mixture of fascination and

3

horror: "there must be in their social bond something singularly captivating and far superior to anything to be boasted of among us; for thousands of Europeans are Indians, and we have no examples of even one of those aborigines having from choice become Europeans!"[2] He concludes his concerns with an example of an Indian raised by a European, who, though trained to a "genteel trade," disappeared back to an Indian village.[3]

Crevecoeur, writing in 1782, with his mixture of fascination and horror, reflects a widespread cultural anxiety of the times. Already in 1707, John Williams's *The Redeemed Captive* has at its moral center the fate of Williams's daughter, Eunice, who refused to return to colonial society. Benjamin Franklin writes that "no European who has tasted Savage Life can afterwards bear to live in our societies."[4] And Titus King, in his own captivity narrative, writes of the dangers of being incorporated into an Indian tribe: "Nothing seems to be more taking. In six months time they forsake father and mother, forget their own land, refuse to speak their own tongue and seemingly be wholly swallowed up with the Indians."[5] These anxieties circulating around the figure of the "unredeemed captive" cannot be reduced to the fantasy of going native. Most disturbing to Crevecoeur is the asymmetry and nonreciprocity of the symbolic exchange: Europeans become Indians, but Indians do not become Europeans.[6] Crevecoeur and others imagine the "singularly captivating" social bond through which colonial settlers held on to their Indian ways. Their interpretation centers on the social bonds that wholly transform persons as a particular threat to the genealogical terms of national and cultural borders. For these observers, the boundaries that are meant to secure personhood have been overrun — "wholly swallowed up with the Indians." The ambivalence about boundaries is underscored by their difficulty in understanding whether this phenomenon has to do with internal constitutions or external conditions: adoptees are imagined as both passive and active, both "swallowed up" and made to "forget" *and* willfully refusing and forsaking.

The specific terms of this anxiety about unredeemed captives revolve around the transformability of personhood. As colonial historians have demonstrated, prior to the late 1750s and early 1760s, relationships between Euramericans and Natives were fluid and open, a shifting set of political alliances, economic arrangements, and kinship networks that were not characterized by the dominance of Euramerican settlement nor by the strict demarcation of colonial, national, or racial boundaries.[7] One particularly important domain for these relations was kinship.[8] As Jane Merritt explains, "Indians recognized the importance of turning strangers into 'either actual or symbolic kinspeople' to strengthen political alliances or increase access to available resources.... Indians often adopted white or other native captives and refugees into their families to replenish community populations."[9] Richard White elaborates on this act of adoption: "the widespread custom of adoption forged social ties that had nothing to do with birth.... In the case of a captive, adoption supposedly erased the social identity of the captive and replaced it with the preexisting social identity of a dead person."[10] These practices of adoption assumed the transformability and substitutability of persons as the adoptees take on the social identity of the persons they are replacing. The acquisition of a new name during the adoption ceremony refashions the individual into another person. Accounts of adoption by white settlers often recount how they are received as a substitute, showing how this process of adoption incorporates them as kinsmen and as Indians. After his capture and adoption by Caughnewagas in 1755, James Smith's new adoptive family told him: "After what has passed this day . . . you are now one of us by an old strong law and custom."[11]

These kinship practices worked in concert with a larger set of expectations and obligations involving gift exchange, reciprocal acts and deeds, and hospitality that shaped relations between Native Americans and Euramericans.[12] Euramericans participated within these practices in ways that entailed flexibly accommodating different notions of personhood, often infusing kinship principles with political alliances: "on the level of formal political relations, the French and the Indians, and to a lesser degree the Dutch and English, agreed to act as if particular transitory selves were subordinate to enduring persons. Europeans pragmatically agreed to an Indian formulation of politics as a kinship relationship between a limited number of named persons."[13] As White demonstrates, these contexts created the possibility and expectation that Native Americans and whites would create new identities, transform themselves, and fashion social personages in relation to the other.

Colonial historians generally agree that this porousness gave way to hardened national and racial boundaries in the latter half of the eighteenth century. A discourse of racial division increasingly came to be used, and nationalist sentiments became increasingly predominant among both Indian and white populations. Scholarship has pointed to the discourse of savagery and other racially coded descriptors that emerge with particular virulence in the late eighteenth century as a crucial tool for ordering both physical and metaphysical distances between the groups.[14] However, these boundaries took shape, I argue, through a particular conjunction of race *and* kinship, a fixed *and* fluid negotiation with the forms of kinship in the service of constructing an intergenerational form of personhood. These national and racial boundaries are made secure only when an entire history and genealogy of intertwined relations that involve the transformability of personhood are disavowed. Forms of intergenerationality provide connections between past, present, and future for persons and the social worlds that they inhabit. They construct particular rules through which a people know who they are, where they came from, and what they will be. During this time, race is not used simply to secure metaphysical or civilizational differences between Indian and white populations, justifying territorial occupation and encroachment. It is constructed through a negotiation of kinship relations and practices in ways that produce a framework for national personhood whose continuities exist apart from relations with Native Americans.

Unredeemed captives thus take on particular significance in the late eighteenth and early nineteenth centuries and mark specific anxieties regarding borders, not because they are divided between two cultures or because they are hybrids that represent the threat of miscegenation or impurity, but because they represent a different conception of personhood that underlies competing notions of kinship. Read within and against the context of domestic relations as they are mobilized within a developing nation-form, these adopted Indians figure the threat of substitution that disrupts a logic of genealogical identity that is just emerging at the heart of U.S. racial and national formation. Native American adoption practices[15] based on substitution, in which the adoptee substitutes for the death of a loved one, differ from an emerging sentimental notion of adoption that treats adoptees "as if" they were kin. The idea of substitution is one where adoptees are fully incorporated into families and become real kin; adoptees become different persons. In the developing Anglo-American notion of adoption, adoptees are treated as if they were kin; they were to be given legitimacy or the rights of inheritance just *like* their own.[16] Their differences from the family "proper" are still marked. This latter notion of adoption actually achieves its status by negating Native American understandings of adoption, rewriting them in order to draw borders between Native Americans and white settlers in ways that ensure that the two groups cannot identify with each other. Through this rewriting of kinship bonds, various works including frontier romances, unredeemed captivity narratives, children's literature, and legal cases secure the psychic and imaginative borders between Native Americans and white settlers.

Conceptions of kinship, domesticity, and family are used to structure political relations between Indians and settlers. The meanings of cross-cultural adoptive kinship in particular provide a crucial metaphorics for the legal redescription of Native American–U.S. relations. The language of the Marshall trials in 1831 famously rewrote the Indian presence in terms of the possibilities of kinship and its failure. Instead of a discourse of civilization and savagery, or religious enlightenment and heathens, arguments for the extermination or removal of the Indians use kinship as the language to accomplish what Étienne Balibar would call the "internal exclusion" of the Indians — the setting off of the Indians not into a place "outside" or "exterior," but rather into "ubiquitous 'limbos' where those who are neither assimilated and integrated nor immediately eliminated, are forced to remain."[17]

In a trial over legal claims to land, Justice Marshall defines Native Americans as domestic dependents:

> It may well be doubted whether those tribes which reside within the acknowledged boundaries of the United States can, with strict accuracy, be denominated foreign nations. They may, more correctly, perhaps, be denominated domestic dependent nations. They occupy a territory to which we assert a title independent of their will, which must take effect in point of possession when their right of possession ceases. Meanwhile, they are in a state of pupilage. Their relation to the United States resembles that of a ward to his guardian. They look to our government for protection; rely upon its kindness and its power; appeal to it for relief to their wants; and address the President as their great father.[18]

Responding to the difficulty of conceptualizing what it means for something "internal" to be "foreign," Marshall's language transposes a political claim for land into a domestic relationship. Indeed, he directly replaces "foreign" with "domestic dependent," excluding and removing Native Americans from future claims while simultaneously granting them a certain civic status within the rubric of the domestic. Here the figuration of domestic dependency is used to limit the genealogical and historical linkages between Indians and whites. Native Americans become "part" of the United States through the substitution of an imaginary of kinship (domestic dependency) in place of a porousness between groups that threatens the national boundaries of the United States. Like the uncertain status of wards who have no stable relationship with their guardian or adoptive parents, and no legal claim on them as such, Native Americans are placed between the possibility of possession and dispossession. Their antagonistic spatial relationship to the United States is transformed into a familial relationship in which the "independence" of the land claims of the United States is founded on the "dependence" of the Indians.

The language codifying Native Americans as "domestic dependents" is not an accidental use of language, nor is it simple paternalism. Underlying this language is a tension between two kinds of kinship bonds and its effects on how personhood is conceived within the U.S. nation-state. Adoption foregrounds this contestation over the terms of kinship bonds when native and settler cultures converge. The anxieties regarding adoptees in both unredeemed captivity narratives and frontier romances of the 1820s — all published during the development of Indian Removal policies and the Marshall trials — underwrite a shifting familial imaginary in which national form and social reproduction are at stake. In this next section, I first attend to how ideals of domesticity and the nationalization of the family in the United States collide with Native American kinship practices.

The Emerging Sentimental Form of Adoption

The developing notion of adoption in the United States during the nineteenth century serves a function different from the literal and symbolic incorporation practiced by many Native American groups. When the first modern adoption law in history was passed in Massachusetts in 1851, it was something of an afterthought. The law "attracted little public attention. Little or no debate over the issue occurred in the legislature, apparently no social reform movements advocated passage of the law, and, when the law did appear, few newspapers bothered to take note of the event." [19] The law could have been, the legal historian Zainaldin speculates, a codification and formalization of otherwise uncontroversial "placing-out" practices and informal adoptions. [20] But apart from these apprentice-like arrangements, informal adoptions through acts of will and testament were quite common, constructed for purposes of succession, inheritance, or economic benefits. As Yasuhide Kawashima suggests, the words "adopted" or "adoption" were often used to denote longstanding relationships between parents and orphaned children in which the orphaned children were generously provided for in wills. These were not, as Kawashima argues, simply the apprenticeship arrangements that prevailed during the colonial period. Rather, they often combined economic and affective bonds: economic bonds sometimes stabilize what are longstanding affective bonds; or conversely, affective bonds lead to the construction of economic bonds. Both bonds seem to cohere in the language of "as their own child." John Demos notes a situation in which a contract for service is coded in terms of a "virtual adoption": "The Crispes promised to 'provide for the said Samuell in all

things as theire owne Child; and afterwards if hee live to marry
or to goe away from them; to Doe for him as if hee were theire
own Child.'"[21] In another example, a husband on his deathbed
asked friends to see if they would "accept of [his son Josias]
and take him as theire child."[22] These practices also suggest
an interest in securing legitimacy for purposes of transmission
or succession. One man, in giving eighty pounds sterling to a
child who shares his last name, writes, "but the porre little girl
she is not my daughter but as she was born under my Roffe I
was always willing for to do something for her so that I would
not have her to be called a Bastard."[23]

The terms of the 1851 adoption statute seem to formalize
this combination of economic obligations, affective investments, and concerns over legitimacy. But the statute also went
further, constituting a radical break from common law — the
first statute that allowed for a complete break of the legal rights
and obligations of "natural" or "biological" parents to their
child. As E. Wayne Carp notes, the 1851 statute required the
"judge to ascertain that the adoptive parents were 'of sufficient
ability to bring up the child . . . and furnish suitable nurture and
education. . . .' It encouraged adoptive parents to build a family
by assuming the responsibility and emotional outlook of natural parents."[24] It thus further represents the increased role of
the state in the affective construction of families. The early to
mid-nineteenth century was the period in which domestic relations law first gets developed: the state increasingly "took the
condition of the family as its responsibility."[25] This interpene-
tration of the familial and the national creates a relationship in
which "heightened emotional and affective bonds and socialization duties were seen by almost all Americans as crucial to
national well-being."[26]

This familial–national apparatus comes to be conjoined with
a child-centered ethic that secures the child in some act of sentimental possession in the popular discourse on domesticity in

the early nineteenth century as seen in various treatises on the home, domestic governance, motherhood, and child rearing. This expansive construction of domesticity crafted a notion of adoption as an act of sentimental possession and legitimation that supplements the more provisional act of caring for a child due to indigency or familial circumstances. In her didactic fictional portrayal of an ideal family, *Home* (1835), Catherine Sedgwick anticipates the ethos of adoption as it becomes codified in law sixteen years later. In the chapter "Home for the Homeless," Sedgwick narrates a debate within the Barclay family about whether or not to take in two recently orphaned children. While Harry is welcome to be adopted because he writes his arithmetic neatly and can fix things, his sister Emily causes some debate because she "is so hateful."[27] In weighing whether or not to adopt Emily, Mr. Barclay says: "Most persons, my dear boys, have something noble in them, if you but touch the right spring to set it in motion. I think poor little Emily has fine qualities, but her character will depend much on the circumstances in which she is placed, for she is easily influenced" (93). This version of adoption emphasizes the sentimental value of the home and its ability to create a good environment for the fostering of what is inside persons. It focuses on the relationship between character and circumstances, highlighting the power of domestic affections for shaping and molding character. The contours of this vision are displayed in the dialogue that ensues between the critical Aunt Betsey and Mrs. Barclay over this decision to admit the orphans into their home:

> "You are the oddest people," she began, "that ever I came across; with seven children, and the Lord knows how many more you may have, the old lady and myself, and only Martha for help, to undertake these two children that have no claim on earth upon you. Claim! the children of your greatest enemy, the man that has all but ruined you, and in such an underhand way

too, — a pretty reward for knavery! I hope you mean to put up a sign, William Barclay & Co.'s orphan asylum, or alms-house!"

Mrs. Barclay was too much accustomed to her sister's railing to be disturbed by it.

"If it were more the practice, Betsey," she mildly replied, "for those who have homes to extend the blessing to those who have them not, there would be little occasion for orphan asylums, and the charity now done by the public, would be more effectively done in private families."

"I see no advantage whatever in turning private houses into alms-houses and such sort of places. I always thought home was a sacred place, from which it was a duty to shut out every thing disagreeable and unpleasant."

"It is a duty, as you say, Betsey," replied her sister, "to exclude every thing permanently disagreeable from the family; for home should resemble heaven in happiness as well as love. But we cannot exclude from our earthly homes the infirmities of humanity. There are few persons, no *young* persons, who, if they are treated wisely and tenderly, will not be found to have more good than evil in them. In the Nortons, I am sure, the good greatly preponderates. Our children, we think, will be benefited by having new excitements to kindness, generosity, and forbearance." (98–99)

The familial circle becomes a circle of humanity that ennobles and makes children good, useful, and well-behaved. When Mrs. Barclay welcomes Emily into her home, she states: "You have promised to be one of my children, dear Emily . . . I intend to treat you precisely as I do them" (104).

The "precisely as I do them" here emphasizes acceptance and inclusion of the child through equal treatment. But in Sedgwick's fictional scene, though Emily has equal treatment, the question of her economic and labor roles in the household remains up for negotiation: shortly after Emily's arrival one of Mrs. Barclay's daughters begins complaining that Emily is not fit for anything. This unresolved question over the terms of equality and the particular status of the adopted child finds expression, as we will see in chapter 2, in fictions narrating freedom and equality before and after the Civil War. Here it is important to note that this construction of sentimental possession becomes the form through which norms of personhood — who can be a good person and who can be included as a subject within the familial nation-form — are negotiated in relation to familial and national boundaries. Not only were Sedgwick and, as I discuss further, Lydia Maria Child at the center of this domestic discourse. They were also major figures, along with James Fenimore Cooper, in refiguring the Native American presence in the early nineteenth century through both nonfictional tracts and historical romances. Each negotiated the confrontation between developing sensibilities of a familial nation-form and Native American practices of kinship in writing about the possibilities of extending sentimental possession to Native Americans. This confrontation emerged most clearly through the unredeemed captive as a figure through which conceptions of kinship and their implications for national formations of personhood are played out. In this next section, I detail the reframing of Native Americans within a framework of domestic bonds, and the way in which this reframing confronts the figure of the unredeemed captive.

Figuring the Unredeemed Captive

Before Harriet Beecher Stowe constructed her domestic ideology as a way of humanizing black slaves in the context of abolitionism, the long historical conflicts and relationships between Native Americans and colonial settlers were reconstructed through a project of humanitarianism and the romantic sentimentalization of the child. This project is deeply ambivalent. On the one hand, the admiration of Native American kinship practices as caring and affectionate is used to both model the emerging notion of domesticity in American households and argue for Native American assimilation and incorporation according to these domestic norms. On the other hand, Native American practices of adoption threatened the national forms of personhood constructed through these sentimental ethics.

This reframing of Native Americans in terms of kinship norms is crucial to Lydia Maria Child's work. Child singles out Native Americans for admiration because of their loving parent–child relations.[28] Her imagination of Native Americans in these domestic terms both argues for their civility and humanity and provides a model for American households. Her stories of Indians often turn on the mother–child relation. In "The Indian Boy," for example, there is a strong sentimental bond between the Maine-resident narrator and an Indian boy who relies on her to help him with his sick grandmother. The Indian boy is singled out for a sentimental representation of his humanity because of his civility and politeness as exemplified in his devotion toward and caring of his grandmother. In this triangulation of familial affection, it is the Indian boy's affection for his grandmother that opens up the affection between him and the Maine woman. Another short story, "Adventure in the Woods," tells a conventional tale of two young children lost in the woods. But they are saved by an old Indian woman, who carries them back safely to their village, showing the level of care that Indians have for children. In both cases, Child suggests that cross-racial bonds are the effect of the sentimental and affectionate forms of bonding inherent in Native American culture.

In her later political tract "Appeal for the Indians," Child draws many of her examples of the Indians' moral and cultural equality, if not superiority, from the way in which they treat their own and others' children. She provides an anecdote of an Indian who moves away from white society because the white people ignore the death of his child. In this anecdote, it is not that the Indians cannot assimilate. Rather, it is the lack of care that they find within white society that drives them away. With Child, the lens of kinship is used to critique American society and households for not upholding the humanity and civility that she finds in Native Americans. At the same time, though, this sentimental humanism operates in the service of a civilizing mission in which the family is the sphere and purveyor of proper civility and conduct. In this same tract, she prescribes an ethic of care and nurture in the government's dealings with Indians, echoing and reproducing the language of the Marshall trials in the service of a different end: "How *ought* we to view the peoples who are less advanced than ourselves? Simply as younger members of the same great human family, who need to be protected, instructed and encouraged, till they are capable of appreciating and sharing all our advantages."[29] In this way, Child romanticizes the kinship ties among Native Americans in an effort to extend sentimental participation toward them and to argue for their ability to be assimilated.

This vision of political relations based on the terms of a sentimental possession relies on rewriting earlier forms of hospitality, exchange, and reciprocity. Nowhere is this tension clearer than in Lydia Maria Child's short story "Willie Wharton" and the figure of the unredeemed captive. "Willie Wharton" begins with a settler family taking in an Indian girl with "justice and kindness."[30] This act is narrated in terms of adoption scenes within the discourse of domesticity as fears of her wild nature are erased by a "charming picture" of domestic accord and love — their son, Willie, and the Indian girl sleeping "as cozily as two kittens with different fur."[31] At the same time, the act is contextualized within the spirit of a network of gift-exchange whereby the Indians can become friends and not harm the settler family. When the girl's parents come to retrieve her, the Wharton family's hospitality is repaid through an exchange of gifts, solidifying relations of peace between the two. However, when Willie Wharton becomes lost in the woods, the specter of Native American adoption emerges: he is possibly lost forever, acculturated by the Indians into their tribes, never to be seen again. Willie's mother falls into depression thinking of him "hopelessly out of reach, among the Indians" and has visions of him wearing Indian attire.[32] When Willie Wharton returns, now married to an Indian woman, the family is reunited and the acts of sentimental possession are emphasized whereby the Indian woman and Willie become part of the family through the civilizing roles of love, affection, and domestic accord.[33] Thus, the threat of Native American adoption to forms of genealogy gets rewritten in terms of the bonds of affection and the ethos of adoption outlined earlier within discourses of domesticity. Child's efforts to codify the sentimental forms through which the Indians are civilized have to confront the figure of the unredeemed captive and overcome the logics of personhood implicit in that figure.

This encounter with the unredeemed captive as a threat to emerging familial and national norms of personhood, reproduction, and filiation does not appear in Child's work alone. While the idea of being "adopted" into an Indian tribe is persistent throughout the captivity narrative tradition, it takes on greater resonance in the 1820s, which saw the publication of the narratives of John Dunn Hunter (1823), Mary Jemison (1824), and John Tanner (1828). These "unredeemed captive" narratives foregrounded the experience of incorporation and adoption. All three narratives are both praised and criticized for their ethnographic "knowledge" of the Indians, for the light that their sympathetic treatment of Indian life might shed on the issue of "civilizing" or "domesticating" the Indians (the problems of Indian policy that were much on the national mind during the 1820s), and for the possibility of treating Indians as humans, not savages. Richard Drinnon

argues that these "unredeemed" captive narratives posed difficulties for a nation struggling with the "Indian Problem": "a
'restored captive' could conceivably contend the Indians were
human beings. The bearer of such tidings could clearly expect
no warm welcome from white America."[34] Indeed, Hunter's
narrative became a sparkplug for a transatlantic debate over
U.S. Indian policy: English social commentators decried the
abuses of a U.S. policy that purportedly "civilized" the Indians, while U.S. proponents of Indian removal, like General
Lewis Cass, disparaged and discredited John Dunn Hunter as
an imposter.[35] Likewise, Tanner is discredited as a "savage,"
thus ignoring any border crossing threat he might pose. And
Mary Jemison's narrative, as Susan Scheckel has demonstrated,
has been contained over the years in terms of a domestic ideology that mitigates possible threats to U.S. ideologies of race
and power.[36]

These narratives raise specific generic and textual issues, for
they are all as-told-to narratives with varying degrees of framing on the part of editors. But while these textual problems
have been read productively in terms of problems of cultural authenticity and appropriation, I analyze how distinct
forms of kinship are registered in these narratives' negotiations with genealogy.[37] Gordon Sayre notes that "the captivity
narrative genre and its criticism have been slow to recognize
that most captives were adopted into tribes and families and
that native kinship, unlike Euramerican custom, regarded such
adoptees as real kin and did not define identity phylogeneti-
cally."[38] The openness of kinship and the hospitality of Indian
communal ties are often employed in these narratives as justifications for the captives' respective decisions to remain with
the Indians over and against the "humanity" and "civilization" of white settler culture. They implicitly defend against
the charges of national and cultural disloyalty by emphasizing

the ties of kinship within their respective tribes and the broken ties of their previous families. But these kinship networks that secure belonging are not the same as the "family" in the sentimental humanism of the bourgeois family form. Interpretations of the unredeemed captive are suspended between Native American notions of substitutability and belonging and Euramerican notions of genealogy and racial and national lineage. Kinship becomes a strategic border on which the constructions of "white" and "Indian" oscillate.

Each of the unredeemed captives describes their adoption into the tribe in terms of their understanding of Native American practices based on substitution. Mary Jemison describes the adoption ceremony itself:

> I was soon surrounded by them, and they immediately set up a most dismal howling, crying bitterly, and wringing their hands in all the agonies of grief for a deceased relative. . . . "Oh our brother! Alas! He is dead — he has gone; he will never return. . . . Though he fell on the field of the slain, with glory he fell, and his spirit went up to the land of his fathers in war! . . . His spirit has seen our distress, and sent us a helper whom with pleasure we greet. Dickewamis [Mary Jemison's Indian name] has come. . . . Oh! She is our sister, and gladly we welcome her here. In the place of our brother she stands in our tribe." [39]

After this description, she explains how it is a custom of the Indians, when one of their number is slain or taken captive, to take a prisoner and "receive and adopt him into the family, in the place of him whom they have lost" (77–78). John Dunn Hunter is similarly aware of his place in the world as a matter of exchange and substitution: "I was adopted into the family of Kee-nees-tah by his squaw, who had lost a son in one of their recent engagements with the Pawnees." [40] Yet in both of these narratives, the logics of kinship as based on substitution are revised in terms of sentiment. In Hunter's narrative, Hunter explains his affections for Indian life through the kindness and affection that he receives from the various families into which he is adopted: "The treatment I received from Hunk-hah and her daughter chimed in harmonious concordance with the vibrations of my bosom: I gave loose to their indulgence, and sincerely loved and respected them, as much, it appears to me, as if they had really been allied to me by the strongest ties of consanguinity" (24). This "as if" language differs from his explanation of his Osage mother's understanding, which is much more in line with practices of Native American adoption based on substitution: "She used to weep over me, tell me how good her son had been, how much she loved him, and how much she mourned his loss. 'You must be good,' she would say, 'and you shall be my son, and I will be your mother'" (23). Hunter translates a practice of substitution into an idea of emotional bonds that are understood in relation to the primacy of blood ties — "as if they had really been allied to me by the strongest ties of consanguinity." Similarly, Mary Jemison writes shortly after describing the customs of Native American adoption: "It was my happy lot to be accepted for adoption; and at the time of the ceremony I was received by the two squaws, to supply the place of their brother in the family; and I was ever considered and treated by them as a real sister, the same as though I had been born of their mother" (78). The emphasis in the latter half of this statement is on her treatment "as though" she had been their mother's daughter. The logics of kinship as based on substitution are revised in terms of sentiment that is always measured against the primacy of consanguinity.

Notions of substitution suggest that the persons adopted become someone else: they take on a new name and must take on the qualities and reputation of the person for whom they substitute: "You must be good . . . and you shall be my son." Native American kin relations act out a logic of belonging that transforms notions of identity and genealogy based on consanguinity. According to John Fierst, in certain Native American adoption practices, "the captive would eventually gain full status within the adoptive society" and "the race of the captive...did not stand in the way of cultural acceptance."[41] This form of kinship is so threatening because adoption here completely changes the adoptee's social status and affiliation. If one child can just as easily substitute for another, then he or she can take on different attributes and characteristics — be they national or racial. Substitutability means that the borders between peoples dissolve. The sentimental construction of "as if" kinship on the other hand relies on the unchanging origins of a child no matter where or what position she is in. It relies on the child's uniqueness and unsubstitutability, maintaining firm boundaries between one family and another: we love you as if you were one of our own. It thus allows for adoption but uses the sentimental family form in order to preserve distinctions between peoples.

When John Dunn Hunter reflects on the other "unredeemed captives" that he met, he registers the threat that Indian customs pose to personhood defined through Euramerican notions of genealogy: "They appeared, like myself, to have been at first forced to assume the Indian character and habits; but time and a conformity to custom had nationalized them, and they seemed as happy and contented as though they had descended directly from the Indians, and were in possession of their patrimony" (11). The danger for Hunter is that customs and habits become descent and "patrimony," replacing a non-Indian genealogy. Hunter is thus careful to distance himself from these other unredeemed captives even as he meditates on the strong attachments of "kinship" to the Indians. In Mary Jemison's narrative, she attaches bourgeois notions of sentiment to the Native American forms of kinship that provide her with a sense of legitimacy and belonging. This is evident when she legitimates Native American kinship by modeling it on how she would feel with her "own" sister:

> We were kindly received by my Indian mother and the other members of the family, who appeared to make me welcome; and my two sisters, whom I had not seen in two years, received me with every expression of love and friendship, and that they really felt what they expressed, I have never had the least reason to doubt. The warmth of their feelings . . . rivitted my affection for them so strongly that I am constrained to believe that I loved them as I should have loved my own sister had she lived, and I had been brought up with her. (88–89)

A feeling of kinship based on reciprocity and exchange of emotion is supplemented with the ideal of affection embodied by her "own sister." At the same time, the language of how her Indian family's warmth of feeling "rivets" and "constrains" reveals some of the tensions in Jemison's feelings about Native American adoption practices and their appropriation of identity.

Both Hunter's and Jemison's narratives rewrite the substitutive bonds of Native American kinship in terms of a bourgeois sentiment that still privileges bloodlines and ancestry as something possessed and transmitted through a genealogical lineage. For Tanner, on the other hand, the fact of his entering into kin relations as a substitute constitutes the very plot and rhythm of his story, rewriting his genealogical place in the world. His personal narrative often revolves around his perceived place within kinship — whether or not he is the favored son. In one example, Tanner is confronted by a relative of Net-no-kwa's, Pe-shau-ba, and "recognized" in terms of the boy he was meant to replace:

> He [Pe-shau-ba] looked at me very closely, and said, "Come here, my brother." Then raising his blanket, he showed me the

mark of a deep and dangerous wound on the chest. "Do you remember, my young brother, when we were playing together, with guns and spears, and you gave me this wound?" Seeing my embarrassment, he continued to amuse himself for some time, by describing the circumstances attending the wound, at the time he received it. He at last relieved me from some suspense and anxiety, by saying, it was not myself who had wounded him, but one of my brothers, at a place which he mentioned. He spoke of Ke-wa-tin, who would have been of about my age, if he had lived, and inquired particularly to the time and the circumstances of my capture.[42]

Pe-shau-ba makes explicit the substitutive relation. As Gordon Sayre argues, "Peshauba saw Kewatin as alive in the person of Tanner, who took on the responsibilities, status, and even the memories of the boy he had requickened."[43]

This is not an isolated incident. Tanner's negotiations with various others are marked by receiving a hurt or responding to a challenge because of the actions of another of his family. Though Net-no-kwa tells her son, Wa-me-gon-a-biew, about a dream in which she finds a bear, Tanner deliberately takes up Wa-me-gon-a-biew's position and kills the bear himself. He substitutes himself for the other son who does not believe his mother's dream. At another point in the narrative in which Tanner demonstrates his Indian-ness, he again calls up the substitutive relation:

There is on the bank of that river, a place which looks like one the Indians would always choose to encamp at.... But with that spot is connected a story of fratricide, a crime so uncommon that the spot where it happened is held in detestation, and regarded with terror.... As I approached this spot, I thought much of the story of the two brothers who bore the same totem with myself, and were, as I supposed, related to my Indian mother.... I wished to be able to tell the Indians that I had not only stopped, but slept quietly at a place which they shunned with so much fear and caution. (92)

As Tanner specifically thinks about his status as an Indian, he constructs his self in terms of its substitutability. It is his ability to occupy the same place as these "two brothers who bore the same totem with myself" that secures his status as an Indian. Throughout the narrative, this substitutive relation makes him the target of others' malice, but it is also how he takes up his position in Indian society as kin.

When Tanner returns to white society, he similarly experiences misrecognition. But unlike the earlier incidents in which the misrecognition is simultaneously recognition of Tanner's status as a substitute, this moment of misrecognition is a denial of kinship. His brother does not at first recognize him and then attempts to transform him in order to make him more recognizable — "he [Tanner's brother] gave me a hasty look, and passed on. . . . He next cut off my long hair, on which, till this time, I had worn strings of broaches, in the manner of the Indians" (248). His continual misrecognitions in white society are a denial of his social status and his capacity to share in white society.

The endings of all three narratives reveal this negotiation of different understandings of kinship. Hunter rewrites his relations with whites in terms of the idea of kinship that marks his experiences with the Indians:

> unknown to a single human being, with whom I could claim kindred, except from common origin. . . . I crossed the Alleghany Mountains, and, as it were, commenced a new existence. By this, however, I intend no local reflection, for wherever I visited, hospitality and friendship have been inmates, and often hailed me in the silent though expressive language of the heart, "thou art my brother." (80)

Kindred means a whole lot more than *just* common origin; it is made substantive only through the "hospitality" that remakes relations. Genealogically defined identity does not give him his place in white settler culture, but rather the "expressive language of the heart" that he receives from everyone regardless of kin as defined by blood. On the other hand, Tanner returns only to remain unrecognized within the terms of white society, terms that are unable to reconcile the tension between Native kinship practices and some genealogically-embedded cultural identity.[44] And finally, the representation of Jemison ends by placing her genealogically — giving a full account of her descendants by consanguinity.[45] This formal device itself expresses a specific notion of kinship and its role in sanctioning the meaning of one's life and identity.

Life on the Borders of Kinship

These memoirs reveal the relationships between differing notions of kinship and conceptions of personhood that underlie the formation of nationality and shifting relations to Native Americans. Historical romances preoccupied with constructing national genealogies similarly fix on the figure of the unredeemed captive at this time.[46] Written in the 1820s, but set in the early colonial period of the late seventeenth century, both James Fenimore Cooper's *The Wept of Wish-Ton Wish* and Catherine Maria Sedgwick's *Hope Leslie* are historical novels that have shifting definitions of kinship and adoption at their center. Melding a historical narrative of Indian–Euramerican relations with domestic discourses and their attendant anxieties regarding inheritance, transmission, and genealogy, these novels negotiate competing meanings of adoption in ways that secure the national-familial form of intergenerational personhood.[47] In this way, kinship bonds become a key site for the historicization of Native American–U.S. conflict in relation to contemporaneous struggles over defining Native Americans as a group.

These two novels have often been read in relation to the conjunction of familial and historical romance.[48] These arguments suggest that kinship, as opposed to some religious identification or modern/primitive distinction, becomes the discursive field out of which distinctions between persons are made; it becomes the ground for norms of inclusion and exclusion. But in much of this criticism, kinship is taken for granted as an undifferentiated category. Kinship bonds may connote distinct logics of belonging and identity depending on historical period and cultural context. Adoption — formal or informal, sentimental or substitutive, suspended between Native American and Euramerican practices — becomes a fraught site for these novelists. Though several critics[49] have noted the frequency of adoption in the work of this period, its consequences for thinking about personhood have not been fully developed. Cooper and Sedgwick's novels blur seventeenth-century practices of kinship, early nineteenth-century ideals of domesticity, and Native American customs of kinship. Rather than focus on the Heathcote family as a stable, patriarchal structure that promotes a narrow ideal of the family, or the family as a nuclear structure in *Hope Leslie,* these frontier romances use the shifting distinctions between "kin" and "non-kin" to rewrite the logics of belonging and identity for Native Americans and white settlers alike. In this way, the particular terms of these frontier romances do more than revise the historical memory of King Philip's war or relate it to current policies of Indian removal.[50] They help constitute the representational shift from a policy and political practice based on the division between "civilization" and "savagery" to a politics of "domestic dependency."[51]

Both historical romances highlight the process of drawing kinship boundaries. In *The Wept of Wish-Ton Wish,* the family is explicitly defined as a wide circle of people that includes not just biological kin but also servants, retainers, and others. At the same time, the novel is structured by the opposition between family and strangers, prompting the question of where to draw the line. Cooper writes, as if to highlight this juxtaposition: "The family of Mark Heathcote, the lowest dependant included, saw these strangers depart with great inward satisfaction." [52] The departing men are strangers, presumably, because they have come to determine whether or not the Heathcote settlement is disloyal to the king. But how to determine who "strangers" are at the borders of the Heathcote settlement is a question that the novel returns to again and again, especially in relation to Native Americans who are in some sense both strangers and kin. Central to the plot of the novel are the captivities of members by both the Native Americans and the settlers. But these captivities do not so much highlight two peoples at war as two peoples thoroughly entangled historically and genealogically.

Early in *The Wept of Wish-Ton Wish*, an Indian, Conanchet, is captured as an enemy of war. But when it is found out that the captured Indian mourns for his father, who was likely killed by one of the members of the Wish-Ton Wish settlement, Mark Heathcote lays out his designs for the child — a mixture of parental and religious desire:

> I see the evident and foreordering will of a wise Providence in this. . . . The youth hath been deprived of one who might have enticed him still deeper into the bonds of the heathen, and hither hath he been led in order to be placed upon the straight and narrow path. He shall become a dweller among mine, and we will strive against the evil of his mind until instruction shall prevail. Let him be fed and nurtured equally with the things of life and the things of the world; for who knoweth that which is designed in his behalf? (82)

Heathcote opens up the possibility of a religious family — one that derives part of its logic from the development of affective bonds and part of its logic from the idea of religious destiny that can make the child part of one family or part of another based on some larger will. Heathcote self-consciously acts as a substitute father, not in terms of inheritance or economic arrangements, but in terms of both affective bonds and the religious status of family. He attempts to civilize Conanchet, summoning him during the hour of prayer, impressing upon him his own customs and habits. Moreover, this adoptive act substitutes an act of care justified by providential design for a history of violence and parricide — the murder of the boy's father by a member of the settlement.

In *Hope Leslie*, Sedgwick similarly depicts the acts of exchange based in war turning into a familial connection. A discussion at the beginning of the novel turns on the fates of two Indian children captured in war and two other orphaned children, all of whom will be joining the Fletcher household. The comparison of the statuses of these children is telling. Of Hope and Faith Leslie, Mr. Fletcher says, "These children will bring additional labour to your household; and in good time hath our thoughtful friend Governor Winthrop procured for us two Indian servants. The girl has arrived. The boy is retained about the little Leslies; the youngest of whom, it seems, is a petted child; and is particularly pleased by his activity in ministering to her amusement."[53] Several overlapping descriptions attend this transaction: the Leslies are brought in for labor at the same time that one is a "petted child"; the Indian children are to be "servants" at the same time that they are something of playthings *for* the children. Though brought in for labor, these children are obviously already something more: invested with affect, they become the main characters in the drama to follow. In response to this description, Mrs. and Mr. Fletcher argue about the "use" of the servant, which turns on whether or not Native Americans are the same as the English settlers. When Mrs. Fletcher responds — "I am glad if any use can be made of an Indian servant," Mr. Fletcher replies, "How any use! You surely do not doubt, Martha, that these Indians possess the same faculties that we do" (20). The status of these children immediately turns into a conversation about sameness and equality at a social and political level between Indians and whites. Determining how these children are to serve varying familial functions becomes the site for the national question of inclusion.

The question about the norms of kinship reframes the representation of Native American–settler relations in the novel as a whole. When one of the Native American children, Magawisca, faces the ethical dilemma of whether or not she should warn her adopted family about her Indian father's vengeful designs, the moment turns toward an implicit negotiation of the terms of Magawisca's inclusion into family. Here different notions of adoption are in conflict.

> Tears fell fast from Magawisca's eye, but she made no reply, and Mrs. Fletcher observing and compassionating her emotion, and thinking it probably arose from comparing her orphan state to that of the merry children about her, called her and said, "Magawisca, you are neither a stranger, nor a servant, will you not share our joy? Do you not love us?"
>
> "Love you!" she exclaimed, clasping her hands, "love you! I would give my life for you."
>
> "We do not ask your life, my good girl . . . but a light heart and a cheerful look." (64–65)

Not knowing that Magawisca is fearful for the lives of her adopted family, Mrs. Fletcher misreads Magawisca's tears, framing them within a sentimental notion of family. Her interpretation represents an ethic of sentimental family feeling that identifies consanguineous ties with affective bonds and assumes that Magawisca is feeling different from the other children. As a sentimentally defined object, she is defined as kin through negation: she is "neither a stranger, nor a servant." Magawisca's status as an equal is *created* through the sharing of emotion and tears. However, the extension of sentimentality is simultaneously a demand, and a disciplinary demand at that: "Will you not share our joy? Do you not love us? . . . We do not ask your life . . . but a light heart and a cheerful look." The sentimental extension of humanity is thus also a demand by the subject to be loved, a demand that still places Magawisca apart.

But Magawisca's response alerts us to a discrepancy between this sentimental mode of kinship and politics, and the idea of kinship and adoption that gets constructed through Native American forms of kinship. For Magawisca responds with the logic of sacrifice and substitution: "I would give my life for you." This statement seems to supplement the sentimental feeling of love. It both adds to the sentimental bond and represents a displacement of it, pushing it beyond its own boundaries.[54] Mrs. Fletcher, of course, responds by translating the terms of their relationship back to the commonality of shared feeling: "We do not ask your life . . . but a light heart and cheerful look." But this dialogue and misunderstanding over the terms of kinship represent two different modes of relation: Fletcher's is based on affective bonds while Magawisca's is based on reciprocity and exchange. A notion of reciprocity and exchange demands ties that link the fate of the Fletcher family with the fate of Magawisca in ways that supersede distinctions between them. The affective bonds, on the other hand, demand a sharing of joy because she loves and is loved "like" kin. The sentimental form of kinship bonds preserves the difference between the adopted child and the family and maintains the distinctions between filiation and affiliation. Whereas in Native American practices of substitution, identity becomes a function of belonging, in "as if" kinship, identity privileges the self-sufficiency and self-sameness of one's person and the singularity of one's history.

Uncertain Distinctions

This negotiation of differing notions of kinship thus has to do with the need to create distinct and separable political identities and histories for Native Americans and white settlers, and the simultaneous inability to make these distinctions. As Colin Calloway notes, King Philip's War was not between strangers, but neighbors, and this legacy haunts the revisionist historiography of these frontier romances. The concern with the space of the frontier, issues of borders, and problematic classifications in Cooper's *The Wept of Wish-Ton Wish* is a symptom of this need to create distinctions.[55] Indeed, the English title to the novel *The Borderers,* already suggests this interest in "life on the borders." *The Wept of Wish-Ton Wish* is preoccupied with the ability or inability to describe and recognize what appears on the frontier. Kinship itself as a form of demarcating some people from others is put into question:

> There is one of a certainty, and it should be one of our hunting party, too; and yet he doth not seem to be of a size or of a gait like that of Eben Dudley. *Thou should'st have a knowledge of thy kindred, girl; to me it seemeth thy brother.*
>
> Truly, it may be Reuben Ring; still it hath much of the swagger of the other, though their stature be nearly equal; the manner of carrying the musket is much the same with all the borderers too; one cannot easily tell the form of a man from a stump, by this light, and yet do I think it will prove to be the loitering Dudley. (126, emphasis added)

Even as various standards are used to discern who this person is — "size," "gait," "stature," "manner" — still "one cannot easily tell the form of a man from a stump, by this light." And though "kindred" is seen as a primary relationship by which one should be able to recognize and "know" the other, it does not provide certainty in this case. Kinship is used to maintain the border, even as its stability is called into question.

Kinship is relied on to make distinctions at the boundaries of race and religion: when Ruth warns of having seen something near the edge of the woods, she makes a quick distinction between animal, white settler, and Indian other: "Aye! Creature, formed, fashioned, gifted like ourselves, in all but color of the skin and blessing of the faith" (63). After being upbraided for the fact that it is nearly impossible to make those kinds of distinctions from such a distance or in the dark, she rests her capacities on her position and feelings as a mother: "Thinkest thou, husband, that a mother's eye could be deceived?" (63). In a novel in which even the most vigilant eyes cannot be trusted because it is too difficult to make distinctions on the "borders," what ought to be known, above all, is whether or not someone is kin.

The unredeemed captive occasions a crisis in seeing who is a stranger and who is kin. The reappearance of Whittal Ring, a boy captured and raised by Indians, becomes a pivot point for the assertion of a notion of kinship that redraws boundaries and puts into place a logic of singular identity. At the beginning of chapter 28, the reader is given a scene in which two people descry two others coming from a far distance, and Cooper's penchant to withhold the identity of a person in the story blurs the lines between native and settler again. The men are introduced through various clues, including their dress and what they are doing. Everything about the character is meant to proclaim who they are. In the description, there is an explicit linking of the clue to his actual person: "A musket thrown across his left shoulder . . . proclaimed him one who had either been engaged in a hunt, or in some short expedition of even a less peaceable character" (250). But the details do not necessarily cohere into a clear portrait of who the person is:

"His dress was of the usual material and fashion of a country-man of the age and colony, *though a short broadsword . . . might have attracted observation*" (250–51, emphasis added). Even as materials, cloth, exterior circumstances, etc., do not cohere into a clear picture of character, Cooper blurs distinctions further: "Whether native or stranger, few ever passed the hillock named, without pausing to gaze. . . . The individual mentioned loitered as usual" (251). Everyone — *whether native or stranger* — would do the same thing.

As the scene unfolds, we get more and more clues about the persons in question, but this is not just an exercise in suspense and recognition. One of the men in question is Whittal Ring. When he is taken back to the settlement, the doctor, Reuben Ring, and Dudley all examine him to determine whether or not he is an Indian or a white man. Whittal Ring, who is described in the novel as slow and dumb-witted, presents a living, speaking contradiction to the observers: "He hath the colors of a Narragansett about the brow and eyes, and yet he faileth greatly in the form and movements. . . . He hath been spoken to in the language of a Christian, no less than in that of a heathen, and as yet no reply hath been made, while he obeys commands uttered in both forms of speech" (258–59). The question underlying Whittal Ring's appearance is how to determine appearance — by bodily markings, movements, religion, language, etc. Each determination of difference dissolves in relation to a different measure. The border between Indian and white is already traversed by several kinds of borders: physical borders and lines, like the gate, through which one can be either welcome or unwelcome; mental borders between the sane and the insane; religious and linguistic borders. Seemingly embodying both possibilities of Indian and settler, Whittal Ring embodies the shared relations between the two that cannot be recognized. The fact that borders can be traversed so easily and so quickly at the same time that they are anxiously produced and multiplied is the insistent preoccupation of the novel.

Whittal Ring is ultimately recognized by his sister, Faith Ring, but this recognition is predicated on a certain kind of kinship — one in which his earliest memories and primary, unique, and affective relationships are privileged. Cooper writes: "Faith had endeavored ... to elicit some evidences of a more just remembrance. ... She tried to excite a train of recollections that should lead to deeper impressions. ... Faith artfully led him back to those animal enjoyments of which he had been so fond in boyhood" (227). But this assertion of Whittal Ring's primary ties points to the particular threat embodied by the presence of unredeemed captives.[56] The danger is that identification can work outside of the bonds of kinship or the similarities of racial or religious community, that children can identify with multiple people across races, thus resituating their ties of belonging and hence transforming their identities, loyalties, and allegiances. It is because identification does not rely on similarity that makes adoption so threatening. On the other hand, if the child is unsubstitutable, if the child is formed through affective bonds that guarantee the child's uniqueness as the terms of Whittal's recognition suggests, then persons cannot shift identifications and become different people. The affective, bourgeois form of family is a way to create a notion of identity that gets rid of anxieties about substitution.

The narration of Ruth Heathcote's kidnapping by the Indians and her return as Narra-mattah displays these shifting registers of kinship and their implications for the terms of racial belonging. The capture of Ruth by Conanchet is actually preceded by the problem of substitution. In the confusion and chaos of the Indian attack, bodies get mixed-up, and the Heathcotes think that they have their daughter Ruth hidden underneath their blanket, when in fact they have their friend's daughter instead: "she [Ruth] saw that, in the hurry of the appalling scene, the children had been exchanged, and that she had saved the life of Martha!" (157). The scene is almost deliberately confusing, making it hard for the reader (and the characters) to track who is who in the first place, highlighting the dangers of substitution.

There are thus two parts to this exchange: Ruth is captured by the Indians and taken away from the Heathcote family; and the orphaned daughter of a friend takes the place of Ruth within the Heathcote family. The question that remains is who *is* deserving of kinship. When they learn of the mistake, Ruth (the mother) shrieks, "It is not our babe!" but Martha cries — "I am thine! I am thine! ... If not thine, whose am I?" (214–15). Content attempts to come to terms with the threat of Ruth being incorporated by the Indians through the rhetoric of God's providence and family (echoing Mark Heathcote's language in taking in Conanchet), at the same time that he struggles with the sentiments of "nature" attached to the unique, biological child:

> "Madam — Mrs. Heathcote — mother!" came timidly and at intervals, from the lips of the orphan. Then the heart of Ruth relented. She clasped the daughter of her friend to her breast, and Nature found a temporary relief in one of those frightful exhibitions of anguish which appear to threaten the dissolution of the link which connects the soul with the body.
>
> "Come, daughter of John Harding," said Content, looking around him with the assumed composure of a chastened man, while natural regret struggled hard at his heart; "this has been God's pleasure. It is meet that we kiss his parental hand. Let us be thankful." (214)

This struggle between "natural regret" and "religious" sentiment in these passages reveals a divided notion of family and kinship: divided between an ethos of substitutability and one of sentimentality and nature that hinges on the "natural" affection for one's own child. Even as the religious ideals of the family state allow the orphan to find in Mrs. Heathcote a substitute "mother," the grounds for family shift toward the language of "natural" feeling, which prevents adoption in the sense of a complete inclusion. This moment speaks to the always partial inclusion of the adoptee, based as it is on the singularity and nonsubstitutability of the child.

Following this substitution of one child for another, Ruth (the mother) does not ultimately accept this substitution as Content suggests, but mourns the loss of her child as unsubstitutable. She is not able to imagine her daughter other than through a form of belonging premised on genealogical identity. When her lost child now "nationalized" as an Indian, Narra-mattah, reappears near the end of the novel, the plot virtually stops in order to fixate on the problem of appearance. Her contradictory appearance, like Whittal Ring's, figures the violence of identity, the absolute impossibility of producing a coherent history around such traumatic dislocations and relocations. When she is taken back to the settlement, she is mute and distant from everyone. Ruth is unable to reach Narra-mattah's affections, or to remind her of her childhood affections toward her white family. Her inability to communicate or be heard in relation to her white family creates a separation between the histories and identities of "white" and "Indian" that belies their actual confluence and convergence. Based on the logic of identity and kinship rooted within a "natural" domesticity, the identities of "Indian" and "white" are secured and constructed as if they had nothing to say to each other.

Narra-mattah ultimately dies, and her death is monumentalized as a kind of eternal mourning. But this narrative of mourning is itself dependent on the idea of the unsubstitutable child, the child whose identity is fixed by the primary relations to one's genealogy. When Ruth begins to mourn for her lost daughter, this feeling of mourning is contested. Dudley wants her to move on, to rejoice in the saving of Martha: "This is carrying mourning beyond the bounds of reason" (200). But Ruth's mourning becomes legitimized and not narrated as "beyond the bounds of reason." Ruth's mourning fixates on the lost-ness of the lost object, on that primary, early relation as transcending all other relations, a logic that the narrative recapitulates in its representation of the unredeemed captives. The unsubstitutable child privileges the primary relation to consanguinity solidified through sentimental bonds as the sole determinant of identity. It is this notion of primary ties that make Narra-mattah unrecognizable and incoherent to the Heathcotes unless she can become Ruth again. This version of personhood militates against Native American conceptions of adoption and readoption (such as what we see in John Tanner), which do not tie personhood to the consanguineous relation as primary.

Personhood as a site of intertwined histories between Native American and white settler is suppressed by a notion of kinship that draws borders. Nowhere is this more apparent than in the mysterious relationship between a character named Submission and Conanchet, the captured Indian whose uncertain status began my analysis. When Submission first appears at the Heathcote settlement, he announces himself as "a brother in the faith, and a subject of the same laws" (143). He is greeted by Content, "Here is truly a Christian man without...enter of Heaven's mercy, and be welcome to that we have to bestow" (143). He arrives without a name and is "known" only in terms of his proclamation of faith. Hospitality toward those of the same religious faith becomes the way to mediate the unstable boundaries between "home" and "wilderness," family and stranger. When Submission comes again, he announces that Conanchet is sitting outside and requires Christian hospitality. Conanchet had somewhat earned the trust of the Heathcotes and was no longer a captive, but had disappeared from the settlement days earlier. The stranger states:

> I found this native child near thy gate, and took upon me the office of a Christian man to bid him welcome. Certain am I, that one, kind of heart and gently disposed, like the mistress of this family, will not turn him away in anger," to which Ruth replies, "He is no stranger at our fire, or at our board." (149)

The stranger himself is not forthcoming here: he has a long history with Conanchet, which we find out only later. So underlying the act done in the name of a "Christian man" are ties of unknown kinship. Moreover, the history of their relationship to each other is submerged: they have something of an adoptive father–son relationship, which is never unfolded or elaborated in the novel. We are given only the bare traces of their cross-cultural adoptive relationship — the fact that Conanchet calls Submission "father," and that Submission says that he is "almost Indian" — without the history of their relationship. Conanchet is captured in the end while saving Submission's life.

Likewise, Conanchet's background and intertwined histories are buried. Ruth says that Conanchet is "no stranger," but he is also not exactly kin either. Conanchet, whose history is not fully known until we are well into the novel, moves back and forth between wilderness and settlement, first as captive, then as a child, guest, and trusted guardian of the Heathcote children, and finally as Narra-mattah's husband and chief of the Narragansetts. At the end of the novel, he is captured by the Mohican chief, Uncas, but rather than go off with his wife and live, he chooses to die a death fitting of his status as an Indian chief. His death is not simply an edict against miscegenation or the future separation of peoples. It is a pronouncement against and rewriting of an *already shared* past and interrelation. The adoptive ties that Conanchet shared with both Submission and the Heathcotes are buried in favor of a stricter demarcation of kinship.

Reciprocity versus Identity

Hope Leslie, like *The Wept of Wish-Ton Wish,* reconstructs King Philip's War in terms of a drama of lost family ties. Both family romances reframe these exchanges/adoptions within a logic of kinship in which *substitution is impossible.*[57] But while the tragic deaths of the two adopted figures, Conanchet and Narra-mattah, in Cooper's novel punctuate the erasure of interrelations, the survival of the adopted figures, Oneco and Faith, in *Hope Leslie* is predicated on their remaining unrecognizable within the American familial nation-form. Even though substitution and exchange drive the machinery of the plot, the ultimate outcomes rely on the unsubstitutability of children for others. We can see this in the juxtaposition of the two main figures: Magawisca, an Indian adopted into the Fletcher family and subsequently recaptured by her father; and Faith Leslie, the sister of the title character, captured and raised by Indians.[58]

Sedgwick overlays the captivity plot with a structure of failed reparations and reciprocities — the inability of kinship ties to answer for and repair racial conflicts. For example, Magawisca acts on this logic of substitution, continually putting her life in danger for others. But each encounter is marked by failure. When Magawisca asks her father to show mercy to the family that sheltered her, this is met with bloodshed, death, and capture. When Everell is to be killed, Magawisca throws her body over his and her arm is cut off. Kinship as practiced by Magawisca seems to demand an ethics of reciprocity: Magawisca asks for mercy because of the affective ties that she has formed with the Leslies ("I would give my life for you"); she again puts herself in place of the other because of the kinship bond that she feels for Everell. Taking sentimental compassion to its limit point, she creates a series of debts and obligations that demand to be repaid, creating a reciprocal relationship between Native Americans and white settlers. But this narrative line is in tension with the mode of kinship based on singular relations, which rewrites the relationships of the novel in ways that preserve the "nature" of identity apart from an ethics of reciprocity.

In the figure of the unredeemed captive, we see again a plot of return that is predicated on the singularity of one's "original" history. Faith Leslie is portrayed in similar ways to Ruth Heathcote/Narra-mattah. When she is recaptured by her "original" family, she remains mute and unspeaking; she is often portrayed crouching in a corner of the room. Hope calls Faith over and "the poor girl obeyed, but without any apparent interest, and without even seeming conscious of the endearing tenderness with which Hope stroked back her hair, and kissed her cheek" (279). The Fletcher household calls Faith a poor "home-sick child," thus framing her despondency in terms of bourgeois sentiment. Their design to reincorporate her involves reattaching her to some pure, sentimental past, but even those "early" affections are littered with evidence of the *ties* between Native and settler. When Mrs. Grafton attempts to give Faith all of her old playthings, "some glimmerings of past times came over her; but as ill luck would have it, there was among the rest... a string of bird's eggs, which Oneco [the Indian boy taken in by the Fletchers] had given her at Bethel.... She dropped everything else, and burst into tears" (279). This attempt to recapture Faith's primary ties within the terms of an identity of self-sameness fails because her primary ties embody not singular relations, but a set of shared relations between Native American and Anglo settler. What is absent in this desire to match Faith's early memories with her present state is everything that occurred in the middle: the reader learns nothing of Faith Leslie's upbringing as an Indian, nothing of how she came to be who she is. She remains unintelligible — the missing pieces of her history are never filled in. Faith is, like Narra-mattah, recognizable only as a child, as a person without a history. Only in her responsiveness to the primacy of her "white" family is she a person.

The initial encounter between Hope and Faith fixates on Faith's appearance in ways that reveal the logic of identity put into place by sentimental forms of kinship. The idea of a primary sentimental relation drives Hope's attempts to find in Faith's veiled interior some connection to her past life, only to find the impossibility of any sense of kinship to her white family on these terms. In Hope's initial exchanges with her sister, it is Faith's trappings, clothes, and ornaments that seem to produce the greatest barrier: "She [Hope] thought that if Mary's dress, which was similarly and gaudily decorated, had a less savage aspect, she might look more natural to her; and she signed to her to remove the mantle she wore. . . . Mary threw it aside, and disclosed her person . . . clothed with skins . . . and ambitiously embellished with bead work. The removal of the mantle, instead of the effect designed, only served to make more striking the aboriginal peculiarities" (239). What were once the possibilities of exchange between peoples — trinkets, jewels, dress — become instead markers of racial and civilizational distinction. Indeed, Hope fixates on these elements in order to displace Indianness from Faith as a person. To put it another way, the attribution of dress or ornament as itself "Indian" is a fetishization of race that defends against the knowledge of Faith's difference: you are and are not kin. Clothing and dress stand not for the reciprocal relations between peoples, but as objects that link part of the person to a past time or memory, reconstructing identity along separate racial and historical lines. After being disappointed by her sister's "unnatural" aspect, Hope attempts to reassert family at the level of national dress: "I want once more to see her in the dress of her own people — of her own family — from whose arms she was torn to be dragged into captivity" (239). Instead of being read as a border through which various material and psychic crossings could occur, Faith is figured in terms of the reduction of identity to a logic of appearance. The violence of dislocation is used as a trope to foreground the primacy of a singular heritage — "her own family."

The repeated description of Faith in terms of her deafness and muteness speaks to her disconnect from the frames — religious, racial, colonial — that give persons meaning and properties. She mirrors back nonrecognition. Hope, like Ruth's mother in Cooper's novel, cannot recognize herself in Faith. Her only hope is to return her sister to the past in ways that make her conform to Hope's own internal picture of her: "I want *once more* to see her in the dress . . . of her own family." The dramatic "return" of unredeemed captives foregrounds a notion of identity in which origins are supposed to preserve sameness. The notion of the primacy of early affective bonds — of unsubstitutability — emerges as a key feature of this logic of identity. An early description in the novel of the founders of the colony bears this out:

> Home can never be transferred; never repeated in the experience of an individual. The place consecrated by parental love, by the innocence and sports of childhood, by the first acquaintance with nature . . . is the only home. There is a living and breathing spirit infused into nature: every familiar object has a history. (17)

These terms — *first* acquaintance; the nontransferability of home — create a notion of the individual that has a singular and unchanging relation to the world based on early ties. If "every familiar object has a history," if, that is, history inheres in "familiar" objects through an affective circuit (as in Mrs. Grafton's attempts to get Faith to remember her history through her childhood playthings), then the unfamiliarity of Faith and her incapacity to respond to affect is used at the end of the novel to irrevocably separate the histories of Native and settler.

Unlike Tanner, Hunter, or Jemison, who get adopted and readopted into a network of Native American kinship ties such that they have a sense of their substitutability within a larger set of relations, the narration of these unredeemed captives in Cooper and Sedgwick foreground the discontinuity of history as a problem to be revised and corrected. While Faith never fully "remembers" her infancy with the Fletcher family, Narra-mattah in *The Wept of Wish-Ton Wish* experiences a surge of remembrance through which she is essentially transformed back into the Ruth Heathcote prior to capture. This incredible moment of remembering foregrounds the subject as univocal and singular, only relatable back to a single primal moment. Faith and Ruth, then, function not so much in terms of their place between two cultures, but rather as a way of redrawing histories of violence and conflict in terms of a personal and internal drama of memory and forgetting, effectively cutting one group off from shared relations and connections with the other.

Identities as Border Patrol

As Jill Lepore writes of King Philip's War, the writing of that war drew and redrew continually unstable boundaries between "what it meant to be 'English' and what it meant to be 'Indian.'"[59] The trope of the unredeemed captive was one way in which writers of the 1820s redrew boundaries in terms of kinship. It took up relations and exchanges that had blurred these boundaries and reframed them within the idealizable and universalizable frames of kinship. Distinctions between civilization and savagery, Christian and heathen, give way to or are remobilized through distinctions based on foregrounding the individual's primary ties and singular histories. The effect of this was to replace historical events with the traumas of personal memory, creating the trope of the unredeemed captive as a story of melancholic loss and the impossibility of kinship.

In his recent retelling of the Eunice Williams capture, John Demos recounts the various markers by which Williams's acculturation may have taken place. The awkward reunion scenes between Eunice and members of her family, recounted by Demos and preserved in letters, is quite similar to Cooper's and Sedgwick's accounts of the unredeemed captive. Similar to the novelistic accounts, the story goes that Eunice's Longmeadow relatives pressed Eunice to put off her Indian garments and adopt English dress.[60] What all these accounts have in common is the nightmare that the unredeemed captive can be or has already been secured and appropriated by someone else. The representational logic of identity that underlies this nightmare is based on a notion of kinship that has at its heart the unsubstitutability of the child. Moreover, this anxiety with regard to the unredeemed captive emerges out of a deep asymmetry in understandings about adoption: Native American practices based on incorporation and substitution; the developing notion of adoption and domesticity that preserved the unsubstitutability of the child and constructed affective and emotional bonds based on the impossibility of complete inclusion. It is this asymmetry that pervades the historical romances of the 1820s and reframes problems of contact, exchange, and reciprocity within the politics of domestic dependency, securing Native American and white identities on a new border.

2

UNMANAGEABLE ATTACHMENTS

Slavery, Abolition, and the Transformation of Kinship

In 1858, just three years before the start of the Civil War, Lydia Maria Child published a short story in the *Atlantic Monthly*, titled "Loo Loo," which already anticipated the difficulties in defining and realizing freedom for former slaves after the Civil War. In this story, a northern man named Alfred Noble purchases a slave child, Loo Loo, out of the South and adopts her, ostensibly giving her freedom. In doing so, though, he uneasily "supplies the place of her father."[1] Uneasily, because Alfred does not know how or where to place her, how she will be related to him: in what way is she his own? Is he more like a father or a brother to her? What kinds of desires and intimacy are appropriate or inappropriate in an adoptive relation? Noble's uncertainty regarding his own position is matched by her anomalous status, for in what sense is she now free? She is a quadroon who is nearly white, educated above her prior slave status. She is an adoptee whose quasi-kin position does not change the fact that she was purchased. The realization of freedom in this story becomes hopelessly entangled with issues of possession, dependency, and desire that mark the adoptive kin relation between Loo Loo and Noble. In this story, the uncertainty of the adoptive relation — what kind of kin relation is it? how does it change social and familial status? — indexes the equally uncertain political problem of social and civic relations after emancipation.

Lydia Maria Child's depiction of Native–Anglo relations and her treatment of Native American removal through the lens of sentimental kinship discussed in chapter 1 certainly staged the way in which she was to tackle questions of slavery and abolitionism.[2] Many of the same critiques of domesticating these relations in the service of political domination apply.[3] Indeed, adoption during this time period has been read as a trope that compromises antislavery visions of freedom by sentimentally reinstituting a hierarchy of unequal relations.[4] Here, though, Child navigates the uncertain meanings of adoption in relation to a wide array of bonds and exchanges at the intersections of kinship and slavery: paternalism; benevolence; unrecognized kin; concubinage; various forms of dependency; nursing; child care.[5] In doing so, she reveals how the legitimation of kinship practices mediates the construction of citizenship. For Child, adoption becomes a central trope that indexes the uncertain status of social relationality and social standing even as the nation moves toward ending slavery and codifying the "free person." Acts of claiming others, like Noble's, highlight the division between the construction of the human as kin — so crucial to the sentimental and humanitarian discourse of abolitionism — and the construction of the human as citizen. Her articulation of adoption and emancipation in "Loo Loo" and in her later novel, *A Romance of the Republic,* is a symptom of the paradoxical position of kinship within attempts to construct freedom and citizenship.

For other prominent writers, as I analyze below, the problem of constructing parental relations similarly confuses the plots of freedom and emancipation. Adoption constitutes an important subplot in Harriet Beecher Stowe's *Uncle Tom's Cabin.* It emerges in children's literature that puts forward moral and sentimental arguments for abolition. Finally, the social relations organized by kinship norms complicate trajectories of freedom in the narrations of a former slave: Frederick Douglass shifts the terms of his emancipation narrative in his second auto-biography, *My Bondage and My Freedom,* as he comes to terms with his relationship to the Auld family. For each of these writers, there is no citizenship without a kinship. Throughout this chapter, I set out the particular ways in which adoption and the politics of configuring parent–child bonds articulates the naturalization of personhood at a time when citizens, free blacks, exslaves, orphans, and displaced children are all caught up in the problem of defining citizenship after emancipation.

Specific notions of family played a crucial role in articulating the transition from slavery to citizenship before, during, and after the Civil War. Abraham Lincoln constructed the nation through tropes of family wholeness when he pronounced the geographical territory of the United States to be "the home of one national family" and asserted that the nation shall "care for him who shall have borne the battle, and for his widow, and his orphan." [6] As I explore later in this chapter, these terms are specifically recast by Frederick Douglass when he calls attention to black Americans' status as genealogical outsiders, as "at best only his [Lincoln's] step-children, children by adoption, children by force of circumstances and necessity." [7] Antislavery fiction and nonfiction dramatized slavery as the corrupter and destroyer of families in several ways: the legally sanctioned removal of children from their slave mothers and concubinage of slaves by oppressive white masters; the notion that economic and market principles would invade and destroy the sanctity of the home. Proslavery fiction and nonfiction on the other hand often dramatized the harmonious interplay of family and slavery by naturalizing racial hierarchy as the parent–child relation (slaves as part of the happy plantation family).[8]

But family did not play just a symbolic role in modeling the nation in its own image. The codification of domestic relations was a structural part of postbellum regulations of freedom and the idea of emancipation itself. Nancy Cott's brief history of the Thirteenth Amendment reveals how its advocates were careful not to eliminate the "other" domestic relations in their wording of the law. For this reason, the wording was changed from "All persons are equal before the law, so that no person can hold another as a slave" to "Neither slavery nor involuntary servitude . . . shall exist within the United States."[9] In response to the early version of the amendment, Senator Lazarus Powell of Kentucky "immediately protested that if a constitutional amendment could 'regulate the relation of master and servant, it certainly can, on the same principle, make regulations concerning the relation of parent and child, husband and wife, and guardian and ward,' thus focusing their alarm on the impact of such an amendment on the overall powers of male heads of household."[10] Because of the similarity between domestic relations and slavery, the law as written in the earlier version would have amounted to, Powell implies, a radical erasure of all relations of domestic dependence. The far-reaching language of equality in the previous version is replaced by the naming of slavery in the final version; slavery is made into an institutional practice instead of a condition or position that could be made analogous to other positions (as the wording "no person can hold another *as* a slave" suggests). The conditions of citizenship and freedom, then, were articulated in ways that preserved relations of domestic dependence and subjugation codified in the patriarchal family. The very act of emancipation is one that is haunted by the intertwining of domestic relations and slavery.

At the same time, this intertwining affects not just how the abolition of slavery is defined, but also the substantive definition of freedom. As constitutional scholar Peggy Cooper Davis argues, prevalent within these same debates was the strong belief that slavery destroyed familial rights and that emancipation required a protection of those family rights. Davis quotes Senator Harlan as describing the way in which the "incidents of slavery" denied the marriage relation and the parent–child relation, both of which should be sacred and hallowed rights.[11] Similarly, Angelina Grimké argues how parental authority is undermined under conditions of slavery: "they [parents] have as little control over them [their children], as have domestic animals over the disposal of their young."[12] But during Congressional sessions that attempted to define freedom, the arguments shift from saying that slavery violates the natural affections between parent and child, to stating that it violates parental rights *to* their children. Senator Sumner bemoans the violation of the "sacred right of family" such that "no parent could claim his own child"; and Congressman Kasson wrote that the "three great fundamental natural rights of human society . . . are the rights of a husband to his wife — the marital relation; the right of father to his child — the parental relation; and the right of a man to . . . personal liberty."[13] An African American soldier echoes this logic, stating that "If slavery denied them the right to control their persons and progeny, freedom would confer that right."[14] The right "to" a person is associated with the right "to" liberty. Freedom here encompasses maintaining control and possession over one's family. The "family" thus occupied a paradoxical place in discourses of freedom: it was the condition for citizenship and emancipation — rights of marriage, parental custody and control, were foundational and integral to liberty. But at the same time, it was an obstacle to emancipation, since it codified the rights and claims of someone over another, which was eerily similar to the conditions of slavery.[15]

The postbellum period attests to the ways in which freedom is negotiated through a dizzying array of practices of claiming others. The Freedmen's Bureau became extremely vigilant over the legal regulation and normalization of African American marital and sexual relations in a way that both delegitimated African American kin relations and disciplined exslaves into a normative citizenship that maintained specific hierarchies of labor and consent.[16] But citizenship was regulated not only through bourgeois notions of sexuality and propriety, but also through laws of descent, property transmission, and the capacity to claim someone else as a dependent. This was particularly true in the U.S. South, where claiming others was often part of an economy of maintaining patriarchy and racial divisions. Inheritances left by white men to enslaved women and their children — mainly the offspring of adulterous relationships with slaves — were often contested, revealing how will and testament law become a regulatory structure that produces the claims of whiteness on and as property. In his analysis of a "jurisprudence of inheritance rights across the color line," Bernie Jones writes: "In the view of the greater society miscegenation between white men and enslaved women or free women of color was not a problem. Instead, the color line was breached when white men recognized and accorded enslaved women and their mixed-race children status in white society by bequeathing them property and manumitting them."[17] As conflicts over wills and testaments and the question of illegitimacy make clear, this domain of constructing the rules by which a child has a name and property is one of the forms through which citizenship and race are articulated through each other.

Apprenticeship or binding out practices in the post-emancipation South is perhaps the most egregious example of this formation of citizenship through the regulation of kinship claims. Katherine Franke describes these statutes and practices:

> The greater threat to the integrity of African American families during this period lay, however, in the postbellum apprenticeship system. White southern authorities respected the integrity of Black families only in so far as parents were able to support their children beyond a certain subsistence level. When, however, parents were found to be paupers, were not habitually employed in some honest, industrious occupation, were deemed to be of notoriously bad character, or where it was determined that it would simply be better for the habits and comfort of a child, a court could order that a minor child be bound as an apprentice to some white person, often the family's former owner, until the child reached the age of majority.[18]

As Dylan Penningroth makes clear, the claiming of children became a pitched battle between African Americans and white plantation owners over the exercising of freedom and authority. African Americans claimed children's labor from their old masters so as to maintain their own property and independence and keep them away from the claims of white planters, using the language of kinship in order to do so: "ex-slaves did not deny that children were an important source of labor. . . . Instead, they said that 'kinpeople,' and not white landowners, were 'justly entitled to the benefits of [their children's] services and should control when and where they worked.' " [19] Claims on others were inextricably tied to labor, property, and the formation of citizenship as autonomy.

These are all examples in which the terms of freedom and emancipation are mediated and racialized by intergenerational familial claims regarding inheritance, legitimacy, property, and belonging. These anxieties regarding inheritance and status also surrounded legal definitions of adoption. Writing in 1876, the legal historian and genealogist William Whitmore notes these dangers to the proper transmission of property, name, and descent opened up by adoption law. Whitmore writes that the "whole idea of creating children by act...may even be said to be repugnant to" the common law.[20] He worries that such laws destroy all semblance of family — resulting in "too casual a relationship between adoptees and new parents" — allowing for illegal connections to be made legal, and upsetting lines of descent.[21] These issues are manifest in the differences within adoption laws themselves. For example, some states stated that adoption legitimated an illegitimate child, while other states expressly stated that adoption *could not* legitimate an illegitimate child. This was the case in Louisiana, where the statute reads: "Any person may adopt another as his child except those illegitimate children whom the law prohibits him from acknowledging."[22] And though Whitmore is right to note that this exception refers to "those who are born from an incestuous or adulterous connection," not all illegitimate children are created equally.[23] As Jones notes, Louisiana laws "placed the mixed-race children of white fathers at a disadvantage to white illegitimates when it came to claiming inheritances from them."[24] The jurisprudence with regard to legitimation, inheritance, and race suggests that this provision's language of "illegitimacy" indexes a particular racial anxiety.

Family law attempts to reconcile the economic and affective arrangements of kinship in order to determine the status of persons with respect to inheritance, property, and social legitimacy. Emancipation attempts to remake the social status of persons as if it were separate from domestic relations and its role in ordering social relations and legitimating persons. The difficulty in keeping these two domains apart was already seen in the writing of the Thirteenth Amendment, and is further exemplified in the convergence of the plot of emancipation with the thematics of adoption. How does the familial scene mediate and narrate these contradictory discourses of freedom and ownership? In what ways does thc familial context of psychic emancipation correspond to a political-social emancipation? How does the family romance, which posits the separation from authority as constitutive of freedom, haunt the narrative of freedom? In the following section, I return to "Loo Loo" to trace the narrative logics by which personhood is negotiated in between the capacity to claim another and the freedom of independence and autonomy. The problem of the relationship between the legal and affective formations of kinship plays itself out in the imagination of citizenship.[25]

Emancipating Loo Loo

In this sense, adoption is not just Child's imaginative, utopian solution to the deep divisions of slavery on the nation. It is a meditation on the conditions of citizenship itself. The metaphor of adoption as a way to narrate and set the terms of how a slave becomes free suggests interrelations among the act of adoption, the problems of claiming that it raises, and the plot of freedom. Child's 1858 story exemplifies a crisis in freedom and emancipation through the ambiguity of its ending. At first, the story seems like a straightforward abolitionist tale built on the conventions of sentimental literature: a familiar critique of slavery as an institution that destroys the sacred bonds of family and the imagination of adoption as a symbolic reparation and reconstruction of those familial bonds. But the fundamental opposition between slavery and family — on which the critique of slavery as dissolving familial bonds rests — breaks down precisely through the conventions of sentimentality. Though the title character, Loo Loo, plots an overall trajectory from slavery to freedom, a series of reversals marks her status as uncertainly shifting between slavery and freedom. "Loo Loo" repeats the acts of bondage and freedom so many times that they begin to converge. Loo Loo is first a happy child living with her "father" (though she does not know that she is legally a slave); then she is "inherited" by a relative as a slave after her father passes away; then she is bought and adopted as a "daughter" by the Northern gentleman Alfred Noble; then she is lost again because of debts to a slave-owner, revealing that her adoption did not change her status as slave property; and finally she is "freed" as the wife of Alfred Noble in Canada. Given the questions above regarding legitimacy in Louisiana law, perhaps it is not a coincidence that Loo Loo's mother is from New Orleans, for her freedom is contingent on the legitimacy of paternal transmissions.

But even this telos of "freedom" only returns us to the beginning, as the resettlement of Loo Loo and Alfred in Canada serves to replicate the terms of their initial encounter. The story is structured as a series of seduction scenes in which Alfred is captivated by the image of Loo Loo again and again. This repetition of seduction scenes reveals a fantasy of Loo Loo as sexual object that underlies and problematizes the act of emancipation. When Alfred first sees Loo Loo, he is captivated by her, and his desire to free her is also a desire to capture her as an object. To him, she is origin-less, displaced and unconnected from the past or future, and this displacement, moreover, is constitutive of the act of emancipation. In other words, his emancipatory desire is contingent upon disconnecting her from history and inserting himself genealogically. When he purchases the child out of slavery after seeing her the second time, his desire is articulated in terms of refinding a lost object: "Now, for the first time, she was completely identified with the vision of that fairy child who had so captivated his fancy four years before. He never forgot the tones of her voice, and the expression of her eyes, when she kissed his

hand at parting, and said, 'I thank you, Sir, for buying me'"
(808). The child is found again, but in a way that returns to
Alfred's first vision of her.

Saidiya Hartman has analyzed the role of a discourse of
seduction in antebellum slave law as a way to assert the slave
woman's "complicity and willful submission." [26] By highlighting the ability of the dominated to influence the master, the
discourse of seduction masked and licensed the sexual violence perpetrated by masters on their slaves. In her reading,
seduction facilitated the difficulties regarding consent, coercion, and will inherent in the slave's anomalous status as both
property and personhood by simultaneously identifying the
enslaved as a "will-less object" and as a criminal and morally
corrupt agent. [27] That Child's plot of freedom acts out a seduction narrative points to its crucial role not just in reimagining
black subjectivity to make it amenable to slave law, but also
in displaying the entanglements of will, coercion, consent, and
objectification in emancipation. For the scene of seduction renders indeterminate where agency lies, who is active and who
is passive. In both the psychoanalytic narrative of seduction [28]
and Child's narrative, the child is at the center of these difficulties precisely because she marks a subject that is neither wholly
dependent nor wholly independent.

The family scene at the end of the short story does not manifest freedom, but rather explores how citizenship is acted out
in terms of kinship. Alfred Noble and Loo Loo, now in Canada, have three daughters, and they name the youngest child
Loo Loo. Noble identifies his wife with their child by giving
his wife a picture of "Loo Loo" — the child — and having
her repeat her now iconic phrase: "Her eyes moistened as she
gazed upon it [the picture of her daughter]; then kissing his
hand, she looked up in the old way, and said, 'I thank you, Sir,
for buying me'" (42). Said in the "same tone" and with the

same "look," the phrase is supposed to be a literal reproduction of the earlier moment. But the phrase does not so much resolve the plot, as it repeats the ambivalence of emancipation. Marked with sentimental tears, it is actually a profoundly unsentimental moment, because the humanity recognized by sentimentalism is directly opposed to recognition of her freedom. Loo Loo becomes the adopted child once again. Or put another way, Loo Loo passes into the condition of becoming Alfred's wife without ceasing to be his adopted child. Neither changes the unfree condition of Loo Loo. The gap between past and present, nostalgia and present desire, is collapsed at the moment of possession and purchase. Noble's act of claiming and construction of a fiction of generational continuity is the precondition for her status.

The adoptive relation between Loo Loo and Noble thus foregrounds emancipation not as a problem of liberation but as a problem of attachment and legitimate forms of intergenerationality. It is important to note that Alfred's first thought for saving Loo Loo from slavery is that his mother and sister were living so that they might adopt the child. Here adoption is thought of as a maternal and sisterly act, precisely in opposition to a paternal notion of family that is premised on ownership and sexual property. Through the course of her "adoption," Loo Loo is incorporated into a vision of belonging and home. She becomes attached to and dependent on Alfred Noble. But these conceptions of adoption — caring and protection on the one hand, and succession, legitimacy, and emancipation on the other — cannot be neatly divided from each other. They cannot, as Alfred's thoughts suggest, be divided between a maternal and paternal act. Rather, Alfred's difficulty with adoption and Loo Loo's ever-uncertain status suggests that the act of caring and protection does not easily inhabit the desires of ownership and possession.[29]

This ambiguity is made clear after Loo Loo is adopted. She has no legitimate place in Alfred Noble's home. She fits neither within relations of kinship nor within relations of race based on labor. In struggling over how to provide a suitable home for Loo Loo, Alfred cannot decide how to relate to her:

> After Mr. Noble had purchased the child, he knew not how to provide a suitable home for her. At first, he placed her with his colored washerwoman. But if she remained in that situation, though her bodily wants would be well cared for, she must necessarily lose much of the refinement infused into her being. . . . He did not enter into any analysis of his motives in wishing her to be so far educated as to be a pleasant companion for himself. The only question he asked himself was, How he would like to have his sister treated, if she had been placed in such unhappy circumstances. He knew very well what construction would be put upon his proceedings, in a society where handsome girls of such parentage were marketable; and he had so long tacitly acquiesced in the customs around him, that he might easily have viewed her in that light himself, had she not become invested with a tender and sacred interest from the circumstances in which he had first seen her, and the innocent, confiding manner in which she had implored him to supply the place of her father. She was always presented to his imagination as Mr. Duncan's beloved daughter, never as Mr. Jackson's slave. He said to himself, "May God bless me according to my dealings with this orphan! May I never prosper, if I take advantage of her friendless situation!" (809)

She flips in his thinking from "companion" to "sister," to "beloved daughter," all the while he represses her actual slave status. She is unable to occupy any one position in social life, completely defined by the social norms that govern her relations to others. Indeed, he struggles with how to imagine her apart from the social norms that constitute his relation to her. That she has not yet been able to emerge into social representation is revealed by the fact that she is inextricable from her "situation," her surroundings, or her unhappy circumstances. Her background and the "circumstances" in which she is "invested" completely encompass and efface any claim she might make to personhood.

In acting as the "noble" abolitionist, Alfred attempts to evacuate desire from his adoption of Loo Loo by evoking the moral duties of kinship as the ground for his actions. He effaces his autonomy, making himself into a passive object (she implored him; she was presented to his imagination). Alfred continually represses his own self-analysis — "he did not enter into any analysis of his motives"; his own feelings were "undefined to himself." Noble represses the knowledge of his own desires by suspending the temporality of their relation and sustaining the imaginary dyad of parent–child: "sometimes he felt sad to think that the time must come when she would cease to be a child, and when the quiet, simple relation now existing between them must necessarily change" (809). This fiction of a "simple relation" facilitates a vision of emancipation without changing the terms of social standing. Likewise, Loo Loo's uncertain kin status is linked to the question of freedom. When Alfred asks Loo Loo to be his wife, she responds "in the simplicity of her inexperience, and the confidence induced by long habits of familiar reliance upon him . . . 'I will be anything you wish'" (811). With this statement, "I will be anything you wish" and the idea that she was "completely satisfied with her condition," Loo Loo displays the gap between freedom as agency and the conditions that construct one's status (812). "I will be anything you wish" expresses her freedom of self-determination as consent. But her consent here is also uncertain because we do not know if it issues forth as an autonomous declaration of freedom or if it is an effect of her *lack* of autonomy. It binds her status to the desires of another, prompting questions about the conditions of "her condition."

The historical transition from slavery to freedom provoked a series of questions: whether freedom was to be substantiated at the level of contractual relations or to what degree it retained the legitimating force of social status; whether it could be divorced from social conditions or whether it needed certain social supports; and finally, what its minimal constraints and duties were.[30] The way in which Alfred and Loo Loo's relationship plays out the interrelations between kinship and citizenship prefigures this problem of situating the emancipated subject. The story is a divided one: it gives us a happy ending by imagining emancipation through, first, the act of interracial adoption, and, then, interracial marriage. At the same time, the story turns on Loo Loo's divided status, revealing not the opposition of the institutions of family and slavery but their problematic overlap: she is legally a slave, but also a daughter; she is informally adopted, but also a form of property; she is legally free, but dependent in fact. The narrative of adoption signals an anxiety at the heart of antebellum and postbellum visions of emancipation and liberal citizenship: Is there a citizenship without a kinship?

The status of the child is a perfect emblem for Child's meditations on emancipation and the conditions of kinship. On the one hand, the child is a figure for Noble's fantasy of emancipation as adoption, thus making freedom conditioned on dependency. But her narrative also shows how the figure of the child confuses the distinctions between dependence and independence, passivity and agency, on which our narratives of emancipation depend. Child exploits the figure of the innocent and seductive child to a different purpose: she crafts a narrative of adoption to reveal the difficulties in reconciling our conceptions of citizenship and freedom with our ideas of kinship and attachment. It is to this figure and its role in Child's children's literature that I now turn.

The Paradox of
Abolitionist Children's Literature

The unfolding of various registers of the adoption motif in Lydia Maria Child's children's literature reveals how narratives of freedom are predicated on familial frameworks of personhood. Analyzing Lydia Maria Child's use of interracial adoption in her children's literature adds to recent scholarship focusing on the centrality of figurations of the child for a host of political ideologies and constructions involved in nation-making and racialization.[31] Here we see the reliance of these discourses of freedom on the transformable figure of the child. At the intersection of children's literature and antislavery sentiment, the child is both the iconic figure for emancipation at the same time that it plays out the contradictions of freedom. It questions whether kinship is to be conceived as a contractual relation or one based on inherited status, and the implications for imagining citizenship. Further, it questions the grounds of emancipation itself. On the one hand, the kinship relation is made the basis for the construction of the "human." On the other hand, kinship itself has its norms and regulations, which treat persons as property and subject children to a necessity from which they are trying to free themselves.

The child plays several functions in abolitionist literature. For one, she often stands in for a common sense of humanity — those beings uncorrupted by politics or society who can actually be the agents of emancipation — unlike their parents or other adults who have been socialized by the institutions of slavery. As a famous dictum of the time put it, "children are all born abolitionists."[32] Second, they index the humanness of slaves as a kinship relation: as the object of suffering or unjust separation from others, the reader bonds sentimentally and empathically with the slave, investing in them human status. Philip Fisher, for example, argues not only for the importance

that the child plays as a mediating figure for the sentimentalization of the slave, but also the idea that the conferring of human
status "occurs particularly because the slave is met within the
family itself, within the realm of domestic feeling and intimacy
which are the primary spheres of sentimental experience."[33]
This sentimental device is consonant with humanitarian discourses at the time, and one of the effects is the location of
the human within the kinship relation. The child plays out both
functions — as the subject and agent of emancipation and as
the object of emancipation — through its embeddedness in
kinship relations. But we can already begin to see a difficulty
in the politics of emancipation: If slaves gain their humanness by being the object of sentimentality, by being the object
within a kinship relation, then how does the status of kinship
shape the terms of freedom?

Narratives of orphans and adoption highlight shifts in social
standing: prototypically, the orphan starts from nothing and
makes something of his life. Isaac Kramnick explains the
ubiquity of the orphan in children's literature in terms of
bourgeois individualism and the promotion of a middle-class
ethics of hard work: "Orphans allow a personalization of the
basic bourgeois assumption that the individual is on his or
her own, free from the weight of the past, from tradition,
from family... or their own fate [they are forced back on]
their own hard work, self-reliance, merit, and talent."[34] Child's
use of the [white] orphan figure certainly follows this pattern up to a point, but she also adds to it the element of
adoption, patronage, and reunion. Her story "The Industrious
Family" is a case in point, where Ellen, the eldest in a family of
orphans, works hard to support her brothers and sisters and is
rewarded by their adoption by a rich uncle.[35] Likewise her story
"The Orphans" is a classic rendition of two industrious, hard-
working orphans who in the end are reunited with their lost

brother.[36] Adoption works in these stories to reconcile bourgeois individualism ("the individual on his or her own") with genealogical attachment: their individualism becomes realized in social and political terms only when it is reattached to some form of kinship and the terms of its reproduction, succession, and inheritance. In this way, orphans "earn" their kinship status, which opens up the way to propertied citizenship.

This plot trajectory of a shift in status gets applied to antislavery fiction, but in ways that shape freedom in certain directions.[37] In "St. Domingo Orphans," two nameless white children are caught in the Santo Domingo slave uprising and become fugitives, alternately being hidden and housed by sympathetic blacks.[38] A perfidious white guardian, however, passes them off as mulattoes and sells them into slavery. These orphans are vulnerable to the extent that they are unattached to others who will keep them secure. In this melding of antislavery protest and children's literature, orphans are figures for slaves: nameless, without a patrimony, they are infinitely malleable to whoever gets their hands on them. The St. Domingo orphans become free only through the auspices of a dutiful parent/guardian. The child's innocence, need for care, and ambiguous status become vehicles for identification with the reader, and it is in this way that Child attempts to exercise the reader's sympathies against the institution of slavery. But the change in status from slave to free is mystified through the familial dynamics of separation and attachment. The logic of the story shows how these orphans were always free, but just needed the right guardian to ensure that status.

The plot device of orphaning and adoption by which antislavery sentiment is mobilized thus transforms the acts of slavery and emancipation into a sequence of separation and attachment: the separation from family as a result of slavery and then the recognition of the slave's humanity as part of a kinship relation. But this narrative logic begs the question of whether kinship constitutes the proper ethical relation to the exslave or whether it constitutes a status that is the condition of freedom. "Jumbo and Zairee" (1831), one of Child's earliest children's stories to attack slavery, displays these ambiguities. The story begins when a white man, Mr. Harris, is shipwrecked near the coast of Guinea and is nursed by Prince Yoloo "as if he had been his own son."[39] This act of kindness produces an attachment between Mr. Harris and Yoloo's two children, Jumbo and Zairee. And when Jumbo, Zairee, and Prince Yoloo end up as slaves in the United States, it is Mr. Harris who buys them and frees them, reciprocating the act of kindness he had received from Yoloo.

In this way, cross-racial adoptive bonds provide the ethical framework for freeing slaves. Being treated like a son or daughter is the impetus for reciprocating in kind; adoption models the golden rule: "Do unto others as you would have done unto you." Mr. Harris, upon his act of freeing the slaves, says, "Prince Yoloo, who treated me like a king in his own country, shall never labor for me. . . . I have tried to show my gratitude to the Negroes by being a kind master; but I am satisfied this is not all I ought to do. They ought to be free."[40] Prince Yoloo's actions compel upon Mr. Harris the need to show the like obligation to his slaves. It is through these contracts of dependency — Mr. Harris being dependent on Prince Yoloo's act of kindness — by which our unequal situations can be made free and equal. "Jumbo and Zairee" thus models these acts of reciprocation that dehierachize the relations between Mr. Harris and Prince Yoloo.

And yet within this form of emancipation as a reciprocal obligation between white and black peoples that seems to level status, there coexists a notion of inherent status as making one "worthy" of freedom. Mr. Harris is able to recognize Yoloo toiling in the fields after all those years only because he sees something of Yoloo's nobility in his actions. Status *produces* recognition, not the other way around; it is an inherent property of persons that allows the literary trope of recognition to work. The romantic racialism that ennobles Africans and that is a part of Child's romance cuts against the ethics of freedom and equality produced by adoption as a reciprocal act. This is emancipation as an act based on birthright. That adoption is itself somewhere in between status and ethical relation is portrayed in the metaphor of royalty used to characterize the reciprocal acts of kindness. Prince Yoloo takes a stranger into his house and treats him like "his own son," thus displaying his own kingly attributes. The narrator states: "The English king could not have treated a guest with more kindness and generosity." [41] This metaphor is reprised in Mr. Harris's emancipatory declaration: "Prince Yoloo, who treated me like a king in his own country." Instead of being an act that makes family into a set of obligations and duties, adoption reifies and reproduces hierarchical statuses that are metaphorized as royalty and aristocracy. While Child attacks the way in which the slave trade gives the lie to the republican proclamation of "all men are born free and equal," the question of emancipation is placed uneasily between the realm of status (recognition as birth and inheritance) and the realm of ethical relation (duties and obligations as the establishment of equality).

Conditions of Kinlessness

Abolitionist children's literature structures ideas of emancipation within a discourse of kinship that mystifies the change in status that is supposed to occur. If we take a look at the transition from slave narrative to autobiography — as Frederick Douglass's unique publication history allows us to do — we see how norms of kinship haunt the claims for personhood by emancipated persons. Douglass's critique of Lincoln's familial nation mentioned earlier calls attention to the particular conditions of kinship that undercut his vision of social belonging. The terms here — "step-child, children of adoption, children by circumstance and necessity" — point to the contingent place occupied by freed slaves: contingent both on the nation's projections of itself and on the rules and formation of kinship. Emancipation makes exslaves into dependents but not children, outside of the conventions of personhood performed through kinship. As Nancy Bentley remarks in her articulation of the condition of kinlessness as an effect of slavery, "being consigned to any degree of blackness meant having a more tenuous claim to the bonds of kinship."[42] Race operates in this way to attenuate the capacity of some people to claim others. It is this negotiation with the "claim to the bonds of kinship" that especially marks the narrations of personhood in Frederick Douglass's *My Bondage and My Freedom*. It is not that Douglass does not have kinship relations or the feelings of affection and loss that attend kinship. The terms of his narration suggest instead that he has no proper way to claim them, to make these affective and economic arrangements have social standing.

Scholars have identified slavery as the site for the complete deprivation of family ties — a definition made famous by Orlando Patterson's theory of slavery as social death. Slavery destroys the institution of kinship because, as Patterson writes, "total power or property in the slave means exclusion of the claims and power of others in him."[43] At the same time, others have revalorized the great strength and resolve of familial life within slavery — often by showing how slaves formed viable nuclear families.[44] Neither of these responses is surprising given the dual needs of understanding the deprivations to which slavery subjected African Americans and of affirming the humanity and legitimacy of African Americans during and after slavery. More recently, historians have provided a more nuanced picture by demonstrating the diversity of forms that organized family life that were neither simply monogamous and nuclear nor fragmented and pathological.[45] After emancipation, these forms struggle for legibility as a more restrictive notion of kinship sets the terms for the civic norms of personhood. The claims of others and one's attachments condition forms of personhood that are neither completely effaced by slavery nor fully guaranteed in freedom.

The shifts from Douglass's first autobiography, *Narrative of the Life of Frederick Douglass*, to his second, *My Bondage and My Freedom*, index the interrelations among kinship and citizenship. His first narrative is famously punctuated by the pivotal turning point: "You have seen how a man was made a slave; you shall see how a slave was made a man" (60).[46] But while those two categories dominate the first narrative, *My Bondage and My Freedom* introduces the category of the child, framing the narrative by creating a "childhood" where before there was only slavery. Instead of the stark division between slave and man, we now get a much fuzzier transition, asking the question of what emancipation means for the construction of a life history. Several critics have highlighted how Douglass's articulation of personhood in *My Bondage and My Freedom*, in contrast to the first narrative, is in dialogue with the efforts to claim kinship.[47] Building from these readings, I emphasize how kinship becomes a norm for the legibility of personhood that must be negotiated through the capacity to claim others and to be claimed. Kinship in Douglass's text is neither negated through social death nor repressed in the service of a purely abstract notion of freedom. Being a child becomes a site of individuation different from the slave but also not yet the individual subject of freedom, situating freedom within modalities of belonging.

In *My Bondage and My Freedom*, the child enters as a middle term within the binary of master and slave set up by the first narrative. In the first narrative, when Douglass is moved to Baltimore and meets Miss Sophia Auld, her kindness is framed in terms of the difficulty of acting like a slave: "My early instruction was all out of place. The crouching servility, usually so acceptable a quality in a slave, did not answer when manifested toward her" (37). But in *My Bondage and My Freedom,* his new status is clearly equated with the subject of the child: "I had been treated as a *pig* on the plantation; I was treated as a *child* now. . . . I therefore soon learned to regard her as something more akin to a mother, than a slaveholding mistress. The crouching servility of a slave, usually so acceptable a quality to the haughty slaveholder, was not understood nor desired by this gentle woman" (215). In the earlier narrative, the slave-slaveholder relationship predominates throughout, and he becomes a free man through overcoming the brutality of slavery. In *My Bondage and My Freedom,* Douglass inserts this adoptive mother–child relationship more explicitly, laying claim to a humanity that is embedded in kinship. Indeed, Douglass later measures the conditions of emancipation through the ties constructed within the Auld family:

> "Little Tommy" was no longer *little* Tommy; and I was not the slender lad who had left for the Eastern Shore just three years before. . . . He was no longer dependent on me for protection, but felt himself a *man* . . . but I, who had attended him seven years, and had watched over him with the care of a big brother, fighting his battles in the street, and shielding him from harm, to an extent which had induced his mother to say, "Oh! Tommy is always safe, when he is with Freddy," must be confined to a single condition. He could grow, and become a MAN; I could grow, though I could *not* become a man, but must remain, all my life, a minor — a mere boy. (328)

Unlike the first *Narrative,* this scene measures manhood and freedom within and against the status conferred by kinship.

Moreover, there is explicitly no relation between condition and status: the gap between his position as "big brother" and his confinement in a "single condition" is made clear. His growing does not amount to a becoming. At the same time that the child–mother relationship becomes the site for humanity, kinship relations simultaneously construct a division between the humanity within kinship and the citizenship of the public sphere.

In the famous "beating scenes," kin relations similarly become a site through which status is given and taken away. In addition to the beating of Esther, which is recounted in both narratives, we have the additional scene of Nelly's struggle in *My Bondage and My Freedom*. Unlike his Aunt Esther, whose sexual spectacle impresses him with the vulnerability of the child to slavery, Nelly fights back against Mr. Sevier with three of her children. Explaining her conduct, Douglass writes: "There is no doubt that Nelly felt herself superior, in some respects, to the slaves around her. She was a wife and a mother; her husband was a valued and favorite slave. . . . The overseer never was allowed to whip Harry; why then should he be allowed to whip Harry's wife?" (181). This narration of resistance based on the claims of others outside the master-slave relation prefigures Douglass's resistance of Covey. Whereas in the earlier autobiography, his resistance is seen against the backdrop of the negated body of Aunt Esther, here Nelly teaches him the lesson that "he is whipped oftenest, who is whipped easiest; and that slave who has the courage to stand up for himself against the overseer, although he may have many hard stripes at the first, becomes, in the end, a freeman, even though he sustain the formal relation of a slave" (182). In the passage recounting her beating, there is a grammatical move from "her [Nelly's] invincible spirit" to the slave as a generalized "he," and then back to Nelly. Douglass isolates the interiority by which he claims freedom apart from the "formal relation of a slave" by invoking the claims of kinship. The ties of kinship provide the terms by which he fashions his autonomy, thus distancing himself further from slavery as a merely "formal relation." [48] And yet the "beatings" are also ambiguous measures of personhood because of the uncertainty of kinship status. Douglass receives, he recounts, "a regular whipping from old master, such as any heedless and mischievous boy might get from his father" (206). At the same time, Douglass was treated affectionately, "Could the reader have seen him gently leading me by the hand . . . patting me on the head . . . and calling me his 'little Indian boy,' he would have deemed him . . . almost fatherly" (172). His personhood is suspended between a kin relation that cannot be claimed and an affective relation that gives him a sense of humanity and belonging.

The difference in genre between the earlier slave narrative and the second autobiography provides a key to understanding the relationship between kinship as a legitimating form of personhood and the narrative project of marking freedom. In the latter, Douglass begins his section on "Life as a Freeman" with an apology, saying that "There is nothing very striking or peculiar about my career as a freeman, when viewed apart from my life as a slave" (349). The narratability of his life as a freeman derives its justification from his life as a slave; freedom has meaning only in relation to slavery. But this condition of narration imposed by the slave narrative raises the risk that Douglass can never be "viewed apart from [his] life as a slave," that he cannot gain social standing without becoming a slave again. His autobiography becomes dependent on the slave narrative and the figure of the slave for its constitution. While slave narrative is built around animating the subject, making a claim to personhood based on its ability to affect the audience *as* a slave, autobiography makes a claim for citizenship by standing in relation to others. The prefatory remarks to each of the narratives are telling in this regard. William Lloyd Garrison, who provides the preface to the first narrative, emphasizes the voice of the slave and the cause of slavery, while James McCune Smith emphasizes Douglass's free-standing place in society as a function of kinship: he introduces Douglass as one who "in his every relation — as a public man, as a husband and as a father — is such as does honor to the land which gave him birth" (137).

But when *My Bondage and My Freedom* attempts to make claims for freedom apart from slavery, the problem of kinship emerges. For Douglass experiences his freedom as the condition of being orphaned again: "I was without home, without friends, without work, without money..." (351). He writes:

> Some apology can easily be made for the few slaves who have, after making good their escape, turned back to slavery, preferring the actual rule of their masters, to the life of loneliness, apprehension, hunger, and anxiety, which meets them on their first arrival in a free state. It is difficult for a freeman to enter into the feelings of such fugitives. He cannot see things in the same light with the slave, because he does not, and cannot, look from the same point from which the slave does. "Why do you tremble," he says to the slave — "you are in a free state"; but the difficulty is, in realizing that he is in a free state, the slave might reply... I was not only free from slavery, but I was free from home, as well. (352)

In negotiating the conditions of freedom, Douglass creates an ambivalent moment in the text. Douglass represents the direct speech of the "free man," but paraphrases the possible reply of the slave. The "I" that emerges between the freeman and the slave is suspended between the two: is the slave or the free man speaking? The articulation of freedom here is compromised by the inability to be situated in relation to "home."

Redefining Social Reproduction through Adoption

The problem of constituting what freedom *is* repeatedly returns to kinship. Each of the narratives above points to the negotiation of kinship practices in narrating individual freedoms and national belonging. One of the reasons why adoption is such a powerful metaphor for emancipation is that it potentially transforms the social status of personhood. This aspiration to revise the terms of personhood within the family and the state animates Harriet Beecher Stowe's and Child's uses of adoption in *Uncle Tom's Cabin* and *Romance of the Republic*. But while Stowe's model for adoption is one of religious conversion and the possibilities of transcending the problems of citizenship and slavery, Lydia Maria Child registers anxieties regarding emancipation and models of patriarchal authority. In both texts, narratives of emancipation run into the difficulties of reconceiving family. As has often been noted, Stowe articulates the question of emancipation through the dynamics of sentimentality and, in particular, sentimentalized interracial bonds. What interests me especially is the way in which one of the most central interracial relationships in the novel, that between Topsy and Miss Ophelia, constructs a narrative of emancipation as adoption.

Adoption here underscores the problem of the extendibility of the mother–child relationship, which underlies and haunts Stowe's construction of freedom. Miss Ophelia's relationship with Topsy is characterized by the civilizing and salvational ethic of adoption. Stowe's notion of adoption already prefigures the work that would be done later by adoption agencies, in which "rescue" and "salvation" would be the major narratives through which to understand the act of adoption. Topsy is given to Miss Ophelia as an experiment, and Miss Ophelia grows to love and take in the wayward girl. Topsy is

incorporated into the household and a domestic economy outside of the prerogatives of male desire and possession within
a masculine slave economy.[49] Ultimately, however, adoption
does not have as its end the construction of interracial families. Instead, it embodies a salvational narrative in which Topsy
both converts to Christianity and goes to Africa as a mission-
ary. While Topsy does manage to change Miss Ophelia's harsh
ways — thus reversing the direction of agency and transformation — she never gains social membership or standing in
the United States. Rather than intertwine racial and familial
feeling, the process of adoption through which Topsy is made
"good" both familiarizes the "very black" Topsy and makes her
out of place. As Gillian Brown notes, "blacks ultimately remain
outside the orbit of sentimental possession," and "being the
same color as one's owner or employer is in fact the condition
of sentimentalization and upward mobility in Stowe's economy of assimilation."[50] The sentimentalization of property
relations that repudiates and perfects the slave economy ultimately does not allow for the construction of an interracial
society. Women are the primary adoptive "parents," replacing
the market relations of master-slave in this domestic logic of
possession without desire.

But adoption is also not just a trope for a maternal ethic
of "owning," but for the production of maternal authority
itself. Indeed, adoption provides the model for how Stowe
constructs the relationship between the narrator and reader
as maternal identification. The common humanity and sympathetic identification shared between reader and narrator has the
mother–child bond as its foundation. When Stowe describes
Eliza's escape from the slave traders, the reader is made to identify with Eliza's situation through the child: "If it were *your*
Harry, mother, or your Willie, that were going to be torn from
you by a brutal trader. . . . How many miles could you make
in those few brief hours, with the darling at your bosom, —

the little sleepy head on your shoulder, — the small, soft arms trustingly holding on to your neck?"[51] The right of Eliza to run away hinges on the iconic status of the child, and it is secured through sympathetic familial bonds. What the reader identifies and sympathizes with is not Eliza herself, but the act of possession — "If it were *your* Harry." The child himself is substitutable ("Harry . . . or Willie") and finally transformed into parts ("the little sleepy head," "the small, soft arms") that signify complete dependence. The call of Stowe's narrator for empathy is thus an identification between narrator and character based on the act of possession. Sentimental feeling does not really have to cross racial boundaries in this conception. Instead, it engages in an imaginative act of substitution: one learns how to feel for others through the naturalness of our feelings for our own.

Rachel Halliday's home is perhaps the best example of how this heavenly matriarchy organizes all relationality around the mother. When Rachel takes Eliza into her home, she treats her like her own child and daughter. Stowe writes, " 'My daughter' came naturally from the lips of Rachel Halliday; for hers was just the face and form that made 'mother' seem the most natural word in the world."[52] The naturalness of this moment where a mother–daughter bond is forged between a white woman and a black woman hinges on the naturalness of being a "mother" and the spirit of that inclusiveness. The remaking of a mother–child bond along nonbiological lines reimagines the maternal as a transcendent ground for legitimating persons. In *The American Women's Home*, Catherine Beecher and Harriet Beecher Stowe imagine adoption as a way to secure the function of maternal authority without the prior authorization of natural arrangements or a patriarchal prerogative: "But a time is coming when the family state is to be honored and ennobled by single women . . . who will both support and train the children of their Lord and Master in the true style of

Protestant independence, controlled by no superior but Jesus Christ."[53] Adoption becomes a way for the mother to exercise authority that is independent of patriarchalism. Beecher and Stowe carve out a place for the single woman "controlled by no superior but Jesus Christ." Halliday's home models this combination of religious ideals and ethics of adoption in the construction of a "family state."

This model of adoption as religious conversion and the "family state" that it imagines is secure in the transformations that it enacts: Miss Ophelia is transformed from a cold, uptight spinster to a warm, mothering person, and Topsy is transformed from the incorrigible child to a good girl.[54] Child's more secular narrative of adoption is less sure about its transformative potential and what kinds of changes in status and personhood are occurring through the intersection of kinship and citizenship. For Child, the legal fiction of adoption leaves unclear the relationship between legally conferred rights and social status. As Carolyn Karcher notes in her biography of Child, Child's own relationships to others presented a mixture of the informal and the formal. She had longstanding friendships with Anna Loring and Susan Lyman, both of whom were proxies of a sort for Child's desire for a daughter.[55] She dedicated her collection of stories "Fact and Fiction" to Anna Loring as "child of her heart."[56] Child was not shy about the ambiguous status of adoption, either. She developed a relationship with a then-twenty-six-year-old John Hopper, whom she passed off as her adopted son. Their growing, illicit intimacy was unabashedly professed in the guise of a loving mother–adoptive son relationship.[57] The passing off of the risqué relations between a married woman and a man thirteen years her junior as an adoptive relation reveals the way in which adoption is used to manage the relationship between ambiguous affects and social norms. Adoption seems to raise the problem of what kind of legitimacy it constructs.

For Child, adoption is also a site where racial differences are negotiated, transacted, and transferred. It is, at one level, the site for the production of sameness. In a letter to Anna Loring on December 26, 1843, Child speaks of her "very happy Christmas," in which she cares for a vagabond off the street who "had neither father nor mother, and had lost his way" and for whom she eventually finds a home "in the country."[58] She documents how she reshapes the child, cutting his hair, cleaning him, and dressing him up. She also describes him as "nearly white, quite good looking, remarkably bright, and very docile and affectionate."[59] The connection to Christmas was no doubt a self-consciously made construction, positing her narrative alongside a narrative of religious salvation and rebirth. But her description of the child as "nearly white" evokes the ambiguous, in-between racial status of the orphan — often called "street arabs" — and Child's need to valorize a set of present descriptions ("quite good looking, remarkably bright, docile and affectionate") that take the place of the orphan's uncertain past. Her dream of remaking the child is part of this fantasy of adoption that replaces the history and social conditions of the child with his expressive "features."

At the same time that we get a fantasy of sameness being produced through this adoption scene, we also get a fantasy of difference. Here the past of the adoptee does not become erased so much as it becomes a site for the production of romance. Carolyn Karcher documents how Child takes a young Spanish woman named Dolores into her home and quickly identifies with her. Child relates her own Freudian "family romance" fantasy in relation to Dolores, telling her friend Lucy Osgood, "When I was quite a little girl, I remember imagining that gypsies had changed me from some other cradle, and put me in a place where I did not belong."[60] Imagining for herself a "foreign" birth and producing a fantasy of adoption, she identifies with Dolores, saying that because she "ought to have been a foreigner," she was "partial to the excessive warmth of foreigners."[61] Despite the fact that Dolores is not really an orphan (rather, she is a young woman fleeing from her husband in poverty), Child still thinks of her as such, writing to the Lorings, "I am not Quixotic about seeking for such occasions . . . but when God lays a forlorn fellow creature in my arms, and says, 'There! take her and warm her!' I cannot otherwise than do it."[62] For Child the adoptee raises the romance of history — another lineage that forms a crucial part of Child's national fantasy and a nostalgia for origins not her own. Here her self-proclaimed duty in the face of another's helplessness hinges on fantasies of national difference and the "excessive warmth" of the foreign other.

Desire is transformed into sacred duty and necessity in this act of adoption, and it is this "duty" toward others that plays a central role in Child's formulation of a national vision of adoption. Adoption in this sense fits with a sentimentalism that emphasizes familial love within a broader discourse about moral and national responsibility.[63] This is similar to Stowe's ethic, in which familial discourse is made into the religiously transcendent form of feeling for racial others. But as we have seen from "Loo Loo" and the other intersections between kinship and citizenship that we have traced, adoption raises the uncertain relation between affective states and legal statuses that problematize easy familial–national narratives. *Romance of the Republic,* published in 1867, strives to enact a familial–national narrative that both heals the nation after the Civil War and reminds the nation of its slave past. It repeats the adoption story of "Loo Loo" and expands it in order to construct a narrative of a multiracial nation. But in doing so, it highlights particular narrative and representational crises around what kinds of "naturalization" and citizenship could be imagined for former slaves. It shows how she simultaneously attempts to critique and identify with paternalism; how a fantasy of the adopted child both underlies and unsettles her imagination of the newly emancipated subject; and how she struggles to create a genealogical form for the nation even as she tries to revise the very terms of genealogical reproduction.

Romance of the Republic begins with virtually the same scene of fantasy as "Loo Loo" does, except that each of the two protagonists from "Loo Loo" are divided. The tension between sexual desire and the desire to do good in Alfred Noble becomes split in the novel into the more principled Alfred King and the dissolute Gerald Fitzgerald in *Romance of the Republic*. Likewise, the character Loo Loo gets split into the more childlike and dependent Flora and her older sister, the more mature and independent Rosa. This division thus resolves some of the ambivalences *within* each of the characters that plagued the narrative trajectory of "Loo Loo." Both sisters are adopted in ways that displace Child's anxieties about paternalism. Flora is adopted by an independently wealthy woman named Mrs. Delano and subsequently marries Blumenthal; Rosa is adopted by a family friend, Signor Balbino, and subsequently marries Alfred King, a good family friend of her father. Both this adoption and her marriage are defined in explicit contrast to the seductions and desire of Gerald Fitzgerald, who had married Rosa in a sham marriage, fathered an illegitimate son, and sold her. Indeed, when Signor Balbino confronts the deceiving Gerald Fitzgerald, he orders him out of the room, saying — "I am her adopted father . . . and no man shall insult her while I am alive." [64] Gerald responds assuming that the term "adopted father" is just a screen for the exercise of patriarchal desire under slave law: "So *you* are installed as her protector! . . . You are not the first gallant I have known to screen himself behind his years" (236). But this sends Signor Balbino into a rage, for his claim on Rosa is strictly a matter of "familial" honor and duty, and it is associated with the rights of the household.

Thus, whereas in "Loo Loo" interracial adoption and marriage repeat the imaginary "capture" of the "freed" subject in a series of seduction scenes, both of the sisters' adoptions and marriages in *Romance of the Republic* evolve distanced from the scene of desire and seduction that opens the novel. Their marriages are based on duty and platonic, brotherly love, whereby duty and desire are reconciled. Indeed, in this sense, the bonds of adoption are combined with the bonds of marriage in order to reconstruct intergenerational bonds along a different set of ethics. As Child writes, "At the time of [Flora's] marriage, Mrs. Delano said she was willing to adopt a son, but not to part with a daughter; consequently, they formed one household" (286). National bonds of obligation, duty, and reciprocity are modeled on familial bonds in which the affection of adoption transforms families formed through marriage. Child does away with the problem of sexual desire as patriarchal prerogative that haunts Alfred Noble's fantasy of Loo Loo, separating it from the ethics of duties and obligations.

Adoption thus provides a kind of ballast against the vagaries and abuse of biological and sexual reproduction. It is a form of legitimation that corrects against the racialization of illegitimacy under slave law. It is also a mode of transforming persons. This is seen most clearly in the tangled plot-line of Gerald Fitzgerald, which speaks to the legacy of sexual reproduction under slave law that Child both critiques and transforms. Fitzgerald fathers two sons — one born a slave by virtue of his mother, Rosa; the other born a gentleman because of his "legitimate" birth through the white Northerner, Lily Bell. They both carry the same name and look exactly alike but have vastly different statuses due to the convolutions of slavery and kinship. Moreover, Rosa switches them in their infancy, such that her son is bred as a gentleman while Lily Bell's son is raised as a slave. As Shirley Samuels argues, these two half-brothers reveal the dislocations of identity under slavery, the ambiguity of locating identity either through the body ("skin" and "blood") or as transcending the body: "The surface does not indicate — for either son — what status they have as subjects of the republic."[65] The real danger of this mode of reproduction for Child is that it leaves social status arbitrary and gives sexual procreation power over legitimation and delegitimation. As Samuels suggests, "as the novel imaginatively traces the consequences of Southern amalgamation, not knowing the difference becomes both a familial and a national issue."[66]

What I would like to add is that adoption emerges for both sons as a possible mode of stabilizing and reproducing personhood, correcting against these dislocations. Both sons are offered up as potential adoptees for Alfred King as a way of transforming them. After Gerald learns that he is in fact Rosa's biological son and was born a slave, he states, "My prevailing wish now is to obtain an independent position by my own exertions, and thus be free to become familiar with my new self. At present, I feel as if there were two of me, and that one was an imposter" (380). Mr. King praises him for these plans, saying: "I will gladly assist you to accomplish it. I have already said you should be to me as a son, and I stand by my word; but I advise you, as I would an own son, to devote yourself assiduously to some business, profession, or art" (380–81). Likewise, when Alfred meets the other of Fitzgerald's sons who was raised in slavery, he makes plans for him, takes a "lively interest in him," and remarks, "His resemblance to poor Gerald is remarkable . . . there was no obvious stamp of vulgarity upon him. It struck me that his transformation into a gentleman would be an easy process" (413). For both, they move from a condition of divided identity associated with the ties to slavery to a new place in social reproduction predicated on the transformation of status through others' dutiful actions. They are both presented as a kind of blank slate on which Alfred can work.

Child constructs the historical continuity between the slave past and the period of Reconstruction through the generational saga of the breakup and reunion of families. In doing so, she seeks to both remember the past and reconstruct national unity through the trope of family.[67] At the end of the novel, the form of family includes parent–child relationships formed through adoption and/or benevolent patronage as well as biological relationships, producing ties of obligation, dependency, and care between members of different races, and creating "legitimate" ties where slave laws would have forbidden such ties.[68] But this remaking of the family along modes of reproduction divorced from the daemonic desires of kinship within slave law quickly breaks down as Child reinvests in the genealogical form of the nation. The break in the novel between parts 1 and 2 is symptomatic of this uneasy reconciliation. In the second half of the novel, generational biological continuity returns to naturalize the family as based in likeness. Indeed, the children of Flora's and Rosa's marriages literally reproduce previous generations: Flora and her husband name their eldest son Alfred Royal, who "was a complete reproduction . . . of the grandfather whose name he bore" (286). They also name their eldest daughter Rosa, who "was quite as striking a likeness of her namesake" (286). The social convention of naming matches biological reproduction in order to reaffirm continuity along these "natural" lines. Moreover, the meanings of adoption are reworked in service of this form of social reproduction. The biological sons and daughters of Rosa's and Flora's marriages are constructed as if they were adopted, for the information of their ancestry and their family history are hidden from them. Race, slavery, and the problems of emancipation are deleted from the family history told to the children,

and instead they are given a "family romance" of Spanish origins. This transposition from "race" to "national origin" is an
important imaginative displacement. By placing the emphasis
on "foreigners," Child reframes the issue of racial belonging
in terms of mixing national differences. "Colored ancestry"
is expunged from family history in order not to impress the
customs and experiences of slavery upon young, fragile, and
innocent minds. Strangely, while the direction of the novel as
a whole seems to be in reencountering history and understanding the failure of the present moment of reconstruction in light
of the failure to remember the past of slavery, history at the
level of familial reproduction is repressed and erased.

The end of Child's novel is marked by the end of the Civil
War and an exuberant familial and national reunion as "All
the family, of all ages and colors...joined in singing 'The
Star-Spangled Banner'" (441). The reunion of the nation is
imagined in terms of the reunion of family, and it signals
Child's vision for a reconstructed America based on interracial families — divorced, as we have seen, from the history
of Southern racial amalgamation and its illicit desires. Her
utopian ideal of the interracial family as the solution for
the problems of race prejudice and oppression breaks many
of the prohibitions that construct familial "legitimacy." The
end of her novel brings together three generations of family
members connected through racial mixture, adoption, and
incest. Indeed, in a reversal of legal prohibitions that link
together miscegenation and incest in their "unnaturalness,"
the difference that miscegenation creates offsets the dangerous
sameness of incest.[69] As Florimond Blumenthal, the husband
of the octoroon protagonist, Flora, states while contemplating cross-cousin marriage: "nations and races have been pretty
thoroughly mixed up in the ancestry of our children. What
with African and French, Spanish, American, and German, I

think the dangers of too close relationship are safely diminished" (432). Here it is imagined that national differences will offset the "dangers of too close relationship," paradoxically allowing for incest. Child's vision of national and racial harmony relies on denaturalizing the way that the institution of family has produced the terms of legitimacy.

At the same time, the reidealization of family here suffers from the amnesia concerning the role of race in our formations of citizenship and kinship that it seems to be arguing against. The final vision of "family" is strangely reproductive of the initial vision of "family" that we get, which critiques the conflation of family and slavery. "What a polyglot family we are! as *cher papa* used to say," Flora exclaims, explicitly linking the final formation of family to the mixed-race family that begins this romance of the republic (432). The similarities give us pause. In the beginning of the novel, Flora and Rosa were unaware of their mother's slave status and thus did not know about their own uncertain social status. At the end of the novel, their children are raised unaware of their racial histories that went into the making of the republic. Memories of the mutually constitutive relation between race and kinship for the purposes of delegitimation are erased in the service of the transformation of personhood. Child replaces one mode of disavowing race for another.

Incomplete Citizenship

In order to grasp the meaning of emancipation and its impact on constructions of personhood for exslaves, Douglass, Stowe, and Child envision various ways of transforming one's social standing in relation to others. As such, they negotiate the particular interrelations of kinship bonds and formations of citizenship through exploring the various ways in which persons can claim others and be claimed. Douglass registers the lack of home that renders his newfound freedom incomplete; he struggles to construct a narrative of individuation and a trajectory from childhood to adulthood that does not bear the delegitimizing effects of slavery and racism on social relationality. Stowe explores the act of conversion, a transformation of both the emancipator and the emancipated within the terms of a maternal ethic. Child gives us the most ambiguous vision: on one level the aspiration to remake our familial bonds through adoption, amalgamation, and incest, and on another level a strict adherence to the legitimating terms of heritage and continuity at the expense of history and memory.

The appropriation of the terms of citizenship within the form of the parent–child bond can be seen most clearly in Lydia Maria Child's edited volume *The Freedmen's Book*, published in 1865, which was a treatise meant to aid the emancipation and education of the recently freed slaves. In light of the previous discussion, we could read this text as Child's attempt to supply the place of the father and mother to the newly freed slaves. Interspersed throughout this collection of biographies of great black men and women, poetry, sermons, and addresses contributed by several different authors, are Child's paternalist and maternalist pieces of advice on becoming free. In pieces like "The Education of Children" or "Advice from an Old Friend" or "The Laws of Health," Lydia Maria Child emphasizes the conditions and expectations, not the status, of freedom; here freedom is mainly a matter of becoming proper parents and children. In the same collection, Frederick Douglass contributes a short paragraph that could be read as an implicit critique of Child's construction of the emancipated subject. In "A Pertinent Question," Douglass lists off a whole range of ways in which black men and women have already occupied social positions and occupations, and asks, "Is it not astonishing, that while we are ploughing, planting, and reaping . . . acting as clerks, merchants, and secretaries . . . living

in families as husbands, wives, and children . . . is it not astonishing, I say, that we are called upon to prove that we are
men?" [70] The formation of citizenship as social standing relies
on and is shaped by narratives of individuation. Working
within a context of liberal individualism that relies on the
nation–family dyad to negotiate problems of defining citizenship, both Child and Douglass register modes of personhood
based on dependency and attachment that remain invisible
within and yet indispensable to conceptions of freedom. As
constructions of adoption develop and continue to revise the
nature of the parent–child bond, these questions around individuation will reemerge. They do so during the retrenchment
of racial divisions that shape the terms of individuality in the
early twentieth century.

3

THE CHARACTER OF RACE
Individuation and
the Institutionalization of Adoption

Am I not still a Negro?[1]
— Charles Chesnutt, *The Quarry*

If I'm not, damned if I haven't wasted a lot of time.[2]
— William Faulkner, *Light in August*

Though William Faulkner and Charles Chesnutt are not known for engaging with the social history of adoption, both authors describe adoption procedures in their fiction at a time when adoption was just starting to develop as a prevalent institutional practice. Moreover, they specifically address the intersection of adoption and racial formations. Donald Glover asks in Chesnutt's *The Quarry*, "Am I not still a Negro?" when he finds out about his adoption; Joe Christmas's famous line about the possibility of being part-Negro in Faulkner's *Light in August* — "If I'm not, damned if I haven't wasted a lot of time" — follows his admission that he does not know who his biological parents are. Both novels dramatize the anxieties of racial individuation — how race affects the process of becoming a separate and undivided entity — through their adopted characters.[3] These quotes use the fact of adoption to ironize the assumption that racial identification is permanent and unchanging. Here racial identification is not solely a process of learning racial meanings materialized on the body and in the world. It may change from one moment to the next because it is contingent on to whom one is attached and how one relates to another. In

85

Chesnutt's novel, race may change depending on who adopts. In Faulkner's novel, Christmas's disclosure of racial identification is partly constructed through others' anxieties about race and partly constructed through his own fantasies, blurring the distinctions between one and another.

These works do not simply use adoption as a meditation on the fluidity or arbitrary construction of racial classifications. Rather, they index a particular shift in the history of adoption practices and the intertwining of adoption and race in the early twentieth century. We have already seen how the social imagination of adoption operated in conjunction with the racialization of the parent–child relationship to manage issues of legal and national personhood — both through the dynamics of genealogy and substitution in the case of Native American adoptions and through the formations of citizenship and freedom in the case of exslaves. The uncertainty of adoption in which modes of constructing genealogy, affect, and property threaten "legitimate" kinship practices becomes a particularly anxious site for the construction of personhood within a familial nation-form. In order to fully understand the adoption scenarios in this chapter, I look to the institutionalization of adoption in the early twentieth century, which is littered with anxieties about how to locate race. These anxieties regarding the intrusion of racial difference into the "home," into what is one's own, are manifested in social worker manuals, notes from adoption placements, and social discourse justifying and codifying early twentieth-century adoption practices. Moreover, they index larger questions about personhood and racial identification: How does one emerge as an individual when you cannot take for granted the continuity and background of a single identity? Why do racial and religious backgrounds become the primary sites for these anxieties of individuation and family relationships? Through adoption practices, racial difference appears not just in civilizational or hierarchical terms, but as a norm that manages and produces the integrity and unity of persons in relation to anxieties about racial boundaries.

In describing racial difference as a norm, I utilize a notion of norms not as a fixed, static ideal or model that individuals are coerced into approximating, but rather as a range, a flexible and changing set of ways to valorize specific objects in relation to each other. As Judith Butler writes, "The norm governs intel-. ligibility, allows for certain kinds of practices and action to become recognizable as such, imposing a grid of legibility on the social and defining the parameters of what will and will not appear within the domain of the social."[4] In this sense, a norm is not a set of rules, but the background that produces them and regulates how they relate to any given context.[5] It produces the field of possibilities "actively confer[ring] reality."[6] Situating my analysis within anxieties about normalizing relationships is a departure from customary ways of reading racial personhood in these novels through the theme of racial passing, the phenomenon of light-skinned black persons who hide their racial origin and pass as white in society.[7] Analyses of passing reveal race as a construct,[8] even as they frame the problem of racial identity in terms of an individual choice to be black or white.[9] They privilege racial identity as a problem of being true to yourself, because to pass within this tradition of scholarship presumes that you are passing as something that you are not. Despite exploring how race operates as a fiction, then, analyses of passing often still operate within an ethics of individual choice guided by binary assumptions of true or false identity, a drama of loyalty or betrayal. As Philip Brian Harper writes, passing "depends on precisely the binary structure of black/white racial difference whose constructed character the practice of passing is itself meant to reveal."[10]

The theme of passing as applied to these novels thus limits our analyses of race because it misses how race is constituted through producing the particular form of our social relation-ships. My analysis of adoption and racial individuation shifts the scene of racial identity from individual choice to the artic-ulation of race as an effect of negotiating one's dependencies, attachments, and identifications to others. In this way, race is conceptualized as a set of normalized knowledges about proper relationships. Several theorists have questioned dom-inant critical frameworks that theorize race principally as a sociological category that is imposed on subjects by adding the conceptual lenses of psychoanalysis, affect, and normativ-ity.[11] Peter Coviello nicely sums up the dangers of an overly determined paradigm of conflict between social structures of racism (specifically as oppression, denigration, hatred) and sub-jective processes: "To presume... that persons are not so much inflected by social contestation as situated, or given being, by their social position is to adopt the vantage of power as though it were comprehensive, or true."[12] To assume this kind of sub-ject is to ignore racial dynamics at the level of coexistence, on the dimensions of race operating through our attachments between persons, the forms of relationality that are mediated by racial norms. This framework focuses on the relationship between the process of individuation — how one separates from another and becomes a unified individual even as one is bound up with another[13] — and the negotiation of race relations through proximity and closeness.

In the following, I analyze how adoption practices in the early twentieth century do not so much take race as a given as they produce racial difference as a way to construct the proper boundaries for how one relates to another and to guard against how one person might affect another. I then show how this model of racial dynamics unfolded through adoption provides a lens for rereading the literary works with which I began. As we will see, rather than exemplifying racial identity as an indi-vidual characteristic or even personal choice (passing), these adopted characters represent the relational dimensions of racial subjectivity as a negotiation of the social and psychic bonds between persons.

The Registers of Race in Adoption

In the mid- to late nineteenth century, "placing out" was an important precursor to the modern institution of adoption. This form of child transfer was not so much about creating adoptive families as we understand them today. Rather, the goals of these transfers were a mixture of apprenticeship and social reform. The orphan trains are the most famous large-scale movement in this history of "placing out," a system that "emigrated" thousands of orphans from the cities to the country, often taking children from poor, immigrant, Catholic families and giving them to Protestant families in the Midwest.[14] Led by Charles Loring Brace, who founded the Children's Aid Society in the 1850s, these groups "emphasized religious training"[15] and preached work, discipline, and self-help. They employed a rhetoric that treated orphans as goods, property, and as children of sin needing to be reformed. These orphans were demanded for their agricultural labor and were consequently often mistreated and abused. These practices articulated the racial identities of poor Irish and Italian immigrants, blacks and Polish inconsistently and in conjunction with "economic markings of rank" and other descriptions in order to "classify status."[16] For Brace, adoption was primarily a form of conversion.

As adoption became defined through different institutional practices and met up with regional and national sensibilities, race is marked, highlighted, and conceptualized in different ways. Linda Gordon narrates a fascinating clash between two distinct sensibilities toward adoption, each of which defined race in distinct ways. In *The Great Arizona Orphan Abduction*, she tells the story of a group of nuns heading a Catholic orphanage that placed forty Irish orphans with Mexican Catholic parents in a small Arizona mining town. In the eyes of the nuns, the religion of the adoptive parents in the service of a narrative of conversion mattered, and the racial backgrounds of either parents or children were less important. This event however caused an uproar among the white townspeople, who kidnapped the orphans from their Mexican adoptive families and fought legal battles in order to keep them. Here the nuns' assumptions about race and religion in their adoption procedures encountered and were transformed by the local construction of racial borders in Clifton, Arizona. The Supreme Court ultimately decided in favor of the white foster parents who took the children away from their Mexican families. This is not simply a case of one monolithic racial sensibility against an equally monolithic religious sensibility. As Gordon recounts the media coverage and court proceedings, a fluid set of dynamics ensues whereby the competing groups — the New York nuns, the Clifton Mexicans, and the Clifton Anglos — position themselves within and against different racial and religious identifications: "Two of the groups were united by religion, two of the groups by 'race.' But they did not all recognize the alignments." [17] The Catholic nuns were primarily interested in the religious identification of the parents and thus did not necessarily align themselves with the white Anglos from Clifton; the white Anglos did not understand the problems of religious transmission with which the nuns were preoccupied and they denigrated the New York Catholic formation of whiteness that the nuns represented to them; the Mexican women had a different understanding of racial classifications — for them, the children were not simply "white" but were rather light-skinned or fair, a measure of status but not necessarily of a hard division between groups.

Indeed, it is the contingent securing and reproduction of racial identifications that is exemplified through the question of adoption rather than the given-ness of racial categories. In the trial, the argument in favor of the Anglos to have custody of the children relied on a vilification of Mexicans as improper parents to white children: Mexicans in this argument were uncivilized, poor, and uneducated. Much of the witness testimony in favor of the Clifton Anglos attempted to secure this identification of both the Mexicans' character and the whiteness of the children. The argument against the Clifton Anglos, on the other hand, attempted to reformulate the "whiteness" of the children by associating them with the stigma of illegitimate birth, a stigma that is better, it was argued, hidden in the lives and homes of the Clifton Mexicans. Whiteness is negotiated here not just through a highlighting of the children's bodily features, but through several intertwined and contested elements: a politics of citizenship located in the specific history of Arizona; a discourse against New York Catholicism; the politics regarding the stigma of illegitimacy; and the Clifton Mexicans' conceptions of race.

This case is a precursor to the intertwined formations of adoption and race in the beginning of the twentieth century because it shows the ways in which the practice of adoption becomes more oriented around shaping the relationship between norms of familial belonging and conditions of racial individuation. As adoption becomes a public, state-regulated institution explicitly aimed at family-making in the 1910s and 1920s, it more self-consciously produces the norms by which individual lives are cultivated, shaped, and made into proper persons. The shift toward state and federal involvement in the construction of adoption was in part a reaction to the often unregulated practices by evangelical reformers and religious institutions mentioned earlier. The modern twentieth-century institution of adoption was constructed in the context of Progressive reform, changing conceptions of motherhood and children, and the developing social science with regard to families and children.[18] Social work agencies armed themselves with the expertise of social science on issues of heredity, the impact of the environment, and child care in order to justify their work in deciding which babies fit with which families and in ensuring that the parents were fit and proper.

This social science of constructing "fit and proper" families relied on a tremendous production of knowledge about the mental, emotional, and physical fitness of both prospective adoptive parents and potential adopted children. As Barbara Melosh notes, "'Fit' was professional shorthand for the goal of matching — through the skilled application of expert knowledge, social workers would design an adoptive family whose members would flourish together."[19] Adoption becomes the site of what Foucault has called "bio-power": "the right to intervene to make live...a power that has taken control of ...life in general," or as Ann Stoler translates, "the right to intervene...in the manner of living, in 'how' to live."[20] Social workers self-consciously exercised a tremendous amount of power and knowledge over the manner of living and the raising of children — how to live the proper, normal life. One caseworker calls it "playing God."[21] Sophie van Senden Theis's placement guide, which became a standard for the field after its publication in 1921, calls for a "keen, close, and unprejudiced observation" of an applicant, arguing that it is "more important to know of a woman that she is easy going and indecisive than that she is a careless housekeeper. A child may grow up to be a satisfactory citizen in an untidy household...but he has a poor chance of it if his foster mother changes her mind about what he must or must not do every day or so."[22] The exacting standards held by adoption professionals reaches into the motives and interior selves of both prospective adopters and potential adoptees. A sense of this regulatory power is captured in Irene Josselyn's assessment of what a child-conscious adoptive process should look at as opposed to earlier adoption practices:

> From the standpoint of the child, his needs were considered met, according to the policy of certain adoptive agencies, if the adoptive parents were of the proper religious faith and attended church. The meaning of their religion *in their actual living* was not explored.... Children require real parents, not stylized ones. To provide real parents, the adults seeking a child to adopt must be first appraised as real people with a recognition of the probability of their having the psychological needs, potentialities and limitations inherent in human beings. The *total personality* of the adults should be explored, and *only then* the evaluation made as to how that total personality will function in the role of a parent in relationship to a child (emphasis added).[23]

Not only should the parents' religion be known, but how that religion translates to their conditions of living should be investigated. This process seeks to capture nothing less than a holistic understanding of the adult and their modes and manners of living.

This process of shaping the integrity of children's and parents' relations is never free from anxieties about racial difference, framed as fears of unknown heredity — the baby's unknown "stock" or "background." Workers gathered "every scrap of significant information about his family" in the quest for a complete background of the child.[24] A questionable heredity or strange behavior could render a child "unadoptable."[25] Racism here emerges as a matter of degeneracy derived from discourses of social Darwinism.[26] In "The Illinois Adoption Law and Its Administration" (1928), Elinor Nims bemoans the lack of proper prohibition against transracial adoptions. She writes: "It is rather startling to discover that one judge considered the matter of race as of no account and would not make it a question of investigation."[27] She points to a case in 1924—very similar to that depicted in Chesnutt's novel—in which the adoptive mother, Mrs. Dunn, "returned the child to the hospital saying that her friends thought the baby was of negro blood. The management then got in touch with the mother, who admitted that the father was a colored man. The baby was then placed with Mr. and Mrs. Morton, a colored family."[28] Nims remarks that this case "is a striking illustration of the necessity for a careful inquiry . . . into the social and medical history of the child."[29] Likewise, Melosh notes a 1938 case record in which the "prospective adopters repeatedly raised concerns about 'colored blood.' They told their social worker that they knew of a white adoptive mother whose baby had turned out to have 'definite Negroid characteristics.'"[30] But these examples do not simply exhibit a fear of racial mixing or the need to uphold racial separation. Rather, they express a more generalized anxiety of what is "inside" the child—some latent, prior "trait" that will come out only later. The child becomes subject to competing projections and desires, highlighting processes of racial identification—in both the sense of identifying someone *as* "x" and identifying *with* someone—as an effect of anxieties over transmission.

Adoption practices thus produce the norms for who can relate to whom and for the conditions of individuation by regulating the identifications between parent and child. The policy of matching encapsulates this production of race as a negotiation of projections. It developed as a practice of placing children with parents based on similarities in race, religion, intelligence, personality, temperament, and a host of other factors. The idea behind matching is to construct the adoptive family "as if" it were biological, using likeness to sustain identification and deny difference within the family. As Ellen Herman puts it, "[modern] adoption has relied on the paradoxical theory that differences are managed best by denying their existence."[31] A closer look at practices of matching helps us see how race is articulated not as a social category and static given that is imposed on individuals, but rather produced through the interplay of projections among social workers. Far from denying the existence of racial difference, "matching" reproduced it as a condition of the child's potential individuation.

For example, a glance at a list of traits used as the bases for matching — everything from the supposedly empirical traits such as racial and religious background to less definable traits such as temperament, intelligence, and personality[32] — reveals the immaterial, projective quality of the traits in question. The listing of traits seems to suggest an ideal whereby these empirical and specific traits are supposed to add up to some kind of identification between parent and child. There is an odd tension in this list between the single trait and the long list of traits, begging the question: How many traits are needed to make a match? This process seems to suggest both that the whole (person) is simply the sum of these parts *and* that persons are synecdoches for a single trait. And yet the sheer proliferation of factors only highlights the impossibility that these traits could add up to any one thing. Matching is not a purely empirical process, but rather one that often calls upon narrative imagination in order to fill in the gaps. One social worker, for example, highlights her own narrative expectations in stating that she "believed that . . . applicants were not 'unreasonable or neurotic in requesting a child whose intelligence is in the superior group and whose background does not read like a story of William Faulkner's."[33] The fact that race and religion are singled out as more important than other traits suggests how crucial they have become for linking specific conditions of individuation with norms of familial and individual integrity.

It was often the case that orphaned children's parentages were unknown. Placing such children involved social workers, parents, and children themselves in a drama of locating race through how one relates to another. One case detailed by Barbara Melosh exemplifies how race and religion are not so much perceived as they are projected into a narrative that produces the conditions for proper individuation through a regulation of the parent–child relationship. In deciding on the proper placement for a particular child, a social worker and nurse alternate between speculations about the mother and then about the child:

> Anyone familiar with the Moors might recognize her [the mother] as Moorish...but otherwise I suspect that she would pass readily as Caucasian.... Both nurse and I feel we would think he [the child] was completely Caucasian if we did not know his mother is a Moor. Knowing this, however, there may be something just a little "different" about his nose and he has an abundance of thick straight black hair which stands out in all directions.[34]

What is most striking about these statements is the continual oscillation between the visible and invisible, the known and the unknown. What is perceived becomes the basis for seeing the child as "Moorish" ("Knowing this, however, there may be something just a little different...") at the same time that some "certain" knowledge is the basis for producing more perceptions: "Anyone familiar with the Moors might recognize her as Moorish." In other words, Moorishness is produced as both cause and effect. It functions as the unified background accounting for any and all perceptions with which it can be connected — even one as random as an "abundance of thick straight black hair which stands out in all directions." In the quest to fully know the child's background, whole ancestries and histories are constructed based on an upturned lip or a darker shade, and a fragment of biography or gossip make a feature visible. Racism has become a mode of thought that embodies, as Étienne Balibar puts it, "a very insistent *desire for knowledge*" that is "a way of asking questions about *who* you are in a certain social world."[35]

I have considered how the anxieties of adoption as a form of bio-power and regulation are projected onto the child, thus reproducing racial and religious identification as conditions of individuation. But what are the implications of this process for the object of anxiety — the adoptee's own subjectivity? How do children understand themselves in relation to this projective anxiety and insistent "desire for knowledge"? The anxiety of what is "inside" is shared by both adopter and adopted alike. This aspect of projection as part of the *relationship* between two subjects is illustrated by the example of a child who acts within the other's projection. Berebitsky recounts a 1901 case in which an adopted twelve-year-old child, Allen Rogers, shocks his adoptive parents by immediately telling them that "his mother was dead . . . that he had a colored brother[;] that his mother had this boy by a black man [and] he didn't seem to think there was anything wrong about it."[36] Supposing "everything was spoiled," the adoptive mother, Mrs. Widman, nevertheless "calmed her husband by telling him that 'no doubt Allen has misrepresented his mother. . . . I supposed she had a little colored fellow around the house and he thought it was a brother'"; she "admonished her children" — "if we ever heard another word we would punish them severely."[37] Though the boy's statements do not mean that he is black, Mrs. Widman takes this anecdote as if it spoils who he is in relation to her. She reacts to an anxiety about transmission and the fact that there is something prior that might impinge on her capacity to sustain an identification with her adopted child that hinges on race. The repression of any other "word" of the boy's history is the attempt to preserve the mother's identification of the child as something unspoiled, an identification that the child's own projection threatens by reopening the anxiety regarding the ever-present question: "How can we know?"

Psychoanalytically informed work on racial formation has often focused on processes of identification rather than projection, because projection is thought simply to be the imposition of racist images onto persons and not constitutive of how subjects themselves might negotiate forms of racialization. But projection has often been a part of definitions of identification in theorists who pay close attention to ego-formation as an effect of relating to objects. Klein's concept of projective identification encompasses the interrelations between projection and identification. As Hanna Segal puts it: "Projective identification is the result of the projection of parts of the self into an object. It may result in the object being perceived as having acquired the characteristics of the projected part of the self but it can also result in the self becoming identified with the object of its projection." [38] To illustrate: projection of the parent's fears of bad heredity identify the child as exhibiting bad heredity. But the child's response may also result in the projection's return such that the parent identifies *with* the fear of bad heredity that she had tried to expel. In her analysis of various adoption case studies, Helene Deutsch puts her finger on this interaction: "[The adoptive mother] does not realize that it is only her fantasy that leads her to interpret the child's behavior, under the magnifying glass of her fears, as a manifestation of bad heredity. Actually this behavior is mobilized in the child by the suggestive force of her suspicion, and he is driven by that force to a kind of compulsive acting out." [39] The parent's interpretation and identification of the child is marked by her projection; the child lives within that projection and acts out in response to it. As such, projection marks the constant traffic between inside and outside, between our projection of some part of ourselves onto that object and feelings of being intruded on by the projection's return. As in the example above, Mrs. Widman fills in the gap of what the boy does not say; she identifies the boy as a threat to herself through her projection of her anxiety onto the boy.

This understanding of identification as inextricable from the dynamics of projection enables us to analyze the interactions between adopter and adoptee as they negotiate anxieties over the indeterminate knowledge of one's race. By tracing this circuit of projection and identification, we see how race is negotiated at the level of our social and psychic bonds to each other. Widman's projection seeks to make race knowable and manageable, even as the boy's response disrupts these norms by which race is located. The uncertainty of locating race among social workers and adoptive parents alike threatens an imaginary of the unified individual based on managing the ambivalence of racial identification.

This critical framework enables my reading of race and adoption in Faulkner's *Light in August*. In a narrative situation that closely resembles that of the Widmans' adoption dilemma, Joe Christmas in *Light in August* fantasizes that he has some "black blood" in him and imagines telling his adoptive parents.[40] Here the object of projection projects back, blurring the boundaries between subject and object and creating a crisis of individuation that envelops the novel as a whole. Joe Christmas's character construction is a symptom of anxieties surrounding racial individuation illuminated by the dynamics of adoption. While a long critical tradition has treated race as a social category either reproduced or disrupted by Joe Christmas's in-between social position, the peculiar conjunction of adoption and race offers an enlarged picture of the processes of individuation that are shaped by anxieties around race as an object of uncertain knowledge. Only by reading Christmas's peculiar responses in relation to how his character is framed and narrated can we see how the normalization of personhood operates in conjunction with the racialization of our social and psychic bonds.

Adopting Joe Christmas

Though *Light in August* is widely recognized as the novel in which Faulkner writes most explicitly about the social construction of blackness, it more crucially dramatizes how race unsettles the boundaries between persons.[41] Like the scenarios of adoption, the novel demonstrates the inability to locate race securely within the individual and the anxiety that it threatens the distinctions between persons. Race is acted out between the other's projection and one's belated perception and understanding of that projection. To think of Joe Christmas in terms of the problem of racial identity is misleading because identity presumes the self-sameness, continuity, and integration of personhood that cannot be taken for granted. Indeed, Joe Christmas fails to cohere as a character despite various narrative attempts to do so: the narrator inserts his biography in the middle of the book, but it remains incoherent and incomplete; the overarching allegory of his character as a Christ figure is full of gaps; a portrait of his psychology giving Christmas's perceptions registers at the same time the difficulties of accessing his interior. Christmas becomes a figure who is inseparable from other characters. He is mistaken at times for a character named Brown with whom he associates. His name is both general and particular, designating both a single individual and any individual. Lena Grove confuses him with the father of her child, linking him to a series of uncertain father figures who blur together at times — Lucas Burch, Brown, Byron Bunch, and even Hightower. Although genealogy is often assumed to provide the order through which the specificity of an identity emerges into the social world, *Light in August* plays with jumbled genealogy so that no one knows any longer who is who.

If we attempt to link Christmas's character to his actions, he still fails to cohere. Christmas's actions seem to have little motivation or background. Even the most understandably motivated action — his assault on McEachern as an effect of the shame that McEachern makes him feel — is narrated as if it were more an accident than a motivated action. The action is given two perspectives — one from the consciousness of McEachern and the other from the consciousness of Christmas — both of which evade the act itself. Faulkner writes first: "And when, staring at the face, he [McEachern] walked steadily toward it with his hand still raised, very likely he walked toward it in the furious and dreamlike exaltation of a martyr who has already been absolved, into the descending chair which Joe swung at his head, and into nothingness" (204); next, from the consciousness of Christmas: "Then to Joe it all rushed away, roaring, dying, leaving him in the center of the floor, the shattered chair clutched in his hand, looking down at his adopted father" (205). In Christmas, Faulkner works hard to fashion a character that has no context for his actions. We are given the form of the action, but not the psychological state or character behind the action. The lack of backstory disrupts the distinctions between one person and the next; McEachern's actions blend into Joe's consciousness.[42] Indeed, the difficulty of ascribing a singular identity to Christmas culminates in the famous scene where Hightower sees Christmas's face as a "composite": "This face ['of the man called Christmas'] alone is not clear. It is confused more than any other, as though in the now peaceful throes of a more recent, a more inextricable, compositeness" (491).[43]

Christmas's adoption combines two frameworks for adoption, highlighting the problem of Christmas's individuation as a separate and undivided character. At first, McEachern tentatively questions his potential adoptee's parentage, registering anxieties common to modern adoption. But the matron of the orphanage replies: "We make no effort to ascertain their parentage. . . . If the child's parentage is important to you, you had better not adopt one at all," implying the assumptions of Protestant adoption agencies in the 1850s and their disavowal of origins (133). Sounding much like descriptions of Charles Loring Brace, McEachern's response blends the Calvinistic notion that all children are originally perverse and sinful with the idea of illegitimacy as an offence against God: "It's no matter, as I just said to you. I've no doubt the tyke will do. . . . I make no doubt that with us he will grow up to fear God and abhor idleness and vanity despite his origin" (134). This form of adoption is predicated on resolving the problem of origin by erasing and transcending it, at the expense of personhood itself. Exemplifying the logic behind Brace's orphan trains, McEachern approaches the adoption as a market transaction that reduces personhood to property: "It was the same stare with which he [McEachern] might have examined a horse or a second hand plow, convinced before hand that he would see flaws, convinced before hand that he would buy" (142).

The anxiety of adoption on the part of parents, social workers, and children alike revolves around what is absent inside the person. In stating, "It's no matter. . . . I've no doubt the tyke will do," McEachern exhibits both his anxiety about absent pedigree, and his attempt to manage that anxiety. Christmas is given a place in the home only within the terms of a constrained and impersonal likeness between adoptive father and adoptive son. The two become alike in their resistance to each other in ways that parody the contemporaneous notion of constructing adoptive families "as if" they were biological families. Faulkner writes: "There was a very kinship of stubbornness like a transmitted resemblance in their backs.... They went on, in steady single file, the two backs in their rigid abnegation of all compromise more alike than actual blood could have made them" (148). A "transmitted resemblance" creates a *greater* likeness than "actual blood." Reflecting Protestant constructions of adoption in the United States where the orphan is both a child of God (Christ-like) and a child of sin, McEachern defends against the mark of sin and accommodates the "difference" of the adopted child by making him into a known quantity of property and labor.

Yet this process of transmission used to secure sameness also highlights the ambivalence of racial identification. The adoption scenario already shows ways in which Christmas's character is constituted through the other's projection, and it is indeed commonplace to describe the workings of race in the novel through this mechanism of projection. Christmas is the "screen on which the cultural fantasies of race are projected." [44] The reader's ignorance of Christmas's origin constitutes the "blank moment on the screen onto which others project a racial lineage." [45] Christmas is not so much a character as he is the product of collective fantasy. But these definitions of projection have several problematic implications for conceptualizing race. First, they conceive projection as a one-way imposition of a racist fantasy onto the other. Second, it suggests that projection and individuality are mutually exclusive: if one is perceived only through projections, then individuality is distorted. These two assumptions frame discussions of race that inevitably lead to binaries of coercion and resistance. Most importantly, these interpretations fail to address the effective force of Joe Christmas's *own* projection of race. Christmas's fantasy of race — his response to the other's demand and projection — follows the model of projection not as a one-way imposition but as the dual process outlined earlier through the Allen Rogers– Mrs. Widman example, which involves an expelling out as well

as a taking in. As André Green writes, "The projective movement is accompanied by an introjective movement . . . as if the
vacuum created by the expulsion were immediately filled by the
projection's return."[46] Christmas's responses enact this return
of projection through which the separation of black and white
bodies is denied.

Such a two-way model of projection-introjection complicates the influential ideological reading of race in *Light in
August*, which sees the racialized subject as acting only insofar
as he is acted on by the system, practices, and rituals of race.[47]
For example, Philip Weinstein analyzes Joe Christmas as just
such a character who is "acted on":

> In Joe Christmas the necessary line between subjective learn-
> ing and objective training verges upon disappearance, for
> he is incapable of reaccenting (digesting) anything he has
> absorbed. . . . Joe's imprisonment within his culture's religious
> and racial insistences — "She ought not to started praying over
> me" (117), "I think I got some nigger blood in me" (216) —
> reveals glaringly the suffocation of these scripts.[48]

This reading fails to appreciate that the statement "I think I got
some nigger blood in me" is addressed to and acts on someone
else, and is Christmas's own projection outward.

Christmas's fantasized disclosure that the McEacherns have
"nursed a nigger" dramatizes this relational process (168).
While sometimes understood as Christmas's internalization of
racist constructs or others' fantasies,[49] this disclosure reveals
how race emerges through a transactive process that circulates
anxiously within the attachments between persons. His projection of himself as "nigger" occurs in the context of a refusal
of the adoptive relation.

> Sometimes he thought that he would tell her [Mrs. McEachern]
> alone. Have her who in her helplessness could neither alter it
> nor ignore it, know it and need to hide it from the man whose

immediate and predictable reaction to the knowledge would so
obliterate it as a factor in their relations that it would never
appear again. To say to her in secret, in secret payment for the
secret dishes which he had not wanted: "Listen. He says he
has nursed a blasphemer and an ingrate. I dare you to tell him
what he has nursed. That he has nursed a nigger beneath his
own roof, with his own food at his own table." (168)

Christmas's disclosure that "[McEachern] has nursed a nigger"
is a projection outward ("secret payment") of what he had
received passively (the "secret dishes which he had not wanted"
and the shame associated with those dishes). This fantasy acts
out the transactional process of projection and introjection,
materializing and enacting racial difference where before it
had been unlocalizable anxiety. Effectively blurring the lines
between what is within himself and what is within the other
through this identification with the other's projection, Christmas's fantasized knowledge of racial difference becomes an
object that exists, like a secret, between him and his adoptive
mother. The repetition of "it" — "could neither alter it nor
ignore it, know it and need to hide it" — materializes racial difference as a verbal and material obstacle that links him and his
adoptive mother within the shared bind of uncertain knowledge. Racial difference appears as the effect of a set of norms
around the proper relations and exchanges between persons.
Further, though the projection of Mr. McEachern as "nurse"
seems misplaced when one considers the relationship between
McEachern and Christmas (which could hardly be described as
"nursing"), it nicely demonstrates how Christmas recognizes
himself through the other's anxious projections: "Listen. He
says he has nursed a blasphemer and an ingrate. I dare you to
tell him what he has nursed." The repetition of "nursed" in the
following lines shows that this misplaced projection rewrites
his relationship to McEachern in order to articulate himself as
the object of anxiety. Significantly, Christmas's projection of

himself as "nigger" operates by invoking the double meaning of "own" as both "to possess an object" and "to acknowledge as belonging to oneself."[50] He repeats the problem of owning (recall that ownership is a significant part of McEachern's socialization of Christmas as a man) back onto the father-as-owner — "That he has nursed a nigger beneath his own roof, with his own food at his own table" — thus interjecting himself into what McEachern must "own," that is, acknowledge and recognize.

The particularly scandalous way in which Christmas avows race reveals not Christmas's choice, will, or intention, as it is commonly interpreted through the lens of passing. It is better understood as his appropriation of and response to the other's projection — an attempt to meet it and secure his reality.[51] Christmas's projections negotiates the racial norms that "confer" reality, produce a variety of rules that render an action and person recognizable. When Christmas tells his girlfriend Bobbie about his supposed "nigger" blood, he begins the conversation — "You noticed my skin, my hair" (196). He projects his own desire for knowledge onto Bobbie, making her perceive and fantasize what she otherwise may not have noticed. This leads to a guessing game regarding his status as a "foreigner," or as "something even different than that," and he finally responds to her question "What are you?" with "I got some nigger blood in me" (196). She responds by reinscribing the property of blood back into *what* he is by asking again — "You're what?" This cat and mouse game of discovery and recognition acts out the play of projection and introjection in which he projects outward this trait as if it were inside of him, and she projects back onto him the demand for a selfsame identity. Calling attention to this play of projections, we see how the question of Christmas's race emerges through relational exchange, a shared fantasy and desire for knowledge, rather than as a question of "identity."

The back and forth of projection dramatizes how Christmas's social bonds with others threaten their own separateness. Christmas's projections circulate race as an object of uncertain knowledge, undoing distinctions between persons. Instead of Christmas being identified as black, others manifest anxiety around identifying *with* Christmas. It is in this sense that Christmas's racial individuation becomes an anxious object around which much of the narrative and critical energy revolves. This anxiety over Christmas's racial individuation culminates in the repetition of his attempt to designate himself, using the simplest and seemingly most direct of locutions: "Here I am." Christmas repeats this phrase in two critical discovery scenes. The first occurs when he happens on a sexual encounter between the dietician and doctor at the orphanage, an event widely recognized as a primal scene of sorts. Christmas vomits toothpaste he had been eating and is discovered by the dietician. She throws back the curtain and cries, "You little nigger bastard!" (122). This scene plays out the inability to differentiate environment from self, what is a part of Christmas's body and what is not:

> In the rife, pinkwomansmelling obscurity behind the curtain he squatted, pinkfoamed, listening to his insides, waiting with astonished fatalism for what was about to happen to him. Then it happened. He said to himself with complete and passive surrender: 'Well, here I am.'" (122)

With its emphasis on the curtain in relation to the body, orality, and what is taken in and pushed out of the body, the scene calls attention to the exchanges between the surface of the skin and the outside, the orifices that make individual and environment indistinguishable. Christmas continues to eat toothpaste while he passively waits to vomit. It is an odd mixture of agency and passivity, where Christmas both announces and surrenders himself. He emerges exactly at the site of the nurse's fears, as if from her own insides.

This first instance of "here I am" puts into question the boundaries of personhood as the pink toothpaste inside him merges with the "pinkwomansmelling" outside him. The second instance further undermines these boundaries, demonstrating a crisis in his individuation when the community is made to identify with its own projections. Again, Christmas is simultaneously hiding from the community and announcing himself to it:

> "They recognized me too," he thinks... "they all want me to be captured, and then when I come up ready to say Here I am *Yes I would say Here I am I am tired of running of having to carry my life like it was a basket of eggs* they all run away. Like there is a rule to catch me by, and to capture me that way would not be like the rule says." (337)

The community will only capture and incorporate him as "nigger," both producing him as familiar (that is, not a stranger or foreigner), and refusing his legitimacy at the same time. His announcement of "Here I am" is refused because it would require them to acknowledge their projections: "to capture me that way would not be like the rule says." The "Here I am" thus signifies not the identity of being and the capacity for self-designation, but rather the disjunction between the demands of others and the attempt to individuate. It is not a stable designation at all, and here Faulkner seems to be playing with the statement's biblical resonances. For this phrase echoes the instability of the "Here am I" in the story of Jacob and Esau in the Old Testament. The phrase marks the duty and obligation that is exchanged between father and son: between first Abraham and Isaac; then between Isaac and Esau; then mistakenly between Isaac and Jacob, when Jacob disguises himself as

Esau, stepping into his place and stealing their father's blessing.[52] Read in this way, the phrase raises adoption anxieties about dissimulation and the presumed absence of the origin. "Here I am" signifies the instability within sameness itself, the fact that the verbal signifier of claiming and usurping, of placing and displacing, are the same.

These moments of disclosure and discovery are so uncanny because they threaten the loss of distinction not only between what is inside and what is outside, but also between subject and object. The primary problem that Joe Christmas poses is how to individuate and distinguish him from others. That is, once one adopts him, how does one detach oneself from him? The inability to determine the character's background precludes locating race within the individual. The dynamics of adoption show how racial difference is part of a constant exchange between persons. "Nigger blood" in particular loads a process of projection and introjection that renders subject and object inseparable, linked in a shared projective fantasy about what is inside or prior to the individual.

But the narrative as a whole counteracts this more open, projective dynamic of racial individuation with its own conventions for normalizing race. It mitigates against acknowledging race as an effect of the anxieties around identification between two people, and instead relocates race as an aspect of a singular individual, identity, and body. It does so by individuating Christmas through the structure of allegory. In the novel, lawyer Gavin Stevens relates Joe Christmas's identity in terms of a theory of "blood": "And then the white blood above him out of there, as it was the black blood which snatched up the pistol and the white blood which would not let him fire it" (449). This infamous allegorical battle between "white blood" and "black blood" is often read as ironic and not representative of the novel as a whole. Yet Stevens's explanation of Christmas's behavior demonstrates a logic that the novel itself implicitly recapitulates, a logic that links the meaning of character to an abstraction of traits, deploys nominal adjectives, and reduces "what" you are into "who" you are. The text invites allegorical personification as a mode of interpreting character. For example, the lynching scene attaches Christmas's identity to a reification of blood: "Then his face, body, all, seemed to collapse, to fall in upon itself, and from out the slashed garments about his hips and loins the pent black blood seemed to rush like a released breath" (465). The gushing of black blood and the odd deification of Christmas's body (the collapsing of particular body parts into a spirit) is not just Faulkner's racial essentialism reordering the text. This allegorical register achieves its effect by linking Christmas back to his "black blood" as the cause of his character. Following this logic, Christmas is interpreted on two levels: the reader is made to identify "black blood" as a spiritual *and* physical immanence that gives Christmas his final form. It paradoxically individuates Christmas in terms of the specificity of race by relating an inner essence (his supposed black blood) to an external, figurative register (fate, destiny, apotheosis).

The allegorical register of the text is consonant with Scott Romine's argument that the narrative, like the community and Christmas himself, needs "black blood" not only in order to have a story, but also to function as the motivation for Christmas's actions. Romine writes: "Although recent critics have been skeptical of Stevens's causal link between black blood and Christmas's actions, it is fully consonant with the narrative's repeated reification of blood not only as a meaningful social metaphor, but as an *agent* as well. . . . Black blood, then, gains legitimacy as an agent that not only defines social caste, but that also causes and explains behavior."[53] Moreover, various figurative registers are used to plot Christmas's journey along a search for a cause. The chess game figuration of Percy Grimm's hunt for Christmas; the turn toward detective story drama near the end of the novel; and the labyrinthine imagery of Christmas's journey all invite one to wonder what motivates/moves his actions.[54] Just as Bobbie's responses earlier converted the problem of the circulation of black blood into a question of ontology, these formal designs invite the reader to ferret out origins and causes.

The novel invites allegorical interpretation to close off and contain the materialization of racial difference through relational exchanges. It invites characters, critics, readers, and even Christmas himself to resolve the problem when, as in the dilemma over matching, race can neither be attached to any concrete ground nor located in any one place. It does so by making race into a cause, into that which mysteriously moves Christmas toward his predetermined destination. Mirroring the regressive move in matching in which racial designation is produced as both the origin and the effect of projective anxiety, the narrative binds Christmas to the reification of blood as both the origin and effect of his character. Even though race has been detached from such "grounds" as appearance and birth, it is remade as manifest through the allegorical procedure of relating internal quantities to external figurations, thus lending continuity and wholeness to Christmas's character. The narrative figuration of Christmas's character has the same structure as the adoptive identity that arose in the practices of matching, in which the adopted person is carrying some mysterious property (materialized as a past, or as some prior event, or simply as a material cause) that must be fulfilled.

Light in August illustrates anxieties over where to locate race and how to demarcate some persons from others. The parent–child relation is central to this anxiety. It is the privileged form for the transmission of whiteness and blackness not just as a biological and legal inheritance, but as a way of rewriting intertwined histories. The retelling of genealogy is a way of securing legitimacy and illegitimacy as racialized constructions.

But the parent–child relation is never secure in this novel, as evidenced most clearly in the plot of Lena Grove looking for the "father" of her child and getting confounded among the possibilities of Brown, Bunch, and Burch, characters whose names barely distinguish them from each other. Christmas and his adoption are emblematic of this dangerous circulation of race between persons in forms that disrupt the racial form of individuation as enacted through the parent–child relation.

Adoption mobilizes particular worries about the parent–child relation as staging proper or legitimate forms of possession, identification, and transmission. In Chesnutt, as in Faulkner, adoption is the catalyst for anxieties regarding racial individuation. Depicting Glover as a race-conscious individual whose race is unknown, *The Quarry* — particularly in its mode of the *roman à clef* — dramatizes the problem of trying to find a stable referent for racial identification. Racial norms are reproduced in the novel by regulating the parameters of personhood and the possible modes of a character's relations to others. These readings together elaborate an account of race as a norm through which a character becomes intelligible.

Normalizing Racial Identification

The differences between Faulkner's and Chesnutt's models for adoption indicate their differing concerns regarding race as an object of uncertain knowledge. If in *Light in August,* parentage is left indeterminate by decree (recall the matron's words "We make no effort to ascertain their parentage. . . . If the child's parentage is important to you, you had better not adopt one at all"), in *The Quarry,* Chesnutt references the anxieties around adoption as framed within the social Darwinist discourse of race. As we have seen from the examples of social workers, adoption through matching is a powerful imaginative site for converting the gaps in knowledge about a baby's background into the primacy of race, and Chesnutt is fascinated by these ambiguities. For Chesnutt, the emerging social science model of adoption highlights anxieties regarding racial individuation that threaten the social norms governing interracial relations.

Chesnutt's novel begins by depicting a formal adoption, exploiting contemporaneous discourses around the profession-alization of adoption and its claims for expert knowledge. The adoption in the novel is framed in terms of a scientific discourse of hereditary strains, statistics, and empirical evidence, which supposedly works to ensure the right "fit" between child and parent. At City Hospital, the Seatons choose a child; Dr. Free-man, in charge of the orphanage, says, "But we'll first have to look up his pedigree and see whether he's the kind of child you want." [55] This scene echoes the role of expert knowledge and the tacit policy of matching in order to make adoption seem as "natural" as possible.

Chesnutt's description of adoption highlights the impact of assumptions about matching for the construction of the child. In looking over a row of babies at City Hospital, the Seatons come across one of "marked individuality" Dr. Free-man calls "young Booker T" (8). This naming secures the infant's projected identity through an illustrious black ancestry. Mrs. Seaton is struck, though, by another child, and expresses a common reaction of adoptive parents at the time: "I want a child that is all my own. I don't attach a great deal of impor-tance to heredity. This is a good and beautiful baby and I'm willing to take him on faith" (10). She asks the doctor to refrain from "looking [the child] up" and thereby disclosing his his-tory and heredity. Early in the story, then, we see the problem of reference — of what to refer the child to, and thus what predicts his or her future.

Chesnutt represents one way expert knowledge is used to create some certainty, some account for the child's unknown origin in order to relate and narrate a life. But this problem of reference — of constructing persons by matching them to a sign that precedes them — dramatized through the adoption plot is highly unstable, an endless process of figuration without substance. Chesnutt highlights processes of projection that inhabit the scene of adoption, illuminating anxieties about the presumed absence of origin. The language that Chesnutt uses to describe the Seatons' desires for a baby echoes the discourse of adoption at the time: "They wanted a child with no strings on it, no parents or relations in the background who might claim it or grieve because they could not claim it" (6). At the same time, uncertainty surrounding the adoptee's origin raises the specter of adopting a child from a "different" background. *The Quarry* hinges on this anxiety. When Mrs. Seaton overhears one of her friends say that the baby has a dark tinge, the articulation of the unspoken anxiety prompts the Seatons to transfer the baby to a black family. Thus, race becomes a matter of projective anxiety, enacted through the demands of others.

The plot revolves around this unknown quantity, which can neither be verified nor disproved because a mistake in record-keeping leaves a trail of empirical evidence that cannot be corroborated. For nothing is determinate in parents' and social workers' fantasies. When Mr. Seaton learns that Donald's heritage may in fact be rather distinguished and might not bear the mark of black ancestry, he raises the issue with Senator Brown, who facilitated the adoption of Donald Seaton by a black family. Senator Brown argues:

> Race consciousness is a complex thing; it is not entirely a matter of blood. Nature made Donald white; man has made him, in sympathy, in outlook upon life, a Negro. Why spoil a good Negro by telling him this fairy tale, which, however alluring, may be no more true than the other? There was one slip-up in a perfect system. There may well have been another. (263–64)

"Race consciousness" here is neither a product of nature nor nurture; it is a product of overlapping and conflicting projections that cannot be reconciled. However, the immediate temptation is to provide a stable ground for the figure of race. Even as Senator Brown attests to the contingency and fantasy implicit in any "match," he immediately lapses into an argument with Mr. Seaton about the relative contributions of white and black people in history that hypostatize "white" and "black" viewpoints. Challenging Mr. Seaton's claim for white superiority of material advantage, the senator notes, "The page of the white race in history is by no means clean. It is soiled and bloody with a long record of cruelty, of treachery, of greed, of calculated crimes against humanity" (265). Seaton responds defensively, "But with some fine achievements on the other side. The abolition of slavery, for instance, and the enfranchisement of the Negro" (265). Here history becomes the ground for adjudicating claims of blackness or whiteness, transforming the unreadability of race into a series of events coded as either "black" or "white." And yet the object of the argument, Donald Glover, reveals precisely the mistake of thinking about "owning" blackness or whiteness in this way.

Glover evades the referentiality of race in ways that question the logic of "owning" blackness or whiteness as a property within oneself. The novel is hounded by the problem of establishing Donald's character. Indeed the manuscript was rejected for the "lifelessness of the characters and the 'priggishness' of the hero."[56] Chesnutt wrote to the editor, "I suspect you are right about all of this, and ... before I submit the book elsewhere, see if I can put some flesh on and some red blood in the characters."[57] This lack is not simply an artistic failure, but rather a symptom of anxieties about racial individuation. For Donald Glover is playing out a narrative that has already, so to speak, made him. The world in which Donald attempts to individuate himself is a *roman à clef,* filled with characters based on historical persons, facts, and places: figurative representations that are modeled on historical referents. To cite just a few examples as noted by Dean McWilliams: Donald at first attends Athena University (Atlanta University), where he meets Dr. Lebrun (W. E. B. DuBois), a crusader for racial equality who takes him under his wing (294, 290). After a run-in with Atlanta's racially oppressive legal system, Donald moves to Columbia University, where he takes a class with the eminent ethnologist, Dr. Boaz (Franz Boas) (291). Later, he meets Dr. Jefferson (Booker T. Washington) and works for him (294). The list goes on to include lesser-known figures of the present and past — Madame C. J. Walker, cosmetics entrepreneur; Ida Cox, singer; John Patterson Green, a local politician (289, 293, 288). Even those characters who do not directly resemble real-life persons contain in their names some reference to past persons: Donald's college roommate is Abraham Lincoln Dixon.

One of Donald's love interests is Amelia Parker, who, he surmises, may possibly be related to the "famous preacher who had been a great friend of his race," Theodore Parker (126). Here Donald makes the reference *for* the reader, pointing to something quite odd in this rendition of the *roman à clef*. It is not just the reader who is faced with the problem of reference; Donald himself constantly alludes to history and literature in order to represent his experiences. For example, he represents his first love affair through allusions to Keats's ballad "La Belle Dame Sans Merci," resulting in a bad romantic poem in prose: "It was a beautiful summer night. The gibbous moon, visible through the branches of the overhanging trees, was riding high, and the glory of the stars filled the firmament. It was an ideal night for love, of whatever sort" (74). In fact, the problem of reference works metafictionally to question the status of the characters in *The Quarry*. One of the characters claims origins in a Thackeray novel: "one of my ancestors appears in *Vanity Fair*. She was the original of Miss Schwartz, the West Indian fellow pupil of Becky Sharp at Miss Wilkinson's Academy" (193). Finally, Donald's adoption itself raises the problem of reference. In deciding how to "train" Donald, his adoptive mother "never lost sight of the Biblical parallel between Donald and Moses. Moses, though of an enslaved race, was never himself a slave.... He had been the adopted son of the king's daughter, the pet of the harem, instructed from infancy in the learning of the priests and the manners of the court" (96). These references condition the possibilities of Donald's individuation; they constitute a world of comparisons and measures against and through which Donald will appear. It is not that his life has to approximate the leadership of Moses; it is that his life is individualized through this parallel, creating a racial allegory in which he is to emerge.

This anxiety of antecedence finally devolves on Donald Seaton himself, as noted by the narrator's take on his main character: "Much of his own speech [Donald's] was in tropes and similes" (81). Everything in this novel, it seems, even the hero's speech and the language of the novel itself, is explicitly a copy of something else, always a reference to something prior. Racial identification in this novel turns on this anxious relation of antecedence. The *roman à clef* structure of *The Quarry* points to the paradoxes within the figure of the race-conscious individual, for Donald Seaton/Glover's life is trapped in reference to past lives and conventions. The repetition of the site of the library in the novel emblematizes the idealized relationship of mirroring between man and book. Early on in the novel, it is noted that Senator Brown has library shelves lined with works by great Negro authors: "the life of Frederick Douglass held a prominent place, George W. Williams's *History of the Negro* another" (35). A similar library scene is played out when Donald visits a patron in Europe. These library scenes bring man and book together in the idealized way imagined by biography.

The biographical imperative is the desire to train and culti-
vate character through the modeling and imitation of one's
life on another biography. This model of reading biographi-
cally reproduces the mimetic assumptions of a life — that life
can be straightforwardly reflected in books and vice versa. But
even as *The Quarry* gives the biographical formation of a race-
man and can be read as eschewing assimilationist stances or
rejecting the ethics of passing,[58] it also calls into question the
figuration of biography itself. Rather than being the picture
of individual leadership, one who leads his race to the future
as his upbringing and education promise, Donald Glover is
represented as having no character without race providing its
structuring norm.

Throughout the novel, Glover is not only open to his former white father's attempts to reclaim him, but also to various
romantic alliances precisely because of his interlinked status as
racial and family property. Glover is continually referenced in
terms of an economy that mixes familial/domestic ownership
and economic ownership. When Mrs. Glover is complimented
for her rearing of Donald, she responds, "And he's paying
me back with interest.... I certainly thank God that he gave
me that beautiful baby, who has grown up into this beautiful
young man — you needn't blush, Donald, everybody knows
how handsome you are — I know what I am talking about, I
have spent many years of my life in helping to make people
beautiful" (208–9). Beauty is a property of Donald's that is
both an investment and a commodity. These acts of appropriation act out a norm of racial personhood based around
ownership and possession. However, Glover deviates from
these norms of racial personhood because he is *too* open to
multiple appropriations. In Glover's first marriage proposal to
Bertha, she responds that despite her love for him, she could
not marry him: "I fear I couldn't be sure of you, Donald.
You're too good looking, and too white. When, or if, you

tire of me there'll be too many women anxious to take my place" (225–26). Her uncertainty devolves on his skin color and beauty—"You're too good looking, and too white." His racial indeterminacy is illegible not so much because it does not fit into a given category: categories can always be imposed as a long history of Jim Crow legislation testifies. Rather, Glover deviates from the norms of race relations that value race as a singular claim. Glover's openness to multiple adoptions and to various economic and erotic claims across racial boundaries render him inseparable from others and thus not fully individuated: "I couldn't be sure of you."

The ending of the novel seems to remedy this lack of certainty by hinging on Donald Glover's private "choice" to be black, for he refuses to act on the information that he is white and chooses to marry a black woman over a white woman. Indeed, the final line in the novel spoken by Mr. Seaton suggests that Glover expresses his racial identification through his marriage and his family: "Your wife is a beautiful and charming woman and the boy is the image of you at his age. I'm not at all sure that you didn't make the wise choice" (286). But his choice is a peculiar one in that it is not as if he makes the choice, but rather as if it is made for him. He comes back to marry Bertha only in response to a fictitious letter written by her friend whose "handwriting is exactly like Bertha's" (282). Thus, he is drawn back to Bertha through mistaking the identity of the letter-writer. His choice is narrated as if it came from a primary understanding of himself as black, even though its contingency is exposed through the narrative. His choice to be black is the effect, ironically, of mistaking the identity of another. Acting out the logic of the *roman à clef,* Glover is referred back to a "real" blackness only through the lure of fiction. More importantly, the terms of Mr. Seaton's valuation of Glover reveals the norms of racial personhood through which his choice becomes legible and attains meaning. Namely, norms built around proper transmission and identification: "the boy is the image of you at his age." This father–son identification relies on a structure of modeling that reproduces race as "something" that can be mimetically transmitted. Here the model to be duplicated does not "contain" blackness any more than the image does. The function of the model is to stabilize the anxious and anticipatory relationship between a self and the uncertain, unknowable norms by which it is conditioned. Playing out this anxiety of one's relation to what comes before, Donald Glover's final words in the novel are, like the rest of his speech, "a colloquialism now seldom employed, and which the uninformed might easily suppose to be of American origin, but it is found in Molière, and much farther back, in one of the Greek dramatists" (283). In *The Quarry*, the structure of the *roman à clef* genre manages the anxiety about references that blur Molière, the Greeks, and Americans — and by extension, black and white — by sustaining the idea of race as a social norm based on the separation of peoples.

The anxiety about character formation in *The Quarry* suggests that Glover's individuality remains illegible without the reproduction of norms regarding race built on proper forms of possession and owning. These norms reveal both the deviations that dissolve the racial boundaries between persons ("I feel I couldn't be sure of you, Donald") and the values that secure the unity of personhood regarding the concept of race ("the boy is the image of you at his age"). The question of adoption in *The Quarry* marks the struggle to manage the gap between the emergence of persons and the social norms that anticipate and condition their appearance. In this way, the construction of a "proper" form of kinship is inseparable from the formation of a specific notion of race based on a logic of possession.

Adoption and the Racial Form of Individuation

Adoption provides a model whereby one's race is not one's own at all. Instead, race is enacted relationally through processes of projection and introjection that threaten and stabilize the conditions of individuation and the boundaries between persons. But if Faulkner and Chesnutt call attention to the structuring of racial norms that secure certain forms of individual persons through adoption, they ultimately differ in the nature of their anxiety. For Faulkner, the adopted character raises the specter of the inseparability of black and white, the fact that race may be a play of projections that destabilizes who is white and who is black. The reason why Joe Christmas is so disconcerting is because he makes the attachments between blackness and whiteness impossible to deny. For Chesnutt, the adopted character displays the norms through which racial identification becomes a powerful logic for the attainment of personhood itself. In both cases, though, they use adoption to shift our frameworks for analyzing race not as a social category whose construction needs to be exhaustively traced, but as a set of social norms that relate persons to the social world along a spectrum of possibilities. As such, they respond to the dual constructions of race and adoption at the time, which are together oriented around regulating the arrangement of our lived ties and identifications.

This conjunction of adoption and race earlier in the twentieth century helps us rethink the status of race in adoption debates today. In late twentieth-century debates on transracial adoption, race is typically thought of as a given thing: it is something to be matched or not matched; something to be accounted for or ignored. But the adopted characters on which this chapter centers — Joe Christmas and Donald Glover — suggest that it is actually the other way around. Race is not so much a given as it is something that gets materialized through the uncertainty of relating the individual to the social contexts that precede and condition it. It emerges through anxieties about individuation, the need to produce some form of correspondence between one's sense of being and one's sense of the world. Racial identification is reproduced through the dynamics of individuation, through the need to secure character and individuality in a social world that provides its terms of intelligibility. In this way, the dynamics of adoption reveal the particular affective and social investments in reproducing race as something inherent, as something that can securely relate character and context, for both adopter and adoptee alike. Adoption reminds us that racial identification is located in that space of anxiety and insecurity between world and self in which social norms are continually in flux. As we will see in the following chapters, these practices of adoption shape and orient our constructions of normative personhood in the twentieth-century, from human rights to the aspirations of multicultural recognition.

II

BETWEEN RIGHTS AND NEEDS

4

THE RIGHT TO BELONG
Legal Norms, Cultural Origins, and Adoptee Identity

Locating Transnational/Transracial Adoption

In the 1950s, a powerful sentimental rationale began to promote transracial and transnational adoptions. This reasoning combined a Christian religious sensibility of hospitality and "God's family" (much like frameworks used by Harriet Beecher Stowe and Charles Loring Brace to different effect) and a political narrative of post–World War II U.S. humanitarianism and civilization. As early as 1949, Helen Doss writes of her family of twelve adopted children, most of whom were of nonwhite backgrounds, "We are more than an 'international family.' Our home, with its strong ties of mutual understanding and love, is symbolic of that most inclusive family of all, God's family."[1] Pearl S. Buck promoted and supplemented this religious rationale with a world-political vision. Also in 1949, she established the Welcome House, an agency that specialized in the placing of African American, Asian, mentally ill, and disabled children. Well known for her advocacy of the social and civil plight of blacks in America, Buck opened up the possibility of cross-racial adoption as a way to fight racism both inside the United States and abroad and promote an international and interracial family as the model for world harmony after World War II.

Often relating her sympathy for racial minorities through her own experience growing up as a white woman in China, Buck justifies transracial and transnational adoption through political and religious narratives that complement each other. Christina Klein elaborates Buck's narratives of adoption as part of a political and sentimental allegory: mixed-race families "offered a way to imagine Americans overcoming the ingrained racism that so threatened U.S. foreign policy goals in Asia."[2] She raises as an example Buck's praise for a memoir called *White Mother* about the adoption of two black girls:

> When any American asks the question of what he — or she — can do to bring an end to prejudice in our country and in the world, that one has only to read "White Mother." The answer is there. You do what the white mother did. There are children everywhere in deep need of love and faith and opportunity.... I am not saying too much when I declare that were we all to follow in the footsteps of this one white mother, we would need not ask how to achieve peace on earth.[3]

Klein writes that "for Buck, the white mother to the non-white child became the emblem of antiracist commitment and the vehicle for achieving racial harmony on a global scale."[4] I would add that Buck collapses two categories — the black child and the foreign other — in order to imagine this act of adoption. In the same commentary, Buck redescribes the act of the white mother thus: "In the deep South, a white lady, a lady of distinction, took into her care two small Negro girls, so underprivileged they might have been savages in a wild land."[5] The white mother emerges from "the deep South" as a beacon of light in the uncivilized land. Linking the Negro girls to "savages in a wild land," she reimagines them as the objects of U.S. overseas missions, simultaneously projecting U.S. care outside its borders and incorporating outside territories inside its domestic space.

Buck conceives of the parent–child drama as acting out the terms of a new citizenship: "These are the citizens of my new world, the children without parents and the parents without children, pressing eagerly toward each other, and yet unable to reach each other."[6] Hers is a cosmopolitanism that is anchored in the domestic, one that holds international and national attachments as one, mutually constitutive whole.[7] In her autobiography, *My Several Worlds,* she writes that the children of Welcome House "unite my worlds in one"—a love of American ideals and a care for common humanity.[8] This particular logic for transracial and transnational adoption, then, naturalized the figure of the adoptee in ways that managed histories of orientalism and imperialism abroad and racism at home from which adoptees emerged. This projective vision sets the terms on which parents adopted and on which adopted children were imagined. The latter became deterritorialized objects through which boundaries are collapsed into one world. This collapsing of home and world placed adoptees in the service of a narrative construction of U.S. obligation, care, and paternalism for China and Asia more broadly,[9] but also required a figuration of their terms of personhood as "piteous lonely children whom no country claims."[10]

I outline Buck's vision in detail because it undergirds the sentimental, salvational worldview that dominated practices of transnational adoption and created the conditions of personhood for a whole generation of transnational adoptees. Though Buck herself talked often of needing to value the cultural origins of the child,[11] what attended this political imagination of adoption was an ethos of assimilation and erasure of ties facilitated by the legal principle termed by Duncan and Yngvesson as the "clean-break" model: the imagination of children "whom no country claims" through the complete severance and erasure of biological ties; the complete reimagination of the child in terms of the adoptive family.[12] Moreover, it shows the ways in which transracial and transnational adoption were imagined in relation to each other for the purpose of managing the various histories and geographies that traverse the act of adoption itself. While it is common to separate transracial from transnational adoptions in the contemporary moment as different kinds of activities, the former domestic and the latter international,[13] I return to this early rationale in order to underscore the ways in which interracial (black–white) and transnational adoption are fundamentally intertwined and read through each other. This sentimental universalism locates adoptees within a specific configuration of world/home/race in order to produce the conditions of their personhood as claimless children.

Thus the social visibility of transracial and transnational adoptees as anything other than international symbols, "nobody's children," or sentimental devices, began only in the late twentieth century. Adoptees have emerged as writers, filmmakers, and activists narrating their experiences and telling their stories, becoming socially recognizable subjects claiming legal rights. Critics have contested the grand sentimental narrative of salvation, defetishizing these adopted children by reconstructing the material, economic, and political histories that situated them.[14] But perhaps most prominently, adoptees have counteracted the erasure of histories embedded in the sentimental and national framework by demanding what Bastard Nation phrases on their mission statement as the "right to know one's identity."[15] This notion is most often associated with adoptees' struggle to access birth records but is also more generally constructed as the necessity to preserve adopted children's ties to cultural, biological, or racial origin. Whether through political activism, roots trips, or the popularity of the adoption story narrated through the search for one's birth parents, this desire for return has become a dominant narrative through which transracial and transnational adoptees have gained legibility and articulated their claims.

This move has given adoption scholars pause because of its apparent fetishization of biological, cultural, and national origins.[16] But rather than read these search narratives for problematic essentialisms, I prefer to contextualize the "right to know one's identity" in relation to the struggle over negotiating normative conditions of personhood. Roots trips and return narratives rely on a specific placement within the spheres of family, nationality, and race in order to exercise their claims to personhood. The problem of the social legibility of transracial and transnational adoptees is precisely how to locate adoptees in relation to multiple histories that cut across their lives.[17] As such, it reveals the relationships between these processes of situating and the reproduction of legitimate personhood and social standing. Moreover, it shows how this reproduction of personhood does the work, as it does for Buck, of managing the meanings of multiple histories.

The works by and about transracial/transnational adoptees articulate what is ignored by Buck's vision of uniting several worlds into one: an account of the mediations through which one moves from family to strangers to common humanity. I read the search and reunion trope for its stronger account of familial mechanisms and investments in relation to various institutional priorities, frameworks and languages. It represents the negotiation of both intra- and inter-national processes in the making of persons, without collapsing them into a vision that both ignores the traumatic histories before adoption and the racialized formations after adoption. This chapter explores what transnational adoptees' claims to reality and subjectivity — specifically mobilized around the "right to know one's identity" and against "clean-break" principles — tell us about this uneasy process of reconciling the desire to situate oneself in disavowed histories and the need to make claims that are socially legible.

In order to understand the parameters through which transnational adoptees' claims are understood today, I trace the right to identity back to the development of adoptee rights discourse in the 1970s and the pathologization of adoptees within psychology, psychiatry, and social work, which began as early as the 1920s. Psychoanalytic discourse plays a crucial role in constructing the particular version of the adoptee that gets taken up by legal movements and codified through international conventions on adoption and children's rights. More specifically, legal constructions of the priority of one's biological and national origin in adoption depend on psychoanalytic pathologizations of the adoptee as living in fantasy. The ironic effect is that the fitting of the adoptee into a model of the rights-bearing individual is premised on the idea that the adoptee is stuck in fantasy and lacks reality. While these two frameworks have been powerful forms for gaining visibility for the psychic realities and social status of adoptees, they have played equally strong roles in normalizing and naturalizing the transnational adoptee within racial, national, and familial logics. Analyzing this relationship between legal norms and psychological accounts allows us to rethink how adoptees challenge the terms of personhood set up by international rights conventions even as they are incorporated within them. The notion of "the right to know one's identity" is not limited to transracial or transnational adoptees, but it is in this context that we can see the mutually imbricated processes of race, nation, and kinship in the reproduction of personhood.

I then turn to narratives that reflect on and negotiate the desire to "know one's identity." Writing against the declarative language of human rights through which this desire usually gets structured, these narratives take up the formal and social conventions of adoptee identity and translate them into the domain of the counterfactual, which offers distinct ways of framing the lives of adoptees. I take up Jane Jeong Trenka's memoir *A Language of Blood* and Bharati Mukherjee's novel *Leave It to Me*, both of which concern an adoptee's search for her birth parents. But these works cannot be reduced to this prototypical plot of adoption literature, and their engagement with the geographical and territorial politics and psychic dimensions of this plot structure reveal alternative logics of figuring adoptive personhood.

As Laura Briggs notes, the stories we like to tell about transnational and transracial adoption often naturalize certain erasures. The "demographics made me do it" story, as she terms it, which locates transnational and transracial adoption as effects of demographic changes due to factors such as birth control and shifts in attitudes toward mothering, naturalizes a narrative of sentimental rescue of needy orphans that obscures the wars, losses, and traumas that cause the displacement of children.[18] These popular frameworks, I have also suggested, locate adoptees in certain ways that condition the terms by which they become legible. In *Claiming Others,* I have endeavored to tell a different story by reconstructing early histories of transracial adoption. This framework enables an analysis of how transracial adoption highlights the fractured relations among racialization, citizenship, and kinship obscured by these dominant histories and explores the terms of personhood constructed within the parent–child bond. These last three chapters analyze how literature by and about adoptees contests the stories that locate their histories in specific ways and naturalize specific forms of personhood. Here I focus on the mediations among the psychic, political, and legal domains through which the norms of adoptive personhood are constructed.

The Right to Identity

The dominant narratives for why adoptees were psychically and categorically different from the "own" child were provided mainly through post-Freudian psychoanalysis — Anna Freud, Helene Deutsch, and the impact of their work on social workers and adoption agencies. Psychoanalytic discourse constructed the adoptee as exceeding the boundaries of normative identifications and reality in ways that would influence legal formulations. Moreover, in circular fashion, they construct adoptees in ways that reinforce normative models of personhood provided through psychoanalytical models.

Florence Clothier's 1943 article "The Psychology of the Adopted Child" argues for what is distinctive about every adopted child:

> Every adopted child, at some point in his development, has been deprived of this primitive relationship with his mother. This trauma and the severing of the individual from his racial antecedents lie at the core of what is peculiar to the psychology of the adopted child. The adopted child presents all the complications in social and emotional development seen in the own child. But the ego of the adopted child, in addition to all the normal demands made upon it, is called upon to compensate for the wound left by the loss of the biological mother. Later on this appears as an unknown void, separating the adopted child from his fellows whose blood ties bind them to the past as well as to the future.[19]

This is not just a simple drawing of an opposition between biological children and adopted children in order to argue for the distinctiveness of the adopted child. The norm against which the adopted child is measured is the subject as defined through psychoanalysis, the idea that the normative child is ensured through a "strict developmental sequence at the end of which stands the cohered and rational consciousness of the adult mind."[20]

The model for this norm is the child who has a base, hereditary personality, onto which his earliest experiences and identifications are imprinted. Clothier describes this normative model in order to show the ways in which the adopted child both inhabits and departs from it: "Though analogies are unsatisfactory, we might say that, in the construction of the personality, constitution provides the basic metal, infantile emotional relationships and experiences add alloys and temper the metal, and childhood education and environment provide the superstructure, the façade, and the paint."[21] This is a psychoanalytic model of development that emphasizes early traumas and their hidden or latent effects later in life. In this way, the adoptee is the perfect demonstration of the psychoanalytic subject — because they are made to represent the impact of trauma on later life — at the same time that they depart from the norms that are put into place by psychoanalysis. Normal children are continuous, bound to the past and the future, and they build up their personalities steadily through early experiences and identifications. Adopted children, by virtue of their separation from their biological mothers and their "racial antecedents," are displaced from this normative process. The ambiguity of "racial" here — is it just a synonym for family or does it denote a racial heredity — opens up the trauma from being just about the mother–child bond to a larger separation from ancestral, familial, or racial history. It points to the curious slippage at the end of the Clothier quote from the separation between parent and child to the separation between the adopted child and "his fellows." The traumatic void is read in a particular way to suggest that adopted children are separate from other *kinds* of people, that this break introduces a categorical difference between adopted children and other, normal children.

In this way, adopted children are figured as both exactly like other children and categorically different. Clothier's logic that adoptees embody all the normal processes of psychological development, just taken to an extreme, is exemplified in her use of the family romance: "Every child, whether living with his own parents or with foster parents, has recourse to phantasy when he finds himself frustrated, threatened, or incapable of dominating his environment. . . . Children living secure in the love of their own parents can indulge in this phantasy as in a game. . . . For the adopted child it is not a phantasy that these parents with whom he lives are not his own parents — it is reality."[22] Both Clothier and Deutsch, and Betty Jean Lifton after them, describe the psychology of the adopted child in terms of Freud's idea of the family romance, but instead of seeing it as a formative stage whereby the child negotiates his ambivalence to his parents, they see it as a pathological structure in which the child lives in a fantasied, imagined world. Clothier writes: "For the adopted child there is always a question to which he can find no answer in the world of reality — even when every question he can frame is answered with full sincerity. . . . For him there is real mystery as to his antecedent possibilities, and correction of the foundling phantasy by reality is much less likely than in the own child."[23] The adopted child, in this formulation, is stuck in fantasy, and cannot correct its fantasies through recourse to reality. She emerges as having a specific psychology through this pathologization, much like the categorization of persons with neurotic illnesses. The adoptees' distance from reality becomes their defining marker as a person.

Moreover, within this discourse, the distance from reality marks an excessiveness and emotional disturbance within adoptees. In H. J. Sants's coining of the term "genealogical bewilderment," one that has been used to characterize adoptees' struggles with their identity since the 1970s, he writes: "A characteristic of the genealogically bewildered, particularly from adolescence onwards, is their *relentless* pursuit of the facts of their origin" (emphasis added).[24] Viola Bernard, similarly drawing on the family romance scenario, writes that "the most potent antidote to *excessive* and *persistent* pathological recourse to this escapist fantasy is a healthy, secure, satisfying relationship between the child and his adoptive parents" (emphasis added).[25] This *excessiveness* of fantasy means that adopted children have a skewed relation to reality: "reality seems to confirm his [the adopted child] fantasies and thereby strengthens them, in contrast to the non-adopted child's use of reality to neutralize fantasy."[26]

The identification of excess here locates individual adoptees' desires and needs as exceeding the boundaries of reality testing and of the subjective norms put into place for individuals by psychoanalysis and by the institution of the family. The adoptee is made to embody the outer limit of psychoanalytic processes of subjectification. Sants's influential article focuses in particular on the problems of identification and incorporation, restricting proper identification to biological similarity: "Differences in appearance can severely hamper a child's capacity to identify with his parents. . . . If differences in genetic structure between natural father and son can hamper identifications it seems likely that identification will be even more hampered when there is no hereditary link between father and child."[27] The adoptee represents the complete severance from primary relationships, leaving her with an unstable open-endedness to "antecedent possibilities." Without the control of "reality" on the possibilities of relationality or identification, the adoptee's selfhood loses coherence. Marshall Schecter emphasizes how adopted children "roam[ing] around almost aimlessly," concluding: "There is a lack of boundaries constituting a self; rather, what can be seen is a diffuseness in poorly integrated identifications."[28] In this way, the adoptee is rendered abnormal, a person whose life needs to be corrected, and whose early identifications need to be regulated so that these processes of identification do not become too "diffuse." The argument that adoptees make egregious demands on reality that, according to Clothier, can never be answered, makes adoptees into abnormal subjects because they take the "normal" process of integrating identifications with others to its socially undesirable ends. For Clothier, Bernard, and others, what is most disturbing about adoptees is the capacity for fantasy to exceed reality. The adoptee is made to represent the dangers of projection and identification without limits.

This way of imagining adoptees as outside of specific norms of personhood defined through psychoanalysis and social work begins in the early twentieth century and provides the conditions for the emergence of adoptees as subjects. By the 1950s, that the child could be scarred by separation became an accepted truism and paradigm for how to think about the child and the role of psychosocial development. As E. Wayne Carp notes, "By the 1950s, Clothier's tentative suggestion had evolved into a proven conclusion. Writing in 1953 and citing Deutsch's and Clothier's early articles, New York psychotherapist Viola W. Bernard asserted that the adopted child's inability to shake off the family romance fantasy was part of the 'symptomatology of emotionally disturbed adoptive children.'"[29] This use of psychoanalysis was prevalent in social work in the United States and was used to justify and defend adoptive practices of secrecy and the pathologization of the adoptee.[30] Psychoanalytic theory was extremely influential in suggesting for social workers that it was best to withhold information so as not to open up the psychological trauma of displacement for the adoptee and to preserve the psychological parenting arrangement between adoptive parent and

adopted child. Adoption experts went so far as to patholo-
gize adoptees who did return to agencies looking for their
adoption records as "unhappy" and "disturbed."[31] Assumptions about psychic well-being also work in conjunction with
the securing of racial norms. Even before the more perva-
sive sealing of birth records in the 1950s, "social workers,
acting in what they felt to be the best interests of the child,
had always selectively withheld certain facts about the child's
background. If a child was light-skinned, social workers would
deliberately not tell an adopted adult that one of his or her
parents were African American or Native American.... They
believed such information to be 'useless' and potentially dam-
aging to the child. A sincere wish to spare the individual painful
emotions or, as they saw it, social stigma motivated these omis-
sions."[32] In this way, disclosure or nondisclosure is used to
perpetuate and maintain social norms as the condition for the
individual's existence and reality. Psychoanalysis individualizes
and situates the adoptee within the purview of what Foucault calls psychiatric power in which the distinctions between
biological and adopted become not so much hard and fast
distinctions as constituting a set of negotiations with regard
to norms of personhood — own/not own; reality/fantasy;
whole/fragmented; racially marked/unmarked.[33] The normalization of adoptees along these lines constitutes the formative
conditions for their visibility and personhood at the same time
that it renders them unreal.

That the articulation of adoptees' group identities and rights
relied on psychoanalytic constructions of adoptive personhood
is manifest in the history of the adoption rights movement.
The pathologization of adoptees has been not simply a form
of denigration, but a form for instrumentalizing and codifying adoptees' specific claims and rights. Prior to the 1970s, the
argument to open up sealed adoption records was based on
previously existing constitutional rights.[34] Activists analogized

the harms done to adoptees by sealed records statutes to harms protected under the Thirteenth and Fourteenth Amendments. Thus, the argument goes, the inability to know one's parents was similar to the incidents of slavery in which slave children were sold without knowledge of their origins. Or the sealing of records violated the right to privacy protected under interpretations of the Fourteenth Amendment's equal protection clause. After the failure of these attempts, adoption activists took a different angle. E. Wayne Carp notes this shift in the argument to open adoption records:

> During the 1970s, the inability to gain access to adoption records by claiming constitutional rights led AAC [American Adoption Congress] leaders to emphasize arguments based on psychological needs rather than rights. As adoptee rights rhetoric declined, a second ideology arose that soon dominated and legitimized the movement in the public's eyes: the psychological argument that knowledge of one's birth parents was crucial to the adopted person's self-identity. In contrast to the red-hot rhetoric of "adoptee *rights*" that militant activists like Florence Fisher used, the public was presented with the cool, objective, pseudoscientific discourse of social-science research supporting the thesis that searching for one's biological family was of great therapeutic value and of little risk or harm to the participants.[35]

Although earlier manifestations of adoptee activism clearly saw the issue of adoptee rights as specific violations of personhood, this new shift began to put together legal right and psychic need. Instead of constructing the adoptee in the vein of the civil rights subject (the Thirteenth Amendment argument) or the subject of one's own private choices (the Fourteenth Amendment argument), this new angle binds the legal claim with the claim for self-identity.

Betty Jean Lifton played a prominent role in publicly spreading this new psychological approach to adoptee rights, most clearly manifest in her work's emphasis on the "reality" of the adoptee. Lifton echoes Clothier's 1939 thesis about the family romance when she writes that "the adopted child's family romance has much in common with other children's, with the difference that the adoptee lives in actuality the family romance that other children live in fantasy."[36] Similar to Clothier, she compares adopted children to other children based on this negotiation with the boundaries of reality. Lifton values the fantasy world as a positive formulation of how the adoptees struggle for the terms of their existence: fantasies "are an attempt to repair one's broken narrative, to dream it along" (62). But despite her attention to the constructive role of fantasy, she pathologizes adoptees as living fictitious or illusory lives in the pejorative sense of being detached from reality. She isolates the adopted child as living wholly in a fantasy world that threatens to be cut off completely from the real world: "Adopted children spend an exorbitant amount of psychic time in fantasy" (61); "Like Peter [Pan], they [adoptees] are fantasy people" (3). Furthermore, she highlights the adoptee's need for reality specified in terms of biology and some notion of innateness as a condition of their personhood: "The best interests of the adopted child can only be served . . . when the child is seen as a real person — not a fantasy child, not an idealized child, not a special child, not a commodity — but a child with his own genetics, his own talents, and his own identity" (275). When Lifton articulates the adoptees' need to search for their birth parents and know their biological history as a need to be "seen as a real person," she popularizes an already existing discourse that focused on the psychic needs of adoptees in order to make rights claims. Whereas before adoptees were pathologized for trying to find out information about their birth parents, now they are pathologized for *not* trying to find out any information.[37] As lack and excess, adoptees are variously positioned in relation to norms of personhood that do not simply reflect the valorization of biology. The norm of living in reality and not fantasy constructs and values notions of the coherent narrative, the whole person, and the person as historically and socially situated as real.

This genealogy of the adopted subject shows that the claims for legitimation on the part of adoptees rest on a specific psychoanalytically derived notion of adoptees as people who are constitutionally distanced from the real. Claims for rights understandably, then, often take the form of reproducing the norms of personhood in terms of continuity, proper identificatory images, and, as we saw from Lifton, a conflation of biological and historical lineage. Erica Haimes's article "Now I know who I really am" is a good example of this reinforcement of the norm, for even as she attempts to combat the way in which adoptees are pathologized as having identity "problems," she measures what adoptees lack in terms of the norm of a developmental sequence and formation of character oriented toward reality and not fantasy. Haimes suggests that the "issues of identity in adoption have more to do with constructing a narratable self than with crisis":[38]

> the "search for identity" then can be understood as the search for their life story, as an attempt to compile a complete consistent biography. Because adoptees have historically been raised without knowledge of their birth parents and the facts of their origins, and are, by virtue of their adoption, displaced from those origins, they are said to lack a narrative sense of self that is essential for their social recognition and membership. The discovery of their adoptive status leads to a reformulation of their life histories and the need to know the full facts. The importance of having a biography cannot be overstated since this provides the necessary account of one's life that everyone needs, not just adopted people.[39]

The lack of a "narrative sense of self that is essential for their social recognition and membership" suggests that adoptees can only make a claim for real personhood through the construction of this socially recognized narrative, one that requires the "full facts of their origins." Haimes conflates genealogical coherence with narrative coherence; for her, biological norms provide the necessary structure for legitimate narrative self-construction. The material signs of biology — a mother's medical history, birth certificates, a family tree — become the legitimating materials for a narrative sense of self that is socially legible. This way of articulating the rights of adoptees does not rest on pathologization per se, but still maintains the normative conditions of personhood that were in part reinforced through the figuration of the adoptee as abnormal.[40]

The legal struggle to open records and gain access to one's biological identity has been the central issue in legally and socially recognizing transnational adoptees as legible subjects. For example, the organization Bastard Nation has as its mission the construction of adoptee rights in this vein:

> Bastard Nation advocates for the civil and human rights of adult citizens who were adopted as children. Millions of North Americans are prohibited by law from accessing personal records that pertain to their historical, genetic and legal identities. . . . The right to know one's identity is primarily a political issue directly affected by the practice of sealed records adoptions. Please join us in our efforts to end a hidden legacy of shame, fear and venality.[41]

This organization explicitly depathologizes adoptees and makes the right to access records into a condition for their legibility as persons. In another example, the Transracially Adopted Children's Bill of Rights, put forth by the New York State Citizens' Coalition for Children, includes such rights claims as "Every child is entitled to have his or her heritage and culture embraced and valued"; "Every child is entitled to parents who know they cannot be the sole transmitter of the child's culture when it is not their own"; "Every child is entitled to grow up with items in their home environment created for and by people of their own race or ethnicity"; "Every child is entitled to have places available to make friends with people of his or her race or ethnicity"; "Every child is entitled to have opportunities in his or her environment to participate in positive experiences with his or her birth culture." [42] These types of statements that attempt to specify the conditions for a child's acculturation, socialization, and well-being are in line with a larger adoption discourse that translates needs into rights. The entitlement of a child "to participate in positive experiences with his or her birth culture" built around an idea of innateness is a way of ensuring psychological needs like self-esteem and self-acceptance that are crucial, the argument goes, for the child to be real.

Statements and rights claims such as those above play a crucial antiracist function, arguing against adoptive practices that do not respect or even acknowledge where adoptees come from, erase cultural backgrounds in the service of a normative whiteness, and ignore the racisms that endure both within the adoptive family and in society at large. These movements are extremely important in rectifying adoption practices and laws that deny the adoptee's claims for social recognition. What I am interested in teasing out is how this way of constructing rights normalizes certain forms of personhood that might limit the range of possibilities and relations through which adoptees become legible. For this argument often identifies birth with identity in ways that conflate biological processes of reproduction with historical continuities. Adam Pertman for example speaks of adoptees' quest for their "background" as a quest for the "people out there...with whom they had shared...hundreds of years of history." [43] What is imagined inside the child is tied to an idealized essence outside binding the child to a shared legacy, continuity, and deep history that legitimizes adoptees based on the bio-logic of genealogy.[44]

This way of constructing rights has specific effects on how race and nation are figured as ideals in the formation of personhood. It accentuates the importance of nation and race as fixed and bounded entities in determining personhood. Nation and race become repositories for this conflation of genetic and cultural "histories." To make the home into a self-enclosed world that presupposes and naturalizes how transmission and identification operate — as in the provision that "Every child is entitled to grow up with items in their home environment created for and by people of their own race or ethnicity" — already suggests how within this discourse, race and nation as specific spatio-temporal locations provide the boundaries within which transracial and transnational adoptees can lay claim to reality.

This logic is mirrored in the codification of children's rights, which were shaped in many ways by the controversies over transnational adoption. Articles 20 and 21 of the 1989 United Nations Convention on the Rights of the Child specifically concern adoption. Article 20 affirms that in considering alternatives to care from the biological parents, "due regard shall be paid to the desirability of continuity in a child's upbringing and to the child's ethnic, religious, cultural and linguistic background."[45] Article 21 makes it clear that national adoption is preferable to intercountry adoption: state parties shall "recognize that inter-country adoption may be considered as an alternative means of child's care, if the child cannot be placed in a foster or an adoptive family or cannot in any suitable manner be cared for in the child's country of origin."[46] The emphasis on safeguarding the child's national ties in both these articles is echoed in Article 8, which articulates a new right in the history of human rights. Article 8 declares the "right of the child to preserve his or her identity, including nationality, name and family relations as recognized by law."[47]

The problem of intercountry adoption — with its attendant scandals of kidnapping and baby trafficking — arguably forms the backdrop for this language of the right of the child to *preserve* his or her identity against the threat of it being taken away. As Jaime Cerda notes, Article 8 was made in response to the phenomenon of child abduction and child separation from families. The Argentinian delegation and the Polish delegation each put forth these emphases in the articles in response to historical circumstances — the former having to do with kidnapped and disappeared children; the latter having to do with orphans displaced by World War II. An additional provision to the Convention spells out precisely this worry about child trafficking going on under the guise of adoption: "A child shall only be adopted if the competent authorities, on the basis of reliable information have determined his status concerning parents, guardians, relatives and other biological and stable social relations."[48]

These safeguards against adoption as an unlawful practice and as one that fully considers the status of the child are of course necessary and important. What I am most interested in is how these articles conceptualize or, more accurately, leave ambiguous, the notion of identity. Rather than anything positively formulated, the identity to be protected seems to be more an effect of its loss. It is identified as a legal possession that hinges on familial and national origin. The UN Convention props up the family defined in terms of national and cultural origin as the safeguard against the loss of identity entailed by displacement. Many of the provisions have to do with the placement of the child within its proper context, within its proper surroundings — "the importance of the traditions and cultural values of each people for the protection and harmonious development of his or her personality."[49] These documents establish biological, normative kinship (as it provides a special key to cultural and social membership) as the conditions for personhood and the integrity of childhood. Indeed, at one point in the working group discussions for the conventions, there is an argument about whether "natural family environment" should be specified as "biological" or whether "natural" already implies the "biological."[50] These articles refix the identity of the child by reconstructing the conditions of normative kinship. As Sharon Stephens notes, the "family is still privileged as the ideal protective frame for children's well-being."[51]

These declarations, then, enact a logic similar to the "right to know one's identity": they conflate genetic, historical, and legal identities by identifying all three with some notion of birth. These become the terms of legibility for the adopted child whose "continuity" needs to be maintained and the child whose identity needs to be "preserved." Biological identity here stands in for the reality of one's personhood — but not as the simple valorization of genetics. Rather it stands in for a placed-ness in nation, family, and race that exceeds the biological. The biological is a spatio-temporal projection in which the body is situated properly, given the conditions that provide a corrective against displacement and unreality. The legal construction of children's rights implicitly relies on the psychoanalytic construction of adoptees as lacking reality because of displacement and separation from not simply biology but also from the normative development and identifications of personhood.

The psychopathological model of adoptive personhood limits the possibilities of identification and projection, ensuring that these processes do not stray too far from the imperatives of cultural, racial, and sexual boundaries. The legal formulation of the right to preserve identity complements this psychopathological model by conceiving of personhood as produced through given properties and specific relations to nation and race as fixed, spatio-temporal constructs. Both participate in a discourse of fixed cultural categories that act in the service of constructing certain norms of individuality and social relationality, norms that are made necessary by adoption itself, since the contingency of adoption makes possible aberrant forms of identification. Indeed, these two ways of forming adoptive personhood might be seen as responses to the particular threat that adoption poses: disidentification with "birth" and inclusion of multiple histories that fracture the singularity of personhood. But the "right to know one's identity" both as psychic need and legal right also challenges these parameters of personhood in ways that the literature of transnational adoptees begins to excavate.

The right of the child to "know one's identity" is often understood within a tradition of rights that emphasizes spheres of personal immunity from governmental intrusion — the right to liberty, the freedom of choice — that are supposed to be immanent in the assumed or even potential integrity of the person. But precisely because identity is *not* something inherent in the person but is guaranteed by something elsewhere — as these statutes freely display — the right to know one's identity is a right *to* others, a right to a larger community that will ensure the personhood in question. The right to know one's identity, as search stories make clear, is not just a mission of inward self-discovery but a process of making claims on others for protection and preservation. In this way they are more like social and economic rights that impose positive obligations on the part of government and that are organized under collective principles of social welfare and distribution.[52] As Michael Ignatieff writes about the incompleteness of a vocabulary of rights:

> Rights language offers a rich vernacular for the claims an individual may make on or against the collectivity, but it is relatively impoverished as a means of expressing individuals' needs *for* the

collectivity. It can only express the human ideal of fraternity as mutual respect for rights, and it can only defend the claim to be treated with dignity in terms of our common identity as rights-bearing creatures. Yet we are more than rights-bearing creatures, and there is more to respect in a person than his rights.[53]

The articulation of rights for adoptees challenges the framework of rights and personhood founded on the division between public and private precisely because it argues for a right to relations between persons, something that the liberal individualist tradition of rights language disavows in its pursuit of liberty. As Marx suggests in critiquing notions of personal liberty within liberalism in "On the Jewish Question," liberty is "not founded upon the *relations* between man and man but rather on the *separation* of man from man. It is the right of such separation. The right of the *circumscribed* individual, withdrawn into himself." This leads "every man to see in other men, not the *realization,* but rather the *limitation* of his own liberty."[54]

The claims of adoptees to their historical and genetic identities is a right to a certain *relation* with someone or something else. The narrowing of this problem within the children's rights conventions and the fight for birth records into the question of biological or national origin manifests the reduction of these claims to the normative terms of personhood. In this case, the right to know one's identity becomes a burden on the individual in order to be recognizable within certain interdictions. Certainly the ambivalence on the part of adoptees who do not search for their parents is evidence of this risk of assuming that the rights and integrity of personhood are bound up with knowledge of biological origins. Moreover, it limits the very radicality toward conceptions of personhood that transnational adoption poses.

Reimagining Adoption Memoir

Narratives of transnational adoption inhabit these terms of legibility, but also challenge the norms of personhood by registering the need to make a claim on others. The dominant convention in narrating the dilemma of transracial and transnational adoption has no doubt been the search and reunion story, which tends to locate racial or national origin as the key to real, whole personhood. The plot revolves around the adoptees' search for their birth parents, which often entails a journey "home" to their national origins. This has become a predominant form for conjuring the conditions of real personhood in narrative terms.[55] In this way, these stories mirror the logics of personhood and individuality constructed in legal discourse, which places the burden on adopted individuals to ground themselves within a certain national or racial trajectory. But these conventions need not provide the only horizon within which the literature of transnational adoption is measured. In this sense, it becomes important to carefully distinguish the political and public fashioning of the transracial adoptee often speaking in the declarative language of human rights from the stories of transracial adoptees that make claims as "something more than rights-bearing creatures," to return to Ignatieff's phrase. I focus on two works in particular, Jane Jeong Trenka's memoir *Language of Blood,* and Bharati Mukherjee's work of fiction *Leave It to Me,* because they self-consciously work within the conventions and forms of the adoption plot, transforming the declarative language of rights claims through narratives that struggle to ensure a listener, a community, and an external relation that will make the affective lives of which they speak legible. I argue that both texts register the problem of finding something inherent within one's body — an effect of the legal demand to determine who you are. And yet instead of reproducing the norms of personhood as they relate to nation, race, and kinship within the terms above, they outline different modes of personhood built on dependence on the world. Trenka's memoir figures processes of projecting oneself into the world in ways that confound the forms of nation and race, while Mukherjee's novel traces the limits of liberal personhood. Both narratives figure adoptees in ways that cut against processes of national and racial reproduction. They depict the forms and logics of individuality when nation and race as forms of territorialization cease to provide representations of the self.

In *Language of Blood*, Jane Jeong Trenka depicts her life growing up as a Korean adoptee in Harlow, Minnesota, often delivering trenchant critiques of racism and orientalism within the silences of adoption. Interlaced with recollections from her upbringing are Trenka's narrations of her contact with her birth mother and her journey to Korea, where she negotiates not only a set of kinship ties but also feelings of loss, punctuated by the death of her birth mother. In the journeys to Korea, the linkages between the psychic and legal norms in which adoptees are made to identify with some external cultural ground as if it were inside of them becomes powerfully present. For example, early on in Trenka's memoir, she articulates a sense of longing that mirrors the legal discourse built around an innate cultural identity to be preserved. When she visits a sacred temple at Haeinsa, she is filled with the desire to claim: "I must take something from this place, something more meaningful than the plastic tapes of chants, the cheap postcards, the wooden bead bracelets. I must remember what I feel on this day, in this place that swallows me in profuse, deafening color."[56] This scene demonstrates the underlying logic of identity at work in reclaiming one's origins. Trenka's demand on herself to incorporate something external as something inherent and integral to oneself reflects the processes of subjectivity dictated by the legal and psychological constructions of identity. This remarkable moment of willed memory and sensation, of willful binding to a place and time, manifests the demand to fix oneself to a cultural origin and history as the precondition for feeling real. The demand that Trenka places on herself at this geographical site is to take in all of Korea through this sacred site, to take in all of racial memory.

The terms of this trajectory are often couched as a sense of feeling more "real." While on tour in Korea, Trenka writes how she slips away from her tour group:

> I spoke no words and blended in, undetected for at least an hour, enjoying my experience as a "real" Korean. The shoulder-to-shoulder density of the crowd opened up and swallowed me, welcomed me into a sea of people where I could be lost in the sameness. Suddenly, everything seemed more real: edges were sharper, more in focus; colors brighter; sounds cleaner; odors more pungent. The third-person, waterproof luster that blanketed me in the tour group fell away: no longer *miguk saram* but *hanguk saram:* not an American but a Korean.... I joined in the swarm of bodies and no longer stepped carefully to avoid the used wash water, the residue of manual labor that seems to snake its way onto every Korean floor, every sidewalk, every surface where shoes tread. (119)

Replaying the scene of being swallowed noted earlier, Koreanness is personified and projected into space itself: she makes the floor, sidewalk, and "every surface where shoes tread" embody this identificatory desire. This construction of Korea is an idealizing form of wholeness, rendering the feeling of being real as consistent with the terms of idealization.

But if these moments depict Trenka's feeling of historical and national identity in ways that reflect the psychic and legal norms within which adoptees are made legible, she also denaturalizes them in describing these introjective and projective processes.[57] As Eun Kyung Min and Seo-Young Chu argue in different ways, Trenka's notion of blood is not deterministic but rather an open metaphor, a form of transferring meaning or of registering unspeakable and unexperienced loss.[58] If the declarative language of rights names nation, race, and culture as categories that constitute the grounds from which adoptees should speak, the memoir in Trenka's hands treats them as processes open to divergent psychic and material spaces. Trenka reconfigures Korea from being a static, concrete ground and idealization that guarantees her personhood to a shifting negotiation of the boundaries between imagination and reality. The feelings of "reality" mentioned earlier are temporary. After a week of what she calls "bizarre juxtapositions," even Korea as a projected space of wholeness gets broken up:

> temples filled with thousands of golden, compassionate Buddhas; the scene of the orphanage, where the children who could lined up for military haircuts and the five who could not because their hydrocephalic heads were too heavy lay motionless on the floor; the moldy tunnels dug by North Koreans past the border displayed as a tourist site; yellow strings of dried fish hanging in a department store; dancers whirling with pulsating peonies at the Korean Folk Village; exhaustion. (120)

Far from incorporating and taking in all of Korea, Trenka gives us a list of unassimilated material, bits and scraps of history, cultural artifacts, and broken memories. This dual movement neatly captures the tensions at the heart of Trenka's practice of memoir: Korea does not remain still, even as she longs for Korea as a fixed place. Trenka writes: "No matter how much Korea changes, no matter how at home or not at home I feel there, no matter how much I change, one thing will remain: Korea is home to my mother, and now she is buried on a mountain in a Catholic cemetery, her beloved Virgin Mary placed atop the headstone, watching, unblinking, six tiny ceramic musicians playing silently on their harps and trumpets

on the bottom ledge" (247). Even as the sentence strives to
negate change by constructing a fixed presence — her mother's
grave — the materialization of fixity (the headstone) calls
attention to the details and specificities that render any idealization impossible. "Korea" is traversed by various figurations:
the institutions and histories of the Catholic religion, the "six
tiny ceramic musicians" whose music remains unheard. These
details evoke other histories, other forms, that populate this
desire for an unchanging same. In Trenka's notes to the memoir, her playfulness with the "tradition" of naming practices —
crucial to the form of genealogy — is immediately apparent,
again breaking up the idealizations of an identification with
Korea: "As my Korean father did not follow conventional naming rules during his lifetime, I also disregarded tradition when
fictionalizing names. I tip my hat to my courageous Korean-
adoptee friends by borrowing many names from them. . . . I
ask the reader's tolerance in navigating this world in which the
improvisation on tradition is at times deliberate, and at times
the mark of a foreigner" (259). What is foreign and what is
native? Trenka leaves it up to us to distinguish what is a knowing improvisation that signals a "native" intelligence and what
is the mark of a foreigner. She gestures toward the rule of
genealogy even as she shows that these rules are themselves
upset by the supposed rule-makers. She intersperses her characters with her real-life friends, mixing Korean adoptees and
Korean people among the characters of her memoir.

Trenka registers the shifting conditions of relationality —
not wholly determined by psychic and legal norms that fix
the grounds of identity — through her revision of the declarative language of autobiography. When Trenka rehearses the
"my name is" trope of autobiography and its assumptions of
a social identity tied to birth as the proper beginning of one's
story, she iterates instead two names and two beginnings:

My name is Jeong Kyong-Ah. My family register states the date
of my birth, the lunar date January 24, 1972...

I am Jane Marie Brauer, created September 26, 1972, when I
was carried off an airplane onto American soil. (14–15)

While this could be read in terms of the tragic trope of
a "divided identity," the different sites named here — the
"family register," the airplane carrying a person onto American soil, the Buddhist temples in the mountains, the Lutheran
churches in the cornfields of the Midwest — gives the sense
that different names are fashioned in relation to distinct claims
to histories, inheritances, and imaginative trajectories. These
divergent histories are external and contingent. The juxtaposition of different modes of coming into being — "stated,"
"created," imagined, waking up — highlight a dynamic process of attaching oneself or being attached to different
histories.

Thus Trenka frames her life in terms of "facts" and reality just as much as she frames it in terms of fairy tales or
dreams and no framework is "truer" than the other. Indeed,
they merge:

I had been at Umma's apartment for nearly a week, surrounded by the Korean language from the moment I woke
to the moment I went to sleep....By the end of the week,
the Korean language began to permeate even my dreams. The
dream was plotless, a rehash of the day's sounds. Although
I couldn't understand, there it was — a full-fledged Korean-
language dream complete with Korean women talking and me
having no idea what they were saying. And then something
quite extraordinary happened: the dream seemed to dissolve,
although I didn't wake. And what was left was a kind of heightened reality, from which there emerged a very loud voice that
asked, "What is your name?" And I said to it, "My name is
Kyong-Ah." (134–55)

This moment of assuming the reality of her Korean name occurs where dreams buttress and support, rather than oppose, reality. The dream lends a "heightened reality," and language is not described as a communicative mechanism so much as an environment that "surrounds" her. This idea of language as a place, as something that moves between external reality and psychic reality *despite* its lack of material signification, constitutes a shared reality through which she can appear. Rather than being premised on the legal binding of name to the "facts" of background and heritage, the name appears where the opposition between dream and reality break down. Indeed, the final line in her justificatory notes — "Jane Jeong Trenka is my real name" — ironizes this question of names as tied to the certainty and "reality" of birth (259). We have already learned throughout the whole of the memoir the imaginative processes that have gone into the making of that name and that "reality." It is not a reality tied to a specific national or genealogical heritage. Rather it is the effect of a set of divergent idealizations, fantasies, and contingent facts. It is a construction in between the various legal identities of Trenka and her psychic investments — one in which the imaginary functions not as a deficit against reality but as complementary to it.

The form of Trenka's memoir bears out this rethinking of facts and fantasy. One might say that the entire beginning of the memoir unfolds as one framing device after another, as if Trenka is meditating on the ways in which one life can be inflected and conditioned by so many different external conditions. It begins with a letter written by Trenka's biological mother addressed to Trenka and her sister. Then there is a quote from the New Testament, Revelation 2:17. This is followed by a fable about the miraculous curing of a queen at a hermitage. When we finally get to the scene of Jane sitting at the temple at Haeinsa quoted earlier, we seem to have reached the present of the memoir. But the very next section is presented as a play, complete with character list, stage directions, and dialogue. The fragments of dreams, fairy tales, embedded fictional stories and one-act plays materialize a fluid relationship between the imaginary and the real. This insistent use of fairy-tale beginnings and dramatic scenes in the form of first-person narration does not merely fictionalize the construction of a life — what Trenka calls her own "personal mythology." Rather, they are all ways of situating the self as both subject and object, placing and staging the self in different, shifting frameworks.

That readers react to Trenka's narrative as evidence of the pathologies of adoptees as confused, mixed-up, and angry is a sign of the psychological norms against which adoptees continue to struggle, linked as it is with the legal and social imperative to either claim their birth cultures or to remain happy where they are. Unflinching in its depiction of sadness, depression, and anger, *Language of Blood* has, as Kim Park Nelson notes, "gained some notoriety as an 'angry adoptee' publication," often in the service of dismissing or critiquing its sometimes harsh depictions of transnational adoption and small-town America.[59] This characterization of the "angry" adoptee has to do with a disavowal of racism and infantilizing of adult adoptees — as if they can only be recognized *as* children — as Sun Yung Shin notes.[60] It also has to do with an anxiety over maintaining the boundaries and frames in which the adoptee is placed. As the analysis of legal and psychic conventions suggests, the securing of a particular relation to the adoptee relies on producing a particular cultural or national explanation for understanding the adoptee's actions and behaviors and by maintaining a strict boundary between fantasy and reality. Trenka's memoir not only challenges because of its frank expressions of anger and disorientation; it challenges because it disorients the reader's framework for contextualizing the adoptee.

It is with this understanding of Trenka's framing devices that we need to read her most virulent depictions of racism and orientalism. For they take the form of a projection back out onto the audience and reader. In a particularly powerful example, Trenka incorporates dramatic text in order to reenact a scene in a restaurant where "Jane" complains of being looked at. The scene ends with the people in the restaurant— doubling for the audience — shouting out racist epithets at Jane and her sister Carol. In another scene written out as dramatic text, "Don't Worry I Will Make You Feel Comfortable," "Jane" performs a monologue in which she hyperbolically acts out orientalist stereotypes much to the pleasure of the audience. The theatrical form is crucial here, for the text projects out the discomfort of being a spectacle, of being the object of racism, back onto the reader who structurally inhabits the position of the "audience."

Far from simply offering critiques of racism, Trenka overtly highlights the process of being made into an object — one in which she indicts the readers themselves for participating. When she introduces the story about her getting stalked, she frames it in terms of its sensationalism, in terms of her self as a made object: "How about this: I'll tell you a real story about a young co-ed who was almost raped and murdered by a deranged stalker. There are guns and videotapes in this story, police and courts. As the story continues, the young co-ed goes crazy and ends up in the nut bin, drugged and surrounded by real people falling asleep on their lunch trays because they've just had shock treatment. Here's the story, and I won't even charge you admission" (81–82). Trenka's memoir depicts in the act of writing itself the process of being made into an object, into something else. By foregrounding the different desires and projections imposed on her, she makes the readers uncomfortable. At the same time, though, she displaces the frames through which adoptees have been made legible. This appropriation of transracial adoption story conventions (the return narrative, the narrative of happy adjustment) reorients conceptions of personhood. Instead of a process of incorporation that is predicated on seeing the imaginary as lack and cultural/geographical origins as real, the text depicts a process of constituting a shared reality between external world and psychic reality, one in which fantasy and facts are complementary and conjoined.

Liberalism with a Vengeance

In *Leave It to Me*, the protagonist, Debby DiMartino, is an adoptee who, after moving to California, hires a personal investigator to find her birth parents. This search takes her through various relationships and reincarnations of her identity until her birth father — a serial murderer — finds her. Similar to *Language of Blood*, *Leave It to Me* uses the framing device to play on the declarative beginnings of autobiographical narration — the "my name is" and "I was born" that implicitly relies on a background of "facts" made real through norms of legitimacy. The declarative gives way to an uneasy negotiation with what could have happened: "I tell myself I must have been left unattended in the sun... I don't want to believe it was an overcrowded orphanage's scheme to rid itself of a bastard half American."[61] While this reliance on counterfactual thinking when it comes to birth is not peculiar to adoptees, we have already seen the great deal of institutional and imaginative energy that is invoked in order to secure the "facts" of birth for children in their biological families and to associate these "facts" with ownership, belonging, and attachment. Without these norms, every materialization in the world becomes a *possible* fact. This is

palpable in the beginning of the novel in which every perception is a possible recall of the originary fact of birth: "I can
almost touch the diamond-hard light of stars and the silky slip-
periness of leaves, almost taste smoke softer than clouds and
sweeter than memory, almost feel God's breath burn off my
sins" (9). These counterfactual perceptions — what is not there
but almost there — become the sites of possible connections,
continuities, and attachments to the world.

The novel begins with a mythic prologue that invites the
reader to think about how a history or a story becomes a
part of someone when there is no genealogical or biological
link that will place her within a certain group history. If, as
Mukherjee writes in "Beyond Multiculturalism," "One's biological identity may not be the only one," then this novel takes
up that challenge and asks: Without biology, what modes of
putting together a self are there?[62] What formations of identity are possible in this hodge-podge of myth and history? Or
as the adopted protagonist of the novel, Debbi DiMartino,
puts it: "Who are you when you don't have a birth certificate,
only a poorly typed, creased affidavit sworn out by a nun who
signs herself *Sister Madeleine, Gray Sisters of Charity?*" (16).
The response is, like Trenka's, not to valorize biological identity or the right to know one's identity as the telos of proper,
legitimate personhood. Rather, it is to question the underlying
assumptions of biological identity on our norms of personhood — specifically a liberal version that emphasizes property
in oneself and the liberty to make one's own life plan. The
problem here is how to become part of a shared world and
community, which involves a different set of questions about
how one relates to the stories and histories that structure one's
appearance in the world. This problem appears again in relation
to the name. For both *Leave It to Me* and *Language of Blood,* the
name is not something that one possesses and declares easily,

but rather something that makes a claim on others and other histories that may or may not prove hospitable.

Mukherjee articulates this ambivalence of the name when the protagonist, Debbie DiMartino, assumes the name Devi Dee, linking her with the mythic Hindu goddess. At first it appears as if the last lines of this section mark the freedom and lawlessness of the self-created person: "The Golden State offered freaky-costumed freedom, and more: it offered immunity from past and future sins. Goodbye, Debby DiMartino. Long Live Devi Dee. A fresh start; the American myth of self-creation and self-renewal" (65). Creating as she does a character who actively invents herself and seems to indulge in the liberal discourse of freedom and choice in America, Mukherjee's interests here appear to be similar to those of her short story "Jasmine," and her more famous novel of the same title. At the end of the short story, Jasmine characterizes herself as "a bright, pretty girl with no visa, no papers, no birth certificate. Nothing other than what she wanted to invent and tell." [63] Inderpal Grewal articulates a predominant sentiment when she reads the novel *Jasmine* as governed by a trajectory of migration that valorizes America as the locus of freedom, choice, and the realization of individual potential. [64] This reading, among others, uses Mukherjee's polemical statements about claiming America and American citizenship in order to critique the way she erases other histories and geographies in her fiction — depicting India as a site of primitive terror and inexplicable violence, for instance. [65] In this classic immigration topoi, as Grewal interprets it, India is characterized as traditional and unchanging, the site of primordial, fixed ties.

But the situation of adoption in *Leave It to Me* seems to reinterpret this topoi. [66] For Devi's renaming does not exemplify the oppositional binary of belonging and freedom on which allegories of Americanization are based: rather, it reinterprets belonging as a condition of freedom. The freedom of self-creation is not necessarily the product of the separation and autonomy of the individual, but rather something that is in dialectic with the relation to one's past and to other attachments. Debbie assumes the name Devi from the license plate of a blonde woman who passes her on the freeway. Near the end of her self-transformation, she reflects — "I put my money on Wyatt's wish that someday soon I'd be rich and powerful as well as tall, pretty, free" (65). In this sense, she is indulging not so much in an act of originary self-creation as an act of speculation on someone else's "wish" and interest. What drives her are in large part others' words — "I put my money on Wyatt's wish" — and her attachments to others. The reference of her friend's name to Sir Thomas Wyatt furthers this suggestion, for he was a Renaissance poet famous for writing courtly love poems mostly involving the pursuit of the girl and the hunt for a loved object. Devi is just as much searching and trying to discover — the narrative aspect of her energy and freedom — as she is being hunted and pursued herself. This is the twist that Mukherjee puts on the common motif of the adoptee searching for her biological parents. Because as the plot unfolds, we learn that far from being the agent of discovery, Devi is the object of discovery. Her biological father finds her and hunts her down. The trope of the adoption plot is reversed and shows not how one person is trying to discover her roots, but how external conditions hunt and haunt the discovery of personal signification.

Leave It to Me thus depicts the reverse movement of being claimed, the way in which competing connections and desires situate life possibilities. Taking up the adoptee not within the telos of immigration and class mobility, it does not identify freedom and the affirmation of American values as many of the norms around transnational adoption do. Though Debbie moves across the country to California at the beginning of the novel, she remains there for the rest of a novel that becomes more and more littered with broken-up elements of her past, her genealogy, history, and myth, which simultaneously situate and displace her. Mukherjee uses the adoption story not to depict a form of self-invention — one overdetermined by the markers of social ambition and American success — but rather to depict the multiple spaces and histories that inhabit the adoptee's claim to personhood.

Debbie's pursuit of the biological and historical terms of her selfhood highlights her negotiation with the all-too-real counterfactuals that make up her existence. Constantly navigating the relationship between the internal and external conditions of identity, identity is not "preserved" as something inside oneself as it is formulated in Article 8 of the UN Declaration. It is not ensured through the inviolability of origins. Rather, she interrogates the logics of an identity that is produced when neither the nation-state nor biological norms preserve the boundaries of personhood. Identity, far from being the effect of a narrative of freedom and self-determination or the realization of individuality, is a fragile proposition that is open to the different contexts, claims, and displacing effects of the world. Thus, there is a prevailing anxiety around references in this novel and the fact that words might carry around a different history, a different set of connotations. When the investigator Fred Pointer tells Devi about her background, he references Kurtz from Conrad's *Heart of Darkness:* "Two continents went into your making. That means you're one up on Kurtz, Devi" (105). To which Devi responds, "Kurtz was probably a mixed-race local rock star" (105). Kurtz is of course the fictional figure for a colonizer of the Belgian Congo, one who becomes primitivist in his power over the natives. This reference and its implications of violence, of imperialist struggle, are just as quickly dropped as Devi translates it into a contemporary phenomenon without a history of connotation. But of course language is laden with history and change and threatens to impinge on and attach itself to personhood. The connotations within names in this novel manifest this anxiety around reference: the name Devi itself recalls a path of destruction; Romeo Hawk, the name for her biological father, is just one among a myriad number of name changes that hide a history of murder. The problem is that meaning can never be contained and simply preserved within the person. History and references stick to language and displace the supposedly given or inherent meanings that situate one's legal and civic personhood.

The violence in *Leave It to Me* manifests the risks entailed by disrupting the sanctity of the integrated, unified individual so familiar to us from liberal political theory and that undergirds all of our notions of human rights. The status of character in *Leave It to Me* is a good example of these risks of personhood conceived as a matter of claiming others. In the novel, characters are different versions of one another: Frankie is seen through the lens of Wyatt; Ham is seen through the lens of Frank. Though seeing correspondences between characters is common enough in any novel, in *Leave It to Me* this idea becomes a principle of personhood. For these characters are not so much distinct, separate characters, as they are people who have a specific use and function for Devi. They fulfill a certain need of hers. She says at one point of her first lover, Frankie Fong, "I'd made him up out of needs I didn't know I had" (45). The instability of character in the novel is an effect of the role of individual needs and how people make other people. Is Jess really the mother of Devi or is she just made into the mother of Devi by the terms of the narrative, the information around it, and by Devi herself? Jess is made by her relationships with Ham and Romeo Hawk; Devi is made by the histories that precede her. The idea of character in this novel is that you are made by others and in the light of the history of others.

This notion of character is deeply unstable because it conceives of personhood as highly mediated by context and external materials. In her search for her birth parents, Devi is overloaded with various clues and written materials through which she is supposed to "find" them. Meaning does not inhere in the singularity of their bodies but is rather disseminated through different forms: transcripts of reports, legal proceedings. After reading transcript pages of a murder trial implicating her father, Devi states: "My mother'd committed follies on the other side of the moon, and now a lover or blackmailer was hounding her. It could be any flower child's story. . . . She was the perfect daughter of her times" (182). The more she learns, the more she views her biological mother as an effect of history, disrupting the singular relationship between parent and child. This logic is encapsulated in a short section of the novel that is told with anecdotes from a newspaper giving us stories of anonymous, random violence: "a man driving home from work. . . shot by a sniper"; "the proud owner of an Asian-run market"; "a refugee just arrived in San Jose"; "two high school dropouts" (109–10). These stories provoke a common fear whenever one reads about anonymous violence: it could happen to me; I am interchangeable with this unnamed person. These newspaper bits make victims and persecutors into generic entities who could be many people. The final paragraph of this list is "a daughter bumps into her runaway mother," bringing us back to the story proper (110). But this interchangeability of character suggests that personhood is made up of a contingent set of connections rather than anything inherent inside the person, thus compromising our attempt to make meaning inhere in a singular relation between narrative and body.

Instead of an isolation of meaning, a narrowing down to a single person that the search story usually portends, Mukherjee gives us an opening out into too many meanings and histories. She narrates personhood as disseminated across a set of histories and national boundaries rather than located "at one with the world." The relationship between national/territorial boundaries and the borders of personhood are no longer stable. In going over the murderous path and history of her biological father, Debby charts a whirling set of geographical places, all of which are not necessarily imagined through the lens of their geopolitical signs as they are through other imaginative signs:

> I was back in Frankie Fong's Asia: *hot, smoky; full of liars and cheats*. In Bio-Dad's over-crowded Asia, how does even an ambitious killer get himself noticed? No media coverage, no computerized Victim-Net, no milk cartons, no Xeroxed flyers. In Bangkok the lovers quarreled. They made up in Bali, to break up again in Surabaja. In Katmandu he added a Romanian to his harem. In Colombo, a Swiss. In Kabul he spent a day in jail for cursing a policeman. In all these cities, and in Chiang Mai, Srinagar and Taipei, he strangled, he conned, he made love to women he liked and to women he scorned and, who knows, maybe left my half siblings behind. (123)

On this rampage, her birth father keeps changing and adding people. People are picked up and left; intimacy is created and destroyed. Places become merely stops on a larger itinerary, a roadmap determined by other forces. Nationality remains a marker of personhood — a Swiss here, a Romanian there — but it provides no real information about either who these people are or even where they are. In this way, nationality is broken up through interactions and relationships, reduced to a marker that has no relationship to geopolitical meanings.

A similar dispersal and dissemination occurs at the intersection of historical events and national boundaries. The historical event of the Vietnam War is detached from its geographical embeddedness in Vietnam and is instead dispersed into other spaces and locales. Corresponding to this breakup of the historical event is the breakup of a single narrative whole into poetry, installments, and lines:

> Larry spat out his Vietnam stories. They could have been poems. He said things like "I went into *villes* scouting Charlie with twenty-twenty vision / I came out scoping Satan with the hi-res clarity of hallucination. . . . " When Larry got going, his words just popped, they belonged to me as much as they did to Loco Larry, and I didn't know shit about wars or Vietnam except for the Flash kick-boxing Commies. His war poems made me mourn the major job Vietnam had done on boys like him, the tinkerers of vintage cars, the village idiots from movie-set towns . . . the farmers from India, the laborers from Mexico, the crazy Armenians speeding on the shoulders raising dust and shouting insults at Okies like his old man selling corn and beans on the side of the road. All the stuff I'd picked up, all the *things,* stuck to my antennae, like pollen on a bumblebee. (136)

Vietnam becomes a world-historical event, affecting everyone from Armenians to the farmers from India to "Okies." Ceasing to be a narrative with a beginning, middle, and end, the stories are poems that impart what events are all about irrespective of one's local experience or knowledge. Dispersed and disseminated as things and as words, history becomes mobile and lateral, rather than bound within a specific territory or nationality or even within a specific person's experience. As such, they "belong to me as much as they did to Loco Larry," adhering to Devi even though the history is not "hers" in the experiential sense.

It is this spatio-temporal restructuring, this reimagining of what it means to live in displacement that transnational adoption stories imagine. Without the spatio-temporal boundaries of nationality, race and nation register as bits and bytes, as poems and nonnarratives across a range of domains and experiences. They are sometimes reproduced as psychic wholes that promise the idealization of being at one in the world as in the trajectory of the return narrative. For Mukherjee, her characters live existences at the limits of liberal personhood, neither self-contained nor self-possessed within the singularity of their history or genealogy. Neither an immigrant narrative nor simply a celebration of transnational mobility, Mukherjee gives us a character whose psychic itinerary through various references and histories that situate *and* displace her exceed the imperative to create inviolable personal boundaries on which human rights is predicated.

Trenka's and Mukherjee's adoption stories imagine and materialize modes of personhood erased by the legal and psychopathological models of adoption and rights. These latter models construct psychic integrity based on birth. This valorization of birth lays claim to "real" personhood through the legal norms of national origins and social norms of cultural identification captured in Article 8 of the Convention on the Rights of the Child. Despite the various theorizations of deterritorialized citizenship that "critiqued ideas of citizenship or identity based on belonging to one nation, state or even community,"[67] adopted children become figures for the integrity of singular belongings. Unlike Ong's flexible citizens, adopted children mobilize the parent–child dynamic in ways that produce a resurgence in national feeling. If, as I argued, the transnational adoptee achieves recognition, visibility, and agency only within a human rights tradition by being fixed to a single geographical entity or origin, one might say that the transnational adoptee has not been adequately conceptualized as transnational. In order to do so, the right to know one's identity needs to be reformulated in ways that take into account how one attaches oneself to the world.

Trenka and Mukherjee draw on narrative techniques of framing and the structure of address that dramatize the drawing of boundaries implicit in the "placing" of transracial and transnational adoptees. Understanding the history of the child not in terms of a linear trajectory of birth and not in terms of a declarative mode that recognizes what is already there, what is already in place, Trenka and Mukherjee depict the life history of the adoptee with greater attention than legal frameworks to the counterfactual. These works move back and forth between what happened, what might have happened, and what happened to someone else but not to me. Rather than disparage these elements as fantasy or as psychic lack, they utilize them in the service of developing a sense of personhood that is negotiating the knowable and the unknowable. In the effort to make adoptees socially legible subjects, legal and psychological frameworks have taken away the function of the imaginary, rooting themselves not in the multiple frameworks and temporalities in which adoptees exist but in the singular framework of one nation or one culture into which adoptees are projected. Writings that center on adoptees demonstrate the crucial role of the counterfactual in demonstrating their lived realities. They reveal the dilemma of making their protagonists legible within shifting spatio-temporal boundaries. It is to this problem of recognizing the adoptee within at least two distinct temporal frameworks that I now turn.

5

RESISTING RECOGNITION
Narrating Transracial Adoptees
as Subjects

Demanding Recognition

An adoption story lies at the heart of Chang-rae Lee's 1999 novel, *A Gesture Life*. Embedded within a narrative that deals with such politically charged subjects as "comfort women," [1] Japanese colonization, and war trauma, the protagonist and narrator, Doc Hata, recounts his struggles as an adoptive parent of a mixed Korean girl named Sunny. But far from being a secondary consideration, a subplot, or even a domestic version of these "larger" issues of racial and national politics, the adoption story provides a crucial angle on the identificatory politics of race, nation, and kinship in the novel as well as a way for thinking the connections between the national and the global, the domestic and the transnational. I argue that it does so by highlighting the question of recognition both as an aspect of adoption and of minority politics more generally. The ethics of recognition as the problem of how to give a legitimate place to and acknowledge the subjectivity of a person has been an intractable question within the political project of equality and rights-claims voiced by minority groups. The act of recognition is often premised on a liberal model of recognizing the uniqueness and separateness of the individual. As such, it often relies on the stability of histories and categories that can reliably and consistently place a person in the world. Through an attention to the contours of transnational adoption and adoption stories, this chapter reimagines recognition as it encounters the displacements of those very histories and categories on which it depends.

In anticipating his adoption of Sunny, Hata describes himself as a "hopeful father of like-enough race and sufficient means," already registering the difficulties in defining this relationship.[2] The odd phrase "like-enough race" in particular calls attention to, at the same time that it resists, the attempt to make adoption "natural." Indeed, the phrase sits uneasily within the terms of contemporaneous debates between proponents of same-race (a policy of matching the racial background of prospective adopters and adoptees) or transracial (a policy of adoption based on the "best interests of the child" irrespective of race) adoption placements. The reference to some notion of racial compatibility illuminates the inability to define race both between two persons and within a single person. Hata himself passes as Japanese, and we later learn that he is an ethnic Korean who was adopted by a Japanese family. Is he of "like-enough" race so that his daughter can relate to him better, so that others will not see a difference between them, or so that the adoption can be approved in the first place? This hesitation at the moment of familial construction reminds us that recognition is not necessarily a single experience, but something that can "become stabilized or destabilized in the course of a history."[3] After all, what does it mean for Doc Hata to be recognized by his daughter and by the community? How does the concern over "like-enough race" embody Hata's anxieties over recognizing himself as a father? And what does it mean for Sunny herself to be recognized at the nexus of these different demands and desires?

These dynamics of adoption in the novel unfold an anxiety with respect to recognition that links the novel to other

forms of adoption writing — in particular, a growing literature of anthologies, memoirs, and documentaries that attempt
to portray and represent how transracial adoptees themselves
articulate and negotiate who they are. As both Barbara Melosh
and Jill Deans have argued, adoption stories as a recognizable
genre emerge in the 1970s as part of the adoption rights movement.[4] Until the 1970s, the legal policies and social norms
of adoption basically rendered the fact of adoption invisible
and secret. The narrative of adoption as the best solution for
all parties involved denied the pain of relinquishment felt by
mothers, the stigma felt by adoptive parents, and the uncertainty felt by adopted children. Following the struggle for
civil rights, each of these parties began to contest this narrative of adoption as the "best solution." Adopted persons
contested the legal sealing of their birth records and narrated
their attempts to search for their biological parents; women
who had relinquished children for adoption claimed the new
identity of "birth mother" in order to exorcise the stigma of
relinquishment and articulate their psychic needs. Adoption
stories thus emerge as a demand for recognition for adoptees
and birth parents alike — recognition of the personal wounds,
stigma, and loss of belonging silenced by adoption policies.
In this first section, I take up how this demand within adoption stories plays out recognition as a contested site between
different desires and expectations, thus complicating normative accounts of recognition itself. As we will see, the demand
for recognition voiced by the adoptee is often accompanied by
resistance precisely because it interferes with others' needs for
recognition.

    The recent turn toward the transracial adoptee is an effort
to reclaim experiences that have been silenced or marginal-
ized by the attention paid to the dilemmas and positions of
adoptive parents. Stories that center on the transracial adoptee

typically shift focus from the trials and tribulations of adopting to problems of the child's acculturation, recognition, and identity. The move to have adopted children tell their stories is a project to foreground the agency of the transracially adopted child. But it is a complex demand for recognition on two counts. One, because the recognition of psychic loss on the one hand and social recognition of group rights on the other are not equivalent. Adoption stories and the example of Doc Hata above show that recognition cannot "be reduced to its legal dimension or to some 'paternal' or 'maternal' privilege," but is played out between these different modalities.[5] Two, because claims for recognition cannot be reduced to the singular, closed, one-way action in which a given subject confers recognition on an other — what Anne Cheng calls the "subject-based assumption... that 'I' recognize 'you' as a separate, individual, and equal subject (and vice versa)."[6] Rather, claims for recognition are often at cross-purposes and have asymmetrical effects.

For example, with the development of adoptees' rights, adoptive parents are often caught in between the claims of biological parents and adopted children, even as they are seeking recognition themselves. Recent ethnographic accounts of transracial and transnational adoption emphasize the competing demands for recognition made by parents and children on each other. Roots trips, in which adoptive parents and their adopted children return to the site of adoption, are organized in order to help parents and children construct a narrative of origin and beginnings. Culture camps are meant to give adopted children a sense of their culture, but also serve the less explicit purpose of helping adoptive parents "place" their children imaginatively and securely in terms of a socially recognized identity (based on a culture or nationality of origin). Several scholars emphasize the ambivalences and problems of recognition in the context of these practices. For example, Barbara Yngvesson's account of roots trips (in this case, Swedish parents taking their children adopted from Chile "back" to Chile) analyzes how Swedish parents attempt to materially reconstitute their child's origins so as to complete a narrative for themselves and their family and produce a ground of recognition. Even as the parents treasure and memorialize pictures of their child's orphanage in order to replace the lost past and background for their child, Yngvesson notes how it was often the case that the adopted children themselves experienced the trip in much more ambivalent terms.[7] Likewise, Ann Anagnost details the efforts of adoptive parents to "construct a Chinese cultural identity for their child [that] anticipates the problems of identity that emerge when the child begins to question her or his difference."[8] While Anagnost uses her title, "scenes of misrecognition" to refer to the "difficulties that adoptive parents face in their struggle for recognition as parents, a struggle that is intensified for the parent of a child identified as racially other," we see how the parents' struggle for recognition of themselves is inseparable from their desire to construct a socially recognized identity for their child.[9] Both of these attempts collapse the parents' desire to provide the conditions for their child's recognition of themselves (in terms of their cultural origin) with their desire to recognize themselves as parents. Recognition exists in this way as a struggle *between* parent and child.

Recognition is thus not so much a linear movement of self-discovery as a process mediated by others. The search narrative as a particular offshoot of the adoption rights movement provides a case in point. As Melosh notes, search narratives are generated as part of the adoption rights movement at the same time that they act to recruit new participants: "Many authors of published memoirs explain that they decided to search after hearing the stories of other adoptees on radio or television."[10]

Moreover, this particularly powerful reciprocity between adoption stories and adoption rights — one need only observe how stories of search and reunion have become popularized and proliferated through the national media — produces its own peculiar effects of recognition. Those adoptees who previously had not thought of or had not desired to seek their biological origins now feel *compelled* to seek recognition in this form. Kimberly Leighton notes her own ambivalence about the search process: "many people often express their belief that it is 'natural' to want to know" and then "extend this claim of naturalness to (or perhaps even base it on) their own imaginings of what *they* would want to know if they were adopted."[11] It has become unnatural *not* to search, thus limiting recognition to this particular form.

Search narratives not only promise and compel recognition, but also give the lie to this form of recognition as self-knowledge, because the demand for recognition always runs up against other people's demands for recognition. Though the expectation of the search is to find one's biological parents and thus be recognized, self-knowledge is very different from the feeling of being recognized. Reunion stories documented in the films *First Person Plural* and *Daughter from Danang,* where the adoptees "return" to their biological parents, provide examples in which adoptees *do not* find the key to their lives as they were hoping for. Instead, what viewers see is the problematic negotiation of claims for recognition. Moreover, they raise in particular the ways in which forms of racialized personhood become the site of these divergent needs for recognition.

Daughter from Danang centers on an adoptee from Vietnam, Heidi, who returns to Vietnam and is initially extremely excited to see her resemblance to her biological parents. She feels tremendously happy to feel unconditionally loved — a feeling that she never received from her adoptive mother. But she learns a lesson in recognition when her biological family creates expectations that she should be supporting them. Interpellated within a longer narrative of children who go abroad as the rich daughter living in the United States, it is her duty and obligation to send money to her biological family in Vietnam and take care of her mother, even though they barely know each other. She finds herself *too much* in the family; they become *too* attached in ways that she did not understand or desire. This misrecognition has to do with two different sets of expectations, both of which mean something like "family" to both parties. Heidi states at one point: "Cause I didn't come here to be anybody's salvation, I came here to be reunited.... The bond that I was hoping to have with her [biological mother] was acceptance of the little girl that she let go, and when I got here, it was like I was the parent, and the parent was the child. She wants to be with me twenty-four hours a day, and, you know, I'm feeling a little mothered."[12] In these statements, Heidi flips between her need to be "the little girl that she [her biological mother] let go," the uncomfortable feeling that she was in fact "the parent" who was emotionally supporting her mother, and the exact opposite feeling of being *too* mothered. She wants a form of acceptance from her biological mother that she is not getting. Being "mothered" is not the kind of recognition that she was hoping for, forcing her to rethink her own idealization of finding herself. These differing and contradictory emotional registers intersect the mother's need to be both mothered and mothering, and the child's need to both feel like a child and an adult.[13]

First Person Plural similarly focuses on the reunion story of an adoptee, Deann Borshay Liem. Written and directed by Liem herself, it emphasizes as its dramatic high-point the reunion in which her biological parents meet her adoptive parents and the dilemma of divided loyalties that seems to beset Deann. But most crucially it documents the demands for and resistances to recognition between Borshay Liem and her adoptive parents on one level and between her and her biological parents on the other. In both cases, what cannot be reconciled is who she is on the one hand and who she is to them on the other. For example, Liem finds out that the adoption agency switched her with another girl right before being sent to the United States. When she tells her adoptive parents that she is really Ok Jin Kang, her adoptive mother says, "Well, I didn't care that they had switched babies — you couldn't be loved more and just because suddenly you weren't Cha Jung Hee, you were Ok Jin Kang, or Kang, or whatever, it didn't matter to me you were Deann and you were mine."[14] Even as Ok Jin is very happy that she resolved her own mystery and corroborated her earlier sense that she was not who she was supposed to be, she is again denied the experience of recognition because her mother is protecting her own sense of belonging with her adoptive daughter, one that is predicated on her being only and always Deann. A similar scene of this denial of recognition is played out during a dialogue with Deann's sister:

SISTER: What was your other name? Your real name?

DEANN: You don't remember?

SISTER: No.

DEANN: Ok Jin Kang.

SISTER: See? Doesn't mean nothing to me. You're still Cha Jung Hee.[15]

When Deann revisits her depression as a particularly difficult point in her relationship with her adoptive parents, Deann addresses the lack she felt from her adoptive parents:

DEANN: Why didn't you ask me what was going on with me?

DEANN'S MOTHER: I don't know, I don't really remember. Maybe I was afraid you'd tell me, you know. I was afraid to know. Because at that time, it was, um, to me it was quite scary. I was afraid I was going to lose you. I just enjoyed . . . what we had. I never thought so much about us discussing it.[16]

Here Deann's adoptive mother recognizes in herself her own denial of Deann's reality: "I was afraid to know." Wanting to fix a relationship in its immemorial past — "I just enjoyed . . . what we had" — Deann's mother denies present realities, including her daughter.

Likewise, when Deann meets her biological parents, she speaks of the powerful resemblance and visceral feeling of likeness. But at the same time, her biological parents — in order to recognize themselves as having done the right thing by her — continue to produce a distance to her that she desperately wants to narrow. Unlike in *Daughter from Danang*, where family imposes too many demands, here Ok Jin Kang does not feel enough demand from her biological family: "What is startling when I look at my Korean family pictures is that during the past 30 years, they have had a very full, productive life. This is a disturbing and sad realization because I was not and am not part of that life. As I look at these photos, I can see the life I would have had with my family had I not been sent away. And I begin to imagine what I would have been like if I had stayed."[17] Both sets of parents resist recognizing Deann Liem in the way that she wants because her desire for recognition interferes with their own needs for recognition. In both cases, Deann is being taken for someone else, not because she is misrecognized for who she *really* is, but because who she is has everything to do with what she is for someone else.[18]

In these adoption stories, Heidi and Deann desire recognition at the same time that they continually run up against the limitations of recognition — negotiated as it is between different desires and demands that run at cross-purposes with each other. In their attempts to construct the transracial adoptee

as a socially recognizable subject through the literary convention of the search for identity, these stories manifest a specific
narrative problem: how to explain and narrate the emergence
of the adoptee across both the parents' (adoptive and biological) and child's demands for recognition. The predicament of
the "transnational" in these stories is not so much a loss of
original culture as the emphasis on roots would have it, but
rather the difficulty of recognition faced by the adoptee at the
conjunction of two distinct spatio-temporal frameworks for
organizing personhood. This is the nonmeeting between lived
and nonlived history that Borshay Liem observes above: "This
is a disturbing and sad realization because I was not and am
not part of that life. As I look at these photos, I can see the life
I would have had with my family had I not been sent away."

These are some of the difficulties that attend the emerging
voice of transracial adoptees. In addition to the documentaries
above, anthologies like *In Their Own Voices: Transracial Adoptees
Tell Their Own Stories* and *Seeds from a Silent Tree: An Anthology
of Korean-American Adoptees* mark specific attempts to hear the
voice of the transracial adoptee. As their titles suggest, these
texts emphasize the point of view of the adoptee; they are
characterized by the desire to transform transracial adoptees
from objects of discourse into subjects of their own discourse.
As the introduction to *In Their Own Voices* notes, the purpose
of the book is for transracial adoptees to "tell their stories in
their own words."[19] Taken together, these works explicitly link
the demand for others to recognize the experiences and lives of
transracial adoptees with the right to narrate their own story.
As Julie Stone Peters notes, in this age of testimony and human
rights, narrative has become identified with the ability to claim
recognition for the denial of both rights and personhood.[20]
Indeed, the idealization of narrative as a mode of recognition to redress wrongs and heal the self underlies the project
to "hear" the transracial adoptee. Adoption stories, however,

provide an opportunity to disarticulate the taken-for-granted identification of narrative and the capacity for recognition, and thus rethink the modalities of recognition and its impact on the ethics of transracial adoption.

Resisting Recognition

Narrative does not simply express claims for recognition; it mediates them. For example, each of the titles above conditions the project of recognition on a specific subject-position and narrative situation: the transracial adoptee is self-possessive ("in their own voices"); they emerge from a silence conditioned by genealogy ("seeds from a silent tree"). Even as these works focus more on personal narratives, their explicit or implicit participation in a collective project of social recognition constructs what Anthony Appiah calls scripts of personhood. "Collective identities," Appiah writes, "provide what we might call *scripts:* narratives that people can use in shaping their life plans and in telling their life stories.... Part of the function of our collective identities ... is also to structure possible narratives of the individual self."[21] Implicit in these narratives, then, is a narrative of selfhood that conditions the very demand for recognition within certain norms.

These works, and more generally this project to hear transracial adoptees tell their stories, raise several issues regarding the relationship between narrativity and what it means to be recognized. For in structuring "possible narratives of the individual self," these scripts may preclude other possible narratives and thus limit the forms by which the transracial adoptee becomes recognizable. The idea that we use collective scripts in order to fit into wider stories presumes that "narrative gives us the life, or that life takes place in narrative form."[22] Appiah writes, for example, "One thing that matters to people across many societies is a certain narrative unity, the ability to tell a story of one's life that hangs together. The story — my story — should cohere in the way appropriate to a person in my society."[23] But this model acts as if telling our story is a simple self-revelatory act, as in the formulation above "to tell their stories in their own words." It does not take into account the problem that narrative construction takes place within the context of a relationship, an address to someone.[24] The act of narration does not simply communicate "my story" to another, as in some reciprocal exchange. Rather it is marked by what you demand of me, what I project onto you, what we desire of each other, in the act of narration.

This focus on the narrative dimensions of recognition allows us to reconsider the emergence of minority subjects within a contemporary politics of equality and multiculturalism. Charles Taylor's influential model of recognition detailed in "The Politics of Recognition" relies on representing the inter-subjective encounter and the relationship between the self and "significant others." He draws on Mikhail Bakhtin's notions of address and dialogism in order to argue that the construction of recognition is always dialogical:

> We define our identity always in dialogue with, sometimes in struggle against, the things our significant others want to see in us. Even after we outgrow some of these others — our parents, for instance — and they disappear from our lives, the conversation with them continues within us as long as we live.... [Identity] is who we are, "where we're coming from." As such it is the background against which our tastes and desires and opinions and aspirations make sense. If some of the things I value most are accessible only in relation to the person I love, then she becomes part of my identity.[25]

Individual identity is profoundly dependent and relational in Taylor's scheme of dialogism. But it is also based on a process of appropriation or incorporation: "the conversation with them continues *within us* as long as we live"; "she becomes *part of* my identity." Identity, even in this very paragraph, moves between something outside ("the background against which our tastes and desires and opinions and aspirations make sense") and something appropriated ("my identity"). But how exactly does this movement between outside and inside work, and what does the language of appropriation sustain ("she becomes part of my identity")? Taylor acknowledges that the dialogic encounter opens us up to the "things our significant others want to see in us." But then he closes off this danger by suggesting that the self is something onto which one adds his or her encounters with significant others. The disjunction between one's background ("where we're coming from") and his dialogic encounters is stabilized through the acts of possession and ownership underlying the phrase "she becomes part of my identity."

The problem of adoption revises Taylor's notion of recognition by giving us a relation that is asymmetrical, nonreciprocal, and nonsynchronous, one characterized not by the easy appropriation of others into "my identity" but by the disjunctures between "who we are" and "where we're coming from."[26] The struggle for recognition in the context of adoption reveals something more like a dual structure of recognition — two temporalities that overlap but do not necessarily meet in any form of mutuality or reciprocation. This is apparent in the example above from Anagnost, in which parents project an identity for the child "that *anticipates* the problems of identity that emerge *when the child begins* to question her or his difference" (emphasis added). Or in the different constructions of and motivations for the "roots trip" by adoptive parents and children pointed out by Yngvesson. The process of recognition is always working through at least two temporal scenes — the scene of encounter and a later, other moment of emergence. Recognizing the transracial adoptee's cultural difference is not something that is simply performed by a parental act or enacted through the institutional preferences of the social worker. For the adoptee, the moment of recognition is deferred, and is enacted only through contingent processes of development and individuation. The process of recognition is always double: the "initial" moment of the emergence of the transracial adoptee in the family and its projection of the child either as culturally different or assimilated as the same, and a later moment in which the child recognizes herself through contingent processes of individuation. In other words, the problem of recognition continues well past the initial naming and transfer of the baby. The description of recognition according to Taylor is a model of incorporation whereby our dialogical encounters with others help constitute our selves. What this double-scene of recognition suggests, on the other hand, is the persistence of two different frames of reference in and through each other, moving back and forth in an uneasy oscillation.

The transracial adoptee does not emerge transparently as the subject that tells their own stories. The doubling of recognition displaces the singular moment of capture — "it didn't matter to me you were Deann and you were mine" — privileged in accounts of adopting. Notions of reciprocation hide the more complex exchanges between self and other when one person recognizes someone else only within and against other contexts and backgrounds: what I want to see in you requires displacing you into another context or some other imagined relationship. This is close to the psychoanalytic notion of transference — that we invent other persons on the basis of our past relationships, and they likewise do the same to us — and I wish to rethink the model of reciprocation and dialogic encounters as instead marked by transference. The concept of transference will be explored in more detail, but for now it is a useful concept because it raises the tensions between past and present, opening ourselves up to other persons and simultaneously closing off our encounters with other persons. More broadly, transference, as opposed to the dialogic nature of the individual explored by Appiah and Taylor, underscores the notion that we are never simply responding to others as a singular identity. Rather, the self-other relationship is marked by a series of overlapping histories in which self and other are repeatedly being constructed through other relationships.

I have argued so far that adoption stories emerge as a claim for recognition, and that this narrative demand becomes a contested site through which different people's claims for recognition are negotiated. I suggest that an analysis of the enunciatory conditions of narrative — what you demand of me, what I project onto you — allows us to rethink modes of recognition. The rest of this chapter explores the relationships between narrative modes and claims for recognition by comparing some of the efforts to narrate transracial adoption. By paying close attention to the relationship between the scripts of identity that produce and recognize the transracial adoptee as a subject on the one hand, and processes of narrating adoption that intersect several histories in conflicting ways on the other hand, we can see the way in which the transracial adoptee is both part of an emotionally laden intersubjective relation and at the nexus of several contiguous and conflicting processes — immigration, migration, economic exchange, assimilation, domestication — that are in continual negotiation.[27] I use the model of recognition that I have been developing in order to juxtapose stories of transracial black–white adoption with stories of transnational Korean–white adoption. By comparing the narrative dynamics and frames of the anthologies, *In Their Own Voices* and *Seeds from a Silent Tree*, I show that even as the ostensibly separate paradigms of domestic transracial and transnational adoption are kept safely apart in order to secure recognition for the adoptee, the double-scene of recognition suggests how a "national" race politics is never simply divorced from a transnational politics and vice versa.

These anthologies of adoption stories point to the construction of a collective script: the collective identity of the adoptees into which the individual adoptees are made to fit and according to which they shape their life stories. The mode of the anthology is to put fragments together and make them into a new whole. In the examples below, we see how the anthology and autobiography work together to mediate the collective identity and individual narrative of the transracial adoptee in securing recognition within a specific framework of understanding race and nation. The form and frame of these stories, however, reveal fissures within their own constructions. By reading these fissures, we can identify the narrative mechanisms of the scripts and norms of recognition even as those same mechanisms resist and foreclose the difficult asymmetry of the adoptive relation itself.

I then turn to Chang-rae Lee's *A Gesture Life* in order to show how it offers a different model for narrating transracial adoption. Less confined by the need to either justify or condemn the practice of transracial/transnational adoption, or the demand to construct a narrative of identity that is peculiar and particular to the experience of transracial adoption, *A Gesture Life* calls attention to the role that norms of recognition play in fashioning the life stories of transracial adoptees. I pay particular attention to the confusions of temporality and the ambivalence of address in *A Gesture Life* in order to argue how the conjunctions of racial histories figured by adoption are enacted through transference: a relation in which the parent sustains the adoptive relationship only through taking the child as another. The language of Doc Hata — a little *too* obliging, a little *too* familiar — is the perfect vehicle for revealing the ambivalences, erasures, and resistances that are embedded in adoption writing itself.

Anthologizing the Adoptee:
Collective Scripts and Unscripted Responses

In Their Own Voices: Transracial Adoptees Tell Their Own Stories and *Seeds from a Silent Tree: Written by Korean Adoptees* represent two very similar calls to heed and recognize the voice of the adoptee in adoption discourse. Yet they emerge from paradigms of domestic, black–white adoption and transnational, Korean–white adoption, respectively, which have been opposed. Transnational adoption is analyzed in terms of a booming cultural economy that has emerged in places like China, India, and Chile, to name just a few. Transracial adoption on the other hand is analyzed in terms of U.S. race relations, the denigration of black children and continuities with a history of policing black families. Analyses of the former focus on narratives of salvation, the commodification of children, the problems of national histories, while the latter focus more on debates on the propriety of black–white adoptions set off famously by the argument by the National Association of Black Social Workers that white parents would not be able to raise black children with adequate attention to their needs.[28]

Thus black–white adoption is seen as a "domestic" issue either to promote more attention to the problems at home with regard to the state of foster-care and the limiting and disciplining of black bodies or to serve as a foil to the more desirable and consumable form of difference that is the transnationally adopted child.[29] Transnational adoption is seen as a question of foreignness in order to divorce these adoptions from all of the "racial" issues that begin at "home." The rhetorical and narrative choice is often to keep the two separate, each with its own separate issues, one located here at home, and the other located abroad. I put the two together in order to think about the effects of this separation of the domestic from the transnational on the capacity to recognize the adopted child.[30] For example, because of this separation, we tend to see domestic, transracial adoptions in light of the legacy of slavery and the history of the civil rights struggle, and we tend to read international adoptions from Korea, for example, in relation to the devastation caused by the Korean War. It is as if the proper way to recognize and give agency to the domestic, transracial adoptee and the transnational adoptee is to frame them within their own specific histories. What the desire to fix these two modes of adoption within their own "proper" histories misses, however, is the overlap and the intertwining of these histories, the fact that racial issues at home are deeply imbricated with global policies abroad and vice versa. The most obvious manifestation of this is the invisibility of the mixed black–Korean adoptee, a legacy that intertwines American race relations and the important role of African American men in the military history of the United States and the transnational conflict in Korea. Another example is the tendency to see domestic, black–white adoptions as having centrally to do with problems of race "at home," while transnational adoptions do not pose "racial" problems at all.[31] This separation of the domestic and the transnational, black and nonblack, has crucial implications for the forms of identity that are seen to be proper and permissible for certain adoptees.

The anthology *In Their Own Voices: Transracial Adoptees Tell Their Own Stories,* published in 2000, dramatizes the conflict between the scripts of recognizing the transracial adoptee and the demands and desires embedded in the narrative situation itself. *In Their Own Voices* is a collection of interviews with transracial adoptees, whose purpose is for transracial adoptees to narrate their daily lives and experience, and the myriad ways in which they construct and struggle to articulate their identities. These interviews are engaged in a project of individualizing these adoptees and emphasizing the complexities of their identity formation. But the narrative trajectories of these interviews often narrow down the contingencies of identity formation that the subject of transracial adoption raises in their life stories. The social recognition of transracial adoption becomes more and more dependent on fitting within a narrative that ties the recognition of identity to a recognition of cultural difference as fixed origin. In other words, the recognition produced for adoptees depends on limiting "recognition" to the single, initial moment in which the adoptive parent adopts the child *as* racially other. This has the effect of fixing the transracial adoptee within a specific national domestic history of black–white race relations. For example, the introduction begins with the wide-reaching, multiracial possibilities of a study of transracial adoption: "Beginning in the late 1960s studies were conducted of white families who adopted American black, Korean, Native American, and other children whose racial and ethnic backgrounds were different from those of their adoptive parents" (xiii). But as the introduction goes on, the focus narrows to black and mixed-race adults (mixed-race meaning black and white).

Throughout this group of interviews, the collective script of transracial adoption becomes quite clear, as the adoptees' narrative trajectories are geared toward a moment of recognizing that they are black within the domestic framework of black–white relations. At the same time, we can read the responses within the act of narration that interrupt this narrative reconstruction. In an interview with a mixed-race adoptee named Tage Larsen, who has a brother named Peik, who is African American and Vietnamese, we see how race gets singled out as the major component in processes of identification and the formation of identity. For even though Tage insists that his relationship with Peik is strong because of closeness in age, and not race, the interviewer singles out the racial aspect as important, making it both origin and destination:

Did you feel naturally drawn to him [Peik] because he is part black?

No. It was pretty much free reign [*sic*] ...

Once you interacted with society outside of your family, did you then feel a certain connection to your brother Peik because of his ethnicity and skin color?

No, not at all. ... I didn't share a special bond with him because of that. (249)

The direction of these questions locates relationality and identification solely along lines of racial resemblance. They seek to tie together a fictive moment in the future (racial consciousness) with an earlier moment in which racial consciousness is less fixed and contingent — "did you *then* feel a certain connection..." (emphasis added).

Despite the complications that Tage's family suggest regarding the whole notion of family or understanding one's family in relation to race, the interview questions relate race to identity as both cause and effect — race is the primary component of identity in that it is both the originary relation and that toward which one is driven. The interview gradually turns toward issues defined by "blackness": "Were there other African Americans in these groups or were you the only one?"; "How does one excite persons in the African American community, young people specifically, about the world of classical music?" (253). Several times toward the latter part of this interview, different versions of "what does it mean to be black" or "to be an African American, what does that mean to you?" are asked (250–51).

In another of the interviewer's questions, she locates Tage's blackness within and against his family metaphorized as a "melting pot": "In a family that reflected a 'melting pot' of different races and ethnicities, how did you maintain your blackness, or did you?" (249). The metaphor of the melting pot fixes the terms of opposition between a model of ethnic assimilation and the specificity of blackness. This last "or did you" evaluates the arc of Tage's life based on recognizing blackness. As a result of this frame, the contingencies of family formation — through schooling or through sibling relationships — are related back to the "originary" moment of adoption in which the opposition between the "white" family and the "black" community is dramatized and repeated.

What becomes a common refrain through these interviews is the desire for the white family to "recognize" the racial identity or cultural choices of their transracially adopted sons and daughters. In one example, the interviewer asks, "Do you think that a black child has a 'future' in a white family?" The interviewee responds with the familiar refrain, "Yes, if the family recognizes that the child is from a different culture and makes a point of actively engaging themselves and the child in that culture" (125). Here the adoptee rehearses the terms of the opposition between "black child" and "white family" that structures the conceptualization of transracial adoption. But what does recognition mean here? To think of the child as "from a different culture" is to define culture solely as a past origin that somehow inheres in the child. To "engage the child in that culture" is to produce distinct conceptions of what black culture and white culture are, and one that presumes a transparent and deterministic relationship between the child's background or place of origin and what he or she should be. This way of framing the adoptee's story reveals the way in which the projection of recognition relies on relating the different, nonsynchronous, moments of recognition into one seamless whole, built around the transparency of blackness. Race is used as a bulwark against the temporal disjunctions between race and nation that mark adoption itself. At the same time, the claim that these adoptees are telling "their own stories" reduces the interview situation — the projections and demands of the interviewer — from which this story is made. The constant back and forth between question and answer allows us to read some of the intersubjective demands within the narrative situation itself.

In Their Own Voices dramatizes the desire to narrate a certain trajectory of racial recognition and the temporal mechanisms of that desire. The direction of the questions continually dramatizes, repeats and returns us to an "initial" moment of adoption in which the adoptee's origin is fixed in terms of racial and cultural difference. Likewise, the frame of *Seeds from a Silent Tree: An Anthology by Korean Adoptees*, edited by Tonya Bishoff and Jo Rankin, naturalizes the moments of recognition that are then made to be formative of the self. This text is a collection of short stories, poems, and nonfiction essays (mostly in memoir or autobiographical style) written by Korean adoptees. But it specifically reuses and appropriates the family tree in order to frame these adoption experiences. All of the Korean adoptees in this anthology are said to "share a specific common origin," thus remaking a form of family and genealogy for these anthologized adoptees.[32] The selections are grouped into four sections — titled (in sequence) "Roots Remembered and Imagined," "Transplantations," "Reunions," and "Seeds of Resolution" — which mimic a biographical model or developmental model that moves from the explorations of roots to the negotiation of new environments to a return to biology and finally to some form of reconciliation. This framing makes a collective set of experiences into a linear form: the sections chart an individual, teleological journey from beginning to end. In this way, the frame of the anthology makes clear that the social recognition of transnational adoption is premised on the terms of a familiar genealogical model. It relies on imagining one's birthplace as a kind of originary relation that needs to be negotiated at some level.

This formal trajectory that dichotomizes birthplace and the act of adoption also dichotomizes Korea and America and makes the pattern from Korea to America and (sometimes) back into a single, continuous movement. In this way, we see the problems of adoption played out as a series of oppositions. As Catherine Ceniza Choy and Gregory Paul Choy note, "Many of the entries in the anthology border on what are by now considered hackneyed expressions of racialized identity in Asian-American literature — either / or, inside / outside, white / nonwhite binaries; encounters with racists and fetishists; and quotidian orientalism."[33] For example, David Miller in *Seeds from a Silent Tree* writes: "Walking a tightrope / Pulled on both sides / Korea / America / For if I fall either way / I lose a part of me" (107). These "hackneyed expressions" should also be seen, however, in the context of how the frame of the anthology links these oppositions to forms of racial recognition. The frame constructs the Korean adoptee as recognizable only in their difficult relation to a cultural and racial origin (Korea) on the one hand and a white family on the other. *Seeds from a Silent Tree* — from its title to the structure and titles of its four sections — reiterates the terms of public recognition.

None of the authors in *Seeds from a Silent Tree* self-identify as Asian American, but rather refer to themselves as "adopted Korean" in keeping with the collective script set up by the anthology.[34] At the same time that the organizing term of "Korean adoptees" helps codify a narrative of return and origins, or an unresolved movement between the fixed terrains of two national cultures, we can also hear, though, a note of tension within some of the stories themselves. As one of the writers in *Seeds from a Silent Tree* writes — against the grain of this frame — "Being adopted Korean is far more complex than *choosing* racial designation."[35] Rather than recapitulate the terms of choosing "Korea" or "America" or the impossibility of doing so, this writer holds out — if only negatively — for other narratives. Another one of the stories in *Seeds* calls attention comically to the desire for a transparent way to recognize if one is adopted or not: "I have adopted Korean radar, I'm sure of it. Perhaps all adopted Koreans have it built inside" (73). The speculative fantasy that adopted Koreans have some built-in connection to each other begs the question of what exactly constitutes the connection or commonality between adopted Koreans. Instead of basing commonality on the division between Korea and America, as the framing of *Seeds* suggests, the problem of recognizing other adopted Koreans questions the very categories that we are using to narrate and collectivize the adoptees.

The "adopted Korean" has come to be its own identity category at the same time that it has an uneasy relation to other statuses or minority identities. Younghee in her short story "Laurel" writes, "Being adopted into a white family does give one a unique perspective.... I no longer believe I am white, but I still have days when I desire to look white.... I still do not know what it means to be Korean American, but I do have a sense of what it means to be Asian American" (88). At first she recapitulates the framing of her own subject position (her "unique perspective" that the experience of transracial adoption supposedly confers; her grappling with the "whiteness" of her family), but then it is slowly revealed that none of these "collective identities" — "white," "Korean American," "Asian American" — necessarily have a given content. "Knowing" what it means to be Korean American or Asian American poses a problem because these terms do not correspond or even refer to any concrete, given content or experience. Rather they are terms that fail to capture the overlapping histories that condition the appearance of the "adopted Korean." Younghee seems to act out the split between racialized identity as it manifests itself within the context of an Asian American domestic orientation and racialization as an effect of transnational exchange. These two frames meet uneasily, evacuating the familiar contexts and histories in which terms like "white" and "Korean American" have emerged as meaningful terms in the past.

Both these anthologies frame the demand for social recognition. But a close look at the mechanisms of this mediation between collective scripts and individual identities reveals the organizing terms that govern social recognition, and the assumption of a single frame of reference that the adoptive pair rely on in order to make sense of their situations and construct their identities. The collective scripts embedded in the frames of these anthologies condense the uncertainties of the adoptive relationship into a notion of return to an origin as a linear process. The narrative of recognition as return codifies norms of recognition that rely on securing the particular ground of one's own culture or one's own race. But as we have seen, the narrative production of a collective script is marked by its own moments of nonrecognition. The ground opened up by Younghee among the terms "Asian American," "Korean American," and "adopted Korean," which fail to provide a stable reference point, is precisely where Chang-rae Lee locates his engagement with adoption discourse. Lee shows how adoption intertwines lives and histories in ways that problematize the closures of a narrative drive toward recognition. His novel provides a model to think about transracial and transnational adoption together as enacting the relationship of two temporalities that is not a movement from one to the other (black community to white community; Korea to America) but a disjuncture that raises the problem of when to mark difference and what history to inscribe. Indeed, Doc Hata's attempt to be comfortably "at home" is the perfect analogue for an adoption narrative that can never quite settle down in one place.

Adoptive Relations as Transference

A Gesture Life is structured by adoptions. The main character, Doc Hata, is an ethnic Korean adopted by a Japanese family. When he moves to the United States, he lives in a suburb named Bedley Run and is thought of as a Japanese person. He adopts a girl, Sunny, from Korea, who is of ambiguously mixed race — some references are made to her being of mixed black and Korean ancestry. These layers of adoption constantly question "where we're coming from," the relationship between background and identity so necessary for the project of recognition. Doc Hata's adoption of Sunny, at one level, seems to mimic the standard narrative of transracial adoption: raising Sunny in Bedley Run matches the classic setting of transracial adoption — the predominantly white, upper-class suburb. Doc Hata is a good, assimilated immigrant, and his adoption of Sunny takes the form of this narrative of giving the adoptee a better life. At the same time, this mixing and matching of race and nationality makes it unclear whether the adoption is same-race or transracial — in fact, it seems to disrupt these very categories. When Hata adopts Sunny, he wonders if he is of "like-enough race" to adopt her.

I focus on this novel not just because it thematizes the problem of adoption, but because adoption forms a nexus for the relationships among race, personal and national histories, and social recognition. Two narrative drives coexist uneasily within this text: on the one hand, Doc Hata's drive to belong and find closure for his life as an assimilated Japanese American in the suburban town of Bedley Run, and, on the other, his constant returns to and flashbacks of the past, the traumatic events of his participation as a Japanese soldier in World War II. What connects these two narrative movements is Hata's adoption of Sunny. This adoption, moreover, explicitly repeats his relationship with K, a comfort woman whom Doc Hata met while stationed as an officer in the Japanese army, as he works out his feelings and relationship toward the one in terms of the other and vice versa. Adoption thus mediates these two narrative movements: its place as a pivot between past and present exemplifies the nonsynchronous nature of the adoptive relationship. Doc Hata's drive is to normalize experience, to make everything "familiar" — which is, in a sense, the drive of adoption to make a "normal" family. But this rubs up against the difficulty of narrating the event of adoption, the persistent inability to relate Sunny back to an understandable origin. *A Gesture Life* is characterized by how this relationship between two narrative drives embeds the difficulties in narrating transracial adoption.

The story of how *A Gesture Life* was first conceived and then rewritten helps us think about the place of adoption in the novel in relation to the ethics of recognition.[36] As Lee notes in an interview

> I originally wanted to write a book that was told from the point of view of a "comfort woman."...I was doing some reading about Korea, and I found out about what happened to these women, and I was just blown away....I remember being on a bus after reading what was otherwise a pretty dry academic article on the subject, and I had to get off and walk home just to think about what had happened.[37]

As Garner goes on to note, Lee flew to South Korea and interviewed several of these women and returned to write. Lee continues, "I probably wrote three-quarters of a book in that vein.... But I began to feel that what I had written didn't quite come up to the measure of what I had experienced, sitting in a room with these people. I began to feel that there was nothing like live witness."[38] Instead of writing a book from the point of view of a comfort woman and inhabiting her subject-status, he instead tells it from the point of view of a "kind" victimizer, the highly mediated persona of Doc Hata. Too much should not be made of Lee's statements or the narrative that did not ultimately materialize. But these displacements are worth noting, for he moves from the impossibility of "live witness" to an ethically ambivalent position, from the assumption of "reliable" narration and the transparency of truth with justice to unreliable narration.

The politics and ethics of this displacement become clearer in relation to Schaffer and Smith's book on human rights and life writing, which has a chapter on the comfort women and their emergence into subjects of representation through their first-person witnessing of the atrocities committed by Japanese soldiers.[39] Speaking about the grave silence that followed the atrocities of World War II, Smith and Schaffer write:

> After World War II there would be no receptive public for the narratives of former comfort women, no cultural intelligibility to their stories, no urgency attached to their particular acts of remembrance and recovery, no juridical or public recognition of their claims, no identity as victim of a rights violation. "Without recognition," comment Brunet and Rousseau, "there can be no punishment, reparation nor rehabilitation. Worse still, there are neither victims nor aggressors." (192)

In this paradigm, identity and cultural intelligibility are clearly premised on rights claims and the status of victimhood. It is through narrative and the status of victimization that these women can stake a claim for public recognition. By recognizing the impossibility of "live witness" and choosing instead to "adopt" the voice of a compromised, complicit, and benevolent doctor in the army, Lee foregrounds issues of guilt and reparation and mediates the opposition of "victim" and "aggressor." By transferring the ambivalent ethical relation between Doc Hata and K to the adoptive relation between Hata and Sunny, Lee's narrative resituates the question of recognition within the dynamics of adoption. Instead of the witness producing a narrative of rights-claims and voicing the demand for recognition of the victimized in a dialogic relationship with the victimizer, the problem of recognition gets played out across the asymmetry of their relations, the difficulty of acknowledging each other and each other's desires.

Adoptive relations in this sense are best thought of in terms of psychoanalytic notions of transference, which suggest both the invention of others on the basis of our past relationships and the acting out of the past in the present in the form of an unconscious repetition. But this transfer is not simply one-way, where the past is the originary relation that is projected onto the present, or where the present is simply thought through the past.[40] Rather, the transference enacts the difficulty of two subjects ever meeting on common ground. This model of transference is suggested in Freud's essay, "Constructions in Analysis," which deals with the recovery of the past in a present narrative.

There the process of retelling a life in psychoanalytic practice becomes considerably more complicated because of Freud's seemingly simple recognition that the work of analysis "is carried on in two separate localities, that it involves two people."[41] For Freud, analytic constructions proceed in an alternating fashion. The analyst's constructions based on material given by the analysand, its "effect" on the subject of analysis, the production of new material by the subject, and further constructions are "carried on side by side, the one kind being always a little ahead and the other following upon it."[42] Construction and the working-through of life history overlap in an uneven way. There is no simple "possession" of the story. Working toward a story that "makes sense" is always incomplete; the process of retelling a life depends radically on the constructions of the addressee and the continual resymbolization of the past. This way of thinking about the relationship between life history, narrative, and dialogue is quite different from one in which there are already given narratives that "provide models for telling our lives," as Appiah puts it.[43] The latter model presumes a relationality in which the subject and what is outside of it are relatively stable. But Freud's emphasis on the continual construction and reconstruction that never quite meet— "the one kind being always a little ahead and the other following upon it" — destabilizes the dialogic, mutually constitutive relation ("the self is . . . the product of our interaction from our earliest years with others") privileged in Appiah's account.[44]

These thoughts constitute the beginnings of a theory of transference in Freud's work that ultimately would see the patient's construction of the analyst as someone else as a repetition of the past. But I want to hold on to this sense of an uneven dialogue between analyst and analysand, an unevenness that Jacques Lacan elaborates on in his own notion of transference as being "both an obstacle to remembering, and a making present of the closure of the unconscious, which is the act of missing the right meeting just at the right moment."[45] Here Lacan argues counterintuitively that the act of transference is not a way of remembering and restoring a past relationship through another relationship, but rather that it is an *"obstacle* to remembering." The repetition of transference does not repair the past relationship so much as it repeats what was repressed in the past relationship. In other words, it repeats exactly what is *missed* in the past, what is *unable* to be remembered.[46]

I elaborate Freud's essay and Lacan's thoughts here to suggest that transference is not just a displacement from one person to another, from the past to the present, but a process of constantly alternating between past and present, in which the past is misconstrued through present needs and disavowals, and the present repeats past repressions. Adoption as a transferential relation that continually repeats the illegibility of past relations is at the center of *A Gesture Life,* and we see this manifested in the uneasy temporality of the novel. The double-movement of the narrative — oscillating as it does between looking forward and looking backward — enacts the model of transference in narrating the adoptive relation. In this way, it complicates the project of recognition at the heart of our life stories. Unlike the notion of narrative so prevalent in adoption literature based on the reconstruction of a life through the recovery of origin — a narrative that facilitates the "transfer" of the child from one country to another, or one race to another — this adoption narrative continually moves back and forth between two temporal moments, the reconstruction of the past and the construction of the present. This transferential relation destabilizes the frames of reference that are used to capture the movement of the adoptee from one place to another.

A Gesture Life thus rethinks how the adopted child is imagined and made to "fit" into narratives of belonging. It refuses to give us clear-cut categories in which to think of the adopted child: the child is neither a blank slate whose history is erased, thus enabling their fit into the family; nor is the child recognized as simply being from a different culture, thus providing a narrative that reconciles belonging and difference.[47] Instead, Sunny is placed at the intersection of several latent histories and relationships, the site of the transitional space of transference. This occurs in the novel through the technique of flashbacks and flashforwards. By making these correspondences, *A Gesture Life* suggests an identification between K and Sunny, a way in which Sunny is trapped in an earlier, guilt-ridden relationship that involves the Japanese occupation of Korea. As Mary Burns, Doc Hata's neighbor and one-time love interest in the novel, states, "But it's as if she's a woman to whom you're beholden. . . . I don't see the reason. You're the one who wanted her. You adopted her. But you act almost guilty, as if she's someone you hurt once, or betrayed, and now you're obliged to do whatever she wishes, which is never good for anyone, much less a child" (60). Mary Burns cannot understand Doc Hata's relationship to his daughter because it is not commensurate with the usual way in which adoption structures feelings — by locating desire and benevolence within the adopter and gratefulness and obligation within the adoptee.

But I do not wish to read the dynamics of this correspondence simply in terms of Doc Hata reworking and repeating the "guilt" involved in his past relationship with K through his adopted daughter, Sunny. This line of thinking would assume that the past is being repeated in the present relation and would emphasize some form of "cure" or reparation going on in this relationship. Rather, this structure of transference suggests a way in which the adoptive relation inhabits histories and identifications that remain uneasily present. Hata's prior relationship lives on in the construction of his adopted daughter, always displacing how the adoptive relationship gets constituted in the first place.

A Gesture Life repeatedly shows how the attempt to narrate the adoptive relation is confounded by the transferences enacted in the very act of narration. This attempt is revealed to be particularly problematic at the scene of recognition. My first example is a recounting of an emotionally laden scene in which we must attend to the ambivalent voice and position of Doc Hata and track the dizzying array of desires and demands embedded in his narration. While Doc Hata is looking for his daughter in a bad part of the neighborhood, he flashes back to a moment in his past when he failed to help a comfort woman pleading for help. The memory of the comfort woman provides the background for his search for Sunny, which ends in another act of guilty witnessing (repeating the guilt of the prior relationship), in which he sees his adopted daughter engaging in sexual acts through a window:

> I had never seen her move in such a way. . . . I saw her as I
> believe any good father would, with pride and wonder and the
> most innocent (if impossible) measure of longing, an aching
> hope that she stay forever pristine, unsoiled. But to gaze upon
> her like this. She was running her hands over herself. . . . And it
> was then that I wished she were just another girl or woman to
> me, no longer my kin or my daughter or even my charge, and I
> made no sound as I grimly descended, my blood already trying
> to forget, growing cold. (116)

In this scene, his sexual desire for Sunny becomes explicit at
the same time that the infinitive form of "to gaze" absents his
gaze and erases himself from the scene of desire. He looks
on and tries to forget, trying to make himself into someone
who could look on in a neutral fashion by transforming her:
"I wished she were just another girl or woman to me." But
his wish to make her into "just another girl" both makes her
sexually accessible and marks the adoptive relation — one in
which she is not "kin" in terms of blood or descent.

This scene is one example of how Doc Hata is continually
confronted with the question of what he is seeing his daughter
as. What the structure of transference brings into view is the
problem of "taking someone for someone else": the problem,
in short, of how to address the other.[48] Does Doc Hata see her
as "just another girl," or as his kin, his daughter, or his charge?
Or does he see her as "any good father would"? The moment
of recognizing Sunny as a sexual object — "I had never seen
her move in such a way" — is followed by a transformation
of the subject in the act of looking ("I saw her as I believe
any good father would"). This process of "taking someone for
someone else" is both "normalized" and resisted by Doc Hata.
Any father would, he suggests, naturally have these thoughts
and feelings. But this only attempts to naturalize how he sees
Sunny in terms of some hypothetical standard father–daughter
relation, avoiding the uncertainty of his own relation to Sunny.

This problem of address — how one "takes" the other, what one is seeing the other *as* — is repeated in Hata's relationship with K. Here again, adoption figures the uncertain play between background and identification in deciding how one can relate to another. K identifies Hata as a confidant, as someone with whom she can speak, because of his appearance and language: they share a common, originary tie in the Korean language. She first thinks that he is Korean, because his voice is just like her younger brother's, but he denies it, saying that he has lived in Japan since he was born. She insists that he is "different" from the other Japanese soldiers. After she learns about his background, she is fascinated by his status as a Japanese adoptee and likens it to her own marginal status as a daughter in a patriarchal household, in which she is treated "as if [she] were of the most distant blood" (245). Yet as much as their lives intersect, as much as they seem to find "originary" ties to each other, their relationship plays out as a series of missed encounters, continually questioning one's primary relation to the other. She takes him to be Korean, as a sympathetic presence; he takes her for a love-object and wants to save her. But she does not want his help, exposing his difficulty in acknowledging desire: "You think you love me but what you really want you don't yet know" (300). Their relationship is an impossible one, precisely because they cannot address each other: *You are taking me for someone else.*

Instead of symmetry — they are both on the margins of kinship, they both speak Korean — their relationship is characterized by the play between familiarity and unfamiliarity. Doc Hata tells K that he loves her, but what does he love her as? As a comfort woman? As a lover? She is, as she puts it herself, "unaddressable" (245). Likewise, the question of how Hata is to be addressed haunts him throughout the novel. As the "venerable" Doc Hata? Or is he always to be haunted by prior identifications: as a Korean, as someone who is not quite Japanese, as someone whose loyalty and belonging are always in question. The problem of addressing somebody "as" is never just a one-way projection; it is a question of an asymmetric relation that transforms both the addresser and the addressee. Constructing somebody "as if" they are Korean or a lover is simultaneously an act of disavowal. In other words, if Doc Hata sees Sunny as "just another girl," or K as a lover, then what does that make him, and what is he avoiding?

This transferential relation complicates the earlier formulation of thinking about the child as "from a different culture," or, I might add, as having a different history. It figures more largely the problem of how history, culture, or origin are imagined to inhere in a person. In other words, how we relate to another raises the question of how we place that person in a certain history. Hata's, K's, and Sunny's lives intersect through the histories of Japanese–Korean colonization. Hata is a Korean adopted by a Japanese family, who then goes on to fight in World War II; K is a Korean woman captured by the Japanese army; Sunny is a child of the Korean war, of ambiguous ancestry. In *A Gesture Life,* the adoptee becomes a site for the overlapping and intertwining of multiple histories, revealing the disconnect between Hata's imagined (desired) relations and his relation to his "own" history. For example, Doc Hata tells of his own imagined relation to Sunny:

> I was disappointed, initially. . . . I had assumed the child and I would have a ready, natural affinity, and that my colleagues . . . though knowing her to be adopted, would have little trouble quickly accepting our being of a single kind and blood. But when I saw her for the first time I realized there could be no such conceit for us, no easy persuasion. Her hair, her skin, were there to see, self-evident, and it was obvious how some other color (or colors) ran deep within her. (204)

This is one of a few ambiguous references to the possibility of Sunny's black ancestry, but it reveals how histories of racialization crop up, uncannily, to disrupt familial imaginaries premised on a "single kind and blood." Doc Hata's perception of the "obvious" "color" that runs "deep within Sunny" makes present his own blind spots in his desire for a natural affinity with his adopted daughter, which is premised on forgetting the history of relations between Korea and Japan. In other words, just when he thinks he can erase his own participation in the Japanese army's imperial efforts by adopting and forging a natural father–daughter relationship with a Korean girl, another history of war and occupation — the U.S. role in the Korean war — emerges in the very place of that erasure. There is no originary tie, no singular relation possible between father and daughter. What is left is the difficulty of negotiating two temporal frameworks side-by-side.

Several histories intertwine and overlap in Hata's adoption of Sunny: the history of Japanese colonization of Korea; the presence of the U.S. army in Korea during the Korean War; the history of black–white relations and Japanese–white relations in the United States. The adoptive relation in *A Gesture Life* suggests that the child always emerges into preexisting histories. Sunny, as Hata's adopted daughter from Korea, figures these doubled, layered histories, emphasizing the notion that one's story does not begin from a single, whole, origin, but is always preceded by and embedded in other histories. The desire to trace our lives back to a single, whole origin coexists anxiously with the unsettlement of context that is enacted by the adopted child.

Unsettling the Closure of Adoption

The anthologies representing the life stories of transracial adoptees restlessly seek closure by staging the recovery of origins and the act of racial or cultural recognition. But just as *A Gesture Life* decouples the imagination of the transracially adopted child from a narrative project that privileges a singular history and origin, it simultaneously reveals the difficulties in such closures. Indeed, Doc Hata reveals the ambivalences embedded in the language of adoption itself and in its attempts to enact closure. In sounding the well-intentioned voice of adoptive parenthood, Hata gives us a voice often at war with itself over its own desires and imaginative constructions. The fissures and ambivalences in Doc Hata's voice, the problematic affect of this text, betray the avoidance and missed encounters that are at the heart of thinking about adoption as a transferential relation.

Hata's voice reveals a split between affect and language in the narration of adoption. There is a persistent gap in his narrative voice between what he feels and what he does not want to acknowledge. For example, Doc Hata recounts his adoption of Sunny thus:

> My Sunny, I thought, would . . . not be so thankful or beholden to me, necessarily, but at least she'd be somewhat appreciative of the providence of institutions that brought her from the squalor of the orphanage . . . to an orderly, welcoming suburban home in America, with a hopeful father of like-enough race and sufficient means. (73)

While the narrative rhetoric has all the trappings of the standard adoption sentiments, the reader is also made aware of the strangeness, or uncanniness, of the language in which this relation is couched. The language both matches the rhetoric of adoption at the same time that it seems oddly out of place. "Providence" of institutions alludes to the idea of adoption as salvation even as Hata is disavowing the idea that Sunny would be "thankful" or "beholden" to him. The idea of a divine providence makes adoption less arbitrary and more natural, but the idea of "providence" is matched strangely with precisely what it is trying to erase — the social "institutions" that mediate the process of adoption. The phrase "of like-enough race," as discussed earlier, alludes to the norm of matching the parent and child based on racial and/or national background, at the same time that the oddness of the phrase reveals the absurdity of "racial matching" as a concept. Even as Hata's language seeks to close off the ambiguities and anxieties of the adoption process, the words he uses betray the difficulties of closure.

Hata continually defends against his own desires, often reconstructing his relation to Sunny in order to fit this misrecognition. His desire for a child is clouded:

> But I wanted a girl, a daughter — I was (as I think of it now) strangely unmovable on the issue.... My desire for a girl was unknown to me... but I... explained how I'd always hoped for a daughter, the words suddenly streaming from my mouth as though I'd long practiced the speech. I found myself speaking of a completeness, the unitary bond of a daughter and father. (74)

Hata repeats the romantic and sentimental language of adoption as if it were second nature. But this repetition is also a form of avoidance that manifests the entanglements of recognizing desire. The slippage in his prose — moving back and forth as it does between wanting a "girl" and wanting a "daughter" — reveals the inseparability of the act of recounting from the desires that remain opaque to the speaker. Even as Hata recounts his explanation (he is telling the story of his explanation to the social worker), his language is inhabited by his unacknowledged emotions, the projections and demands that he makes on the other, and the desire that confounds his speech.

Likewise, the adoptive relation ambivalently moves between the refusal to acknowledge the other and the desire for an acknowledged relation. While Doc Hata often points to his desire for a real father–daughter bond, he also recounts his willful ignoring of Sunny as part of how he manages his "cherished relations." For example, in convincing "his" Sunny to have a very late abortion, Hata recounts: "I forced her to do it. . . . In a way, it was a kind of ignoring that I did, an avoidance of her as Sunny—difficult, rash, angry Sunny—which I masked with a typical performance of consensus building and subtle pressure, which always is the difficult work of attempting to harmonize one's life and the lives of those whom one cherishes" (283–84). The work of "harmonizing one's life and the lives of those one cherishes" is revealed as a process that avoids the difficult asymmetric nature of the parent–child relationship. *A Gesture Life* gives us both the sentimental language of adoption (which wishes away the problems of kinship) and exposes the ways in which unacknowledged desires are embedded in the language of adoption itself.

The problematic closure of adoption is made evident, finally, in the ambivalent closure of the novel. The first line of this novel — "People know me here" — rubs uneasily against the final line of the novel — "Come almost home" (1, 356). The former announces the project of recognition at the heart of this life story. Doc Hata narrates himself as the example of the good, assimilated immigrant, whose quest for recognition and belonging has been fulfilled. But this process of assimilation is complicated by the ambivalences of the adoption narrative, captured by the latter phrase — "come almost home." Indeed, the ending of the novel unsettles the events and scenes that typify some form of closure in the adoptive family romance: reunion with Sunny and her son; some form of shared understanding with her; property left as a legacy to be transferred to a daughter. Each of these acts of constructing and transmitting family is haunted by the very closures that they wish for. As Hata intones: "We wish it [parent–child relationship] somehow pure, this thing, we wish it unmixed, unalloyed with human hope or piety or fear or maybe even love. For we wish it not to be ornate. And yet it always is" (351). Even the haltings and ambivalences of these sentences, as well as the odd language choice of "ornate," speak to the ways in which the language of family often covers over its own ambivalences and gaps.

Throughout the novel, adoption and the "familial" holds out the promise of the unity of the parent–child bond or of a whole family. But phrases like "as I assumed a real father would or should be," "former daughter," "almost home," or "a 'whole family'" shadow the kinds of closures attempted by the discourse of adoption (275, 58). The meditative, elegiac nature of the ending resists closure, as evident by the series of negations that specifically run against a narrative of recognition as return: "Perhaps I'll travel... to land on former shores. But I think it won't be any kind of pilgrimage. I won't be seeking out my destiny or fate. I won't attempt to find comfort in the visage of a creator or the forgiving dead" (356). Resistant to the narrative closures that mark the search narratives and roots narratives of adoption discourse to the very end, Lee's novel forces us to dwell in the uncomfortable space of being "almost home." Adoptive identity, in *A Gesture Life,* is embedded in the ways we are traversed and criss-crossed by stories, histories, and relations that both precede us and are outside of us. Lee's novel suggests the impossibility of narrating adoptive identity in terms of a single origin or in recognition of where you come from. But it is also finally attendant to the closures that both adopters and adoptees often wish for, but never quite receive.

The dominant paradigm for representing transnational adoption has been a spatial one that maps the itinerary of the adoptee from one country and one nationality to another. In this way, a set of disparate and often contingent relations between various individual and institutional actors — parents, social workers, children, charity organizations — become spatialized as a movement between origin and destination. This spatial logic governs the reproduction and recognition of the identities of adopted children, framing understandings that the adopted child's identity "is produced in the passage from one place (one parent) to another and that this history shapes the 'nature' of the child."[49]

As I have argued above, this spatial paradigm is reflected in the narrative modes through which transracial adoption is represented: the search and reunion/return narrative; the production of recognition as a psychic and narrative end-point that locates the adopted subject in relation to a single origin. Much of this narrative production can be seen as reproducing the transnational adoptee as only legible and recognizable in terms of given places. By looking at some of the narrative processes whereby the adoptee is located and recognized, I specify a transnational subject marked by the collapsing of different times and histories into a discontinuous present. In *A Gesture Life,* the narrative dynamics of transference keep *present* the overlapping layers of history that are erased through the reproduction of the adoptive subject. This time-lag of recognition questions the production of persons within both the national boundaries of citizenship and the singular histories used to validate, legitimize, and recognize individuals. In this vein, what is transnational about transnational adoption is not the movement from one country to another but a temporal displacement that evokes and merges multiple histories of racialization and nationalization.

6

MAKING FAMILY
"LOOK LIKE REAL"
Transracial Adoption
and the Challenge to Family

If the world is undergoing an "adoption revolution" that purportedly challenges the biological norms of personhood, it is
simultaneously experiencing what Janet Beizer calls an "equally
powerful move to readmit biology, genealogy, and genetics
into the adoption picture."[1] According to an article in the *New
Yorker*, genealogy is second only to pornography as the most
searched-for subject on the web.[2] The recent craze over DNA
tests, from the discovery that James Watson was 16 percent
African to the finding of a "risk-taking" gene, have recen-
tered biology and genetics as primary ways of thinking about
who we are.[3] This development is not just a pendulum shift
back to nature in old nature–nurture binaries, although that
is how it is often framed. In the context of my arguments in
Claiming Others, we can see it as part of a negotiation of the
norms of personhood through the parent–child relation, a process that involves not just how notions of biology and culture
shape this relation but also the construction of affective bonds
through sentimental forms, norms of dependency and property transmission, social scientific formations of heredity, and
constructions of the human within children's rights.

Throughout this book, I have concentrated on how the literature and discourse of transracial adoption negotiate two central logics through which specific kinds of personhood are shaped. One is the normalization of individuation in ways that make the securing of racial boundaries a condition for self-possession, singularity, and continuity of self. Narratives of transracial adoption dramatize the ways in which psychic and social identifications do not necessarily follow legitimized modes of filiation and affiliation. These adoptive figures break up norms of individuation that rely on the singularity of national and racial identification at the same time that they reveal the strong pull of the familial nation-form in producing the conditions of legible personhood. The second is the use of family as a metaphor for larger forms of collectivity including race and nation, envisioning all three as homologous. This way of thinking underlies visions of transracial adoption as remaking social integration at the level of the nation. Echoing the ethics of care in such precursors as Lydia Maria Child and Pearl S. Buck, Elizabeth Bartholet declares that "transracial adoptive families constitute an interesting model of how we might better learn to live with one another in this society. These families can work only if there is appreciation of racial difference, and love that transcends such difference." [4] Bartholet follows from a tradition of thinking that the family is a microcosm of the nation, and that social and racial unity at one level can be used to produce unity at the other level. This homological thinking continues to frame transracial adoption debates, situating personhood within the idealizations of family, race, and nation that it reproduces. As we have seen throughout *Claiming Others*, the parent–child relation is structured by social norms, legal regulations, and political sensibilities in ways that naturalize personhood. The complexities of transracial adoption emerge when we account for the mediations between these levels in ways that do not take for granted the internal unity or ideality of familial, racial, or national membership.

In this concluding chapter, I take up the contemporary return to biology in the context of both these logics. As we saw in chapter 4, recent developments in children's rights have articulated a "right to know one's identity," which often conflates knowing one's biological origins with having a historical identity. In that chapter, we saw the linkages between geopolitical boundaries and psychic processes that normalized the conditions for real, socially legitimate personhood. Here I am more concerned with how the desire for biological relations is constructed. In particular, I explore the centrality of the measure of "likeness" — people resembling each other — around which the ideal of unity often hinges. The drive to produce "likeness" fills the lack of a ground for the categorical unities of family, race, and nation. I then explore how transnational adoption stories that grapple with the problem of familial unity engage with, inhabit, and sometimes resist the homology between family and nation.

What Does the Biological Family Look Like?

Far from being used to critique the valorization of biological origins and open up nonbiological modes of relationality, adoption is often used to make even stronger claims to the primacy of biology. Precisely how adoption is used in this way helps us examine the rhetoric through which the desire for biological norms is reconstructed as the grounds of proper personhood. In "Family History," J. David Velleman argues that knowledge of one's biological ancestry is necessary to a meaningful life. In doing so, he highlights in particular the adoptee search narrative as evidence that persons are not coherent without this knowledge: "[Adoptees] go to heroic lengths to find their biological families, impelled by what they describe as a deep and unrelenting need."[5] At one level, this is certainly an exaggeration of the romantic idea of finding one's biological parents in order to suggest that without this knowledge, one is lost.[6] But at another level, the search story models the itinerary of "proper" identification:

> When adoptees go in search of their biological parents and siblings, there is a literal sense in which they are searching for themselves. They are searching for the closest thing to a mirror in which to catch an external and candid view of what they are like in more than mere appearance. Not knowing any biological relatives must be like wandering in a world without reflective surfaces, permanently self-blind. (368)

This description models a notion of identity-formation that hinges on resemblance: biological family members are needed for a proper sense of self because they give you what you are like. Resemblance to oneself is correlated with literal family resemblance to others. It provides the key to something "deeper" than appearance, present without knowing how it is present: "To have such a family-resemblance concept is just to have the ability to know an instance when we see one, without being able to say how we know it" (365). Velleman constructs biological family resemblance as an unknowable trait, thus ensuring that it is both obviously perceivable and compellingly ineffable.

Reconstructing the biological norm, then, requires a careful straddling of the literal (that which can be immediately read) and figurative (that which requires a reading of a deeper, underlying layer). Indeed, Velleman's argument for the primacy of biology is made by suppressing figurative expression and reproducing the family as literal. Throughout his essay, Velleman avoids what he calls the temptation of "symbolic and mythical thinking" in order to point to the literal and the real — "the resemblances that hold within biological families" (376).

His reduction of similarity into sameness relies on the suppression of figuration, for figuration would suggest, according to Velleman's logic, some distance from the real and concrete resemblances founded on biology. He uses Wittgenstein's concept of "family resemblances" not in its technical sense, but to talk about "literal resemblance within families" (365). This literalization of the family creates a sameness out of similarity, a self-identification out of resemblance: "If I want to see myself as another.... I don't have to imagine myself as seen through other people's eyes: I just have to look at my father, my mother, and my brothers, who show me by way of family resemblance what I am like" (368). In this magical way of thinking, resemblance to another provides the substance of *"what* I am like." It is not surprising, then, that it relies on the search narrative, which is precisely the plot that enacts this logic of creating sameness out of similarity, of creating a correspondence between something beyond appearance and appearance itself. Using the adoption search story, Velleman identifies biology as the literal resemblances that are crucial for identity-formation.

But as much as Velleman attempts to suppress the figurative, he relies on it all the same. Though beginning with a warning about indulging in "symbolic thinking," he uses popular and canonical stories from Odysseus to Star Wars to "illustrate a bit of common sense about the self-knowledge drawn from acquaintance with biological relatives. Telemachus, Oedipus, Moses, and even Luke Skywalker illustrate the centrality of this knowledge to the task of identity formation, and the centrality of that task to a meaningful human life" (369). Stories appear in the article as a supplement, adding to the literality of biological origins without disrupting the literal at all—in fact, it illustrates "common sense." But the literal, it would seem, cannot stand on its own. It requires the figurative in order to construct the common sense of biology.

This rhetorical move in reconstructing the biological as literal finds an unlikely counterpart in the work of Betty Jean Lifton, the famous adoptee activist. As I noted in chapter 4, Lifton uses the norms of biological origins in order to affirm the adoptee as a real person and not a fantasy child. This polemical project is accompanied by a desire to typify the meaning and condition of adoption. In *Lost and Found*, she sought to "look at the psychological meaning of adoption from all sides," collecting various general frameworks for understanding adoptees.[7] But she describes the adoptee through a series of similes: "The Adoptee as Mythic Hero"; "The Adoptee as Double"; "The Adoptee as Survivor"; "The Adoptee as Adult." Each of these "as" formulations places the adoptees firmly within the register of the figurative. They are detached from the reality of being survivors because "[they] are kept in ignorance of what it is [they] have survived."[8] They are only "like" adults because they "never fully grew up."[9] This figurativeness of adoptees — the condition, we might say, of always being a simile, always being likened to something else — describes a constitutive lack of reality, an inability to "test [their] fantasies against reality."[10] For Lifton, the reality-testing begins with the search for the biological family: she puts all her writing about search and reunion within a section of the book called "found." Treating biological family as literal, as the space for reality-testing, and adoptedness as figurative is endemic in Lifton's text.

Both Velleman's and Lifton's texts reveal that there is something more going on than the simple valorization of biological origins as an ideology. Biological norms are continually reconstructed through a careful navigation and deployment of literal and figurative in order to read biological relations as "literal" resemblance. It is this move through which biology forms the ground for the claiming of real personhood — whether through a narrative coherence that relies on genealogical origin or through the moment of resemblance in which a person can see "what they are like." As this "return" to biology shows, narrative and fiction are usefully employed not only for the disruption of biological norms but also for their reinforcement and reconstruction. Narrative is used both to open up the possibilities and figurations of selfhood and to revalorize a coherence based on biological origins. Velleman reiterates this equation between narrative, biology, and identity, when he writes: "I am inclined to think that a knowledge of one's origins is especially important to identity formation because it is important to the telling of one's life story, which necessarily encodes one's appreciation of meaning in the events of one's life."[11]

Charlotte Witt rereads the concept of "family resemblances" in order to demystify literal resemblance as a unifying mechanism for families:

> Family resemblances are part of a family's mythology, and they serve various purposes: bonding family members, explaining behavior, assigning blame. Family resemblances attribute relational properties to individual family members.... Family resemblances are relational properties which are biological/social hybrids; they exist only as part of a family mythology and hence are social, but the myth tells a story of genetic inheritance, and hence they are biological.[12]

"Looking like" another family member, she goes on to say, is not straightforwardly "descriptive or observational" but reflects "community norms."[13] Resemblance is as much imaginary as it is "genetic" or "essential"; it is as much the product of storytelling as it is of observable appearances. Witt helps us to see the degree to which family resemblances are dependent on the social, not just something that can be construed and constructed as if it were solely "inside" the family. She points to the interface between family formation and social norms that impinge on and reframe family itself. In this way, figurative resemblance — Lifton's similes and Velleman's supplementary analogies — comes to fill in "where something should be but isn't,"[14] namely, the certainty of the biological constitution of family, an essential, noncontingent connection to other people. It functions more in terms of Lacan's notion of the semblant as an appearance that produces satisfaction precisely because it wards off the anxiety of what is missing: some deep foundation for what constitutes a family. In this fashion, both Velleman and Lifton imagine the biological family as a transparent appearance.

Witt demystifies the ways that "family resemblances" idealize biological familial unity, but we also need to take into account other processes for reproducing the ideal unity of the family in order to understand how the family as a norm operates. Psychoanalysts and psychologists dealing with group processes detail the specific practices of family that reinstitute and re-idealize this norm. R. D. Laing describes the process whereby family members internalize the unity of the family itself:

> Each family member incarnates a structure derived from relations between members. This family-in-common shared *group presence* exists *in so far as* each member has it inside himself. Hence fantasies of the family as preserved, destroyed, or repaired, the family growing, dying, being immortal. Each member of the family may require the other members to keep the same "family" imago inside themselves. Each person's identity then rests on a shared "family" inside the others, who, by that token, are themselves in the same family.[15]

In Laing's model, the family's self-identity is constituted through a mechanism of internalization whereby the family's wholeness and oneness can be reproduced. It rests on a certain conception of the "relations between members." The cognitive psychologist Jerome Bruner writes of a similar dynamic when he notes the family's centrifugal pull through the mode of storytelling: "families are systems for keeping people from being pulled centrifugally by inevitably conflicting interests."[16] And one of the techniques for doing so is "the use of canonical family stories that serve to highlight [family roles]. Every family has a store of these."[17] This capacity of the family to remain singular depends on erasing the other "conflicting interests" that may interrupt the family imago.

Appreciating the multiple ways of reinstituting norms for family enables a different sort of commentary on transracial adoption stories. For analyses of transracial adoption sometimes take for granted, without describing further, how transgressive transracial adoptions are for our normal conceptions of family. Janet Beizer argues that "transracial family structures" are "iconoclastic in the sense that they make visible the irrelevance of consanguinity to family bonds and the reality of alternatives to conventional family structures."[18] But the sheer visibility of a way of doing family differently does not attend to how family operates as a norm. It is not enough to say that adoption breaks with ideologies of consanguinity. The demystification of resemblance does not necessarily mean that biological family will not be reidealized through some other set of practices. Any reading of a challenge to these norms must be attentive to how norms get reproduced through the idealizations that get embodied in social practices and to the possibilities for distancing or reworking these idealizations.[19] As Judith Butler notes in her analysis of gender norms, "the norm only persists as a norm to the extent that it is acted out in social practice and reidealized . . . through the daily social rituals of bodily life"; "the relation between practices and the idealizations under which they work is contingent" and "can be brought into question and crisis potentially undergoing deidealization and divestiture."[20] The fact of adoption continually raises the interface between social norms and family image, and as such, it renders visible the processes of idealization and identification that mark the reproduction of family. Moreover, transracial adoption stories reveal how the reproduction of familial norms often relies on social practices organized around race and nation.

Transracial and transnational adoptive families are constantly reminded of the fact that families are both internally constituted and externally created, and indeed a great deal of conversation about adoption revolves around the uncomfortable gaze of strangers and how to deal with it. This uneasy space of evaluation and judgment is the site of the regulation and the normalization of appearance. I thus read transracial adoption stories for the ways in which they manifest the practices of making family in ways that at times reinstitute norms and at other times deidealize the unities of family, race, and nation that undergird them.[21] I return to the search-and-reunion trope in order to look more closely at how a text both relies on homologous constructions of family and nation for psychic constructions of wholeness and questions the very idealization of familial unity. Inhabiting the search story, Katy Robinson's *A Single Square Picture* reproduces many of the logics underlying biological and legal formulations of personhood. At the same time, it registers crises in idealization that open up the illegibility of adoptive personhood within these governing frames. I then turn to two adoptive family stories that are linked through their shared project in dramatizing the transnational adoptive family as a whole rather than through an individual. This shared project allows us to think about the logic of the family as a metaphor for the nation and how adoption compromises the fantasies of internal unity regulated by the norms of family.

The Comfort of Convention

As we have seen, the reduction of adoption stories to the specific element of search and reunion is a prime example of how one version of personhood is privileged.[22] This reduction does not simply revalorize biological norms of personhood. The search narrative is the perfect plot device for repeating a psychic itinerary in which one finds wholeness through identification with the biological parent and, correspondingly, the birth nation or birth culture. By locating the dynamics of personhood within the question of what is "inside" someone, it facilitates the trope of biology whereby similarity is converted into sameness. It gives the "substance" to identity. Without it, biological identity would be mere similarity, mere appearance. Observing this desire for wholeness, critics have faulted the adoption search story for indulging in cultural and racial essentialisms.[23] But what is criticized as simple essentialism or reification is in fact an intertwined set of logics whereby our notion of individuality itself is predicated on this psychic itinerary of identification. The search story creates a correspondence between that biological unity of self and a national, cultural, or racial idealization of unity. The form of the search story reiterates race and nation as things rather than processes because it uses the model of "the family" in order to retroactively construct those categories *as* whole.[24]

A Single Square Picture: A Korean Adoptee's Search for Her Roots is a good example of this tension between the disruption of expectations within the search and the search story's poetic effects in constructing and identifying race and nation as unities in the world.[25] The plot of this memoir focuses on Katy Robinson's search for her birth parents in Korea. Robinson, adopted at age seven, returns to Korea as an adult, often reifying notions of Korean culture and tradition. However, it is crucial to note *when* culture as an essentialized

thing appears in the narrative. Cultural explanations of differences fill in the gaps of incomprehension, awkwardness,
and nonmeeting between Robinson and her birth father. The
interpersonal dynamics get reinterpreted through the lens of
cultural categories:

> I tried hard to be the person I guessed my father wanted me to
> be. Back and forth, we tried to please each other with growing
> unease as our expectations kept getting in the way. We were
> two strangers, pretending to be a father and daughter and not
> wanting to admit the wide gulf that separated us.... But now
> that my father and I were face-to-face, it was much harder to
> cross the barrier created by language, culture, and lost time.
> Before I came, I had heard about the important role of Confu-
> cian values in Korea's culture.... I interpreted his short Korean
> words as brusqueness reminiscent of my American father and
> found myself retracting on impulse. Even as my Korean father
> searched my face, the booming voice of my American father
> flooded my mind until I was suddenly angry at the man before
> me. Then my father smiled at me. And I remembered that
> I was in Korea, where no two people were ever equal in a
> relationship — least of all a parent and child.[26]

These passages are characterized by a movement back and forth
between the interpersonal and the categorical. How to identify
Katy's birth father — in terms of a structural correspondence
that he shares with her adopted father? In this transferential
moment, he is identified in nonculturally specific ways. But
then right after this moment, he is recontextualized within the
cultural territory of Korea with its specific, hardened, value
and belief systems. Her negotiation of her relationship with
her father *produces* the cultural whole named by "Korea" and
extrapolated outward onto the Korean nation itself. Indeed, a
few pages after this scene, her birth father is identified with
Korea itself: "It was dawning on me that I would never truly
understand my father or the life he led. I despised my father

and loved him with equal strength, as I did Korea itself, for the strong hold it had on me, while at the same time rejecting me as one of its own" (153). Nation and family are made into homologous entities and identified with each other. Robinson's inability to relate to her father as a daughter — the inability to instantiate and reproduce the norms of family — is reinterpreted through the lens of these conceptual categories in order to create a more clear-cut opposition between acceptance and rejection. These idealizations around nation and culture are achieved through this interplay of interpersonal dynamics and social categories.

The conventional language of adoption discourse owes something to this creation of homologies among family, race, and nation. Narratively, these homologies mystify the material relations out of which adoption usually emerges. For what Robinson learns is that her birth family genealogy is a mess — full of illegitimate children, lost fathers, and disconnections. She was born out of wedlock, and her biological father had children with two other women. After meeting her aunt, who is the same age as she is, Robinson writes:

> My mother was like a diseased limb snipped off the family tree. I pictured what my Korean family tree might look like on a diagram — spindly branches spinning off and twisting this way and that, fostering half siblings and half relatives until the whole thing looked like a giant knot of tangled twigs and broken branches. (238)

When she learns that her aunt, Sunny, was the daughter born of an illicit affair by their shared grandfather, just like Robinson, she relates to her aunt not through shared biological resemblance but through shared positionality: "At some point during our time together, it occurred to me that Sunny was to my *halmoni* what I was to my brother's mother. . . . In Sunny, I saw myself, or what I might have been had I stayed in Korea"

(242). Robinson imagines Sunny's life not to tell her what she is like, but to find an appropriate measure for what her life has been: "Each time I studied Sunny, I knew that my life just as easily could have been hers. She looked at me too, with that same knowledge in reverse" (243–44). Katy looks to Sunny not for some more authentic root, cultural origin, or biological connection, but for the possibility of contemplating the conditionality of their lives, the possibility of alternative histories: "'I owe my mother everything,' Sunny mentioned several times during the weekend, as if seeing me — a Korean adoptee — were a reminder of her good fortune" (242); "we both were secretly a little envious of each other and yet eternally grateful for the decisions our mothers had made and the way our lives turned out" (244). This "resemblance" between Katy and Sunny constructs a mode of relation based on the possibility of projecting oneself into an alternate life.

As David Eng argues, transnational adoption is marked by the mourning of lost ideals — a state of suspension in which "ideals of both Asianness and whiteness remain estranged and unresolved."[27] Struggling with this estrangement, Robinson idealizes the unities of family, race, and nation so as to situate herself within recognizable boundaries. The idealization of the father and mother constructs the possibility of a wholeness to be achieved as a condition of personhood. This idealization is reproduced through the formation of race and nation as unified constructs. All of these forms are ways of anticipating persons, making persons fit one's needs. As André Green notes, the ideal object is "never the cause of any frustration" because it anticipates the desires of the subject.[28]

But even as Robinson uses these idealizations in order to smooth out the messiness of meeting her father's needs, she also opens up her familial relations — thought to be primary and static — to projection in ways that recontextualize and remake these relations. When her adoptive mother visits her in Korea, Robinson recontextualizes her relationship to her mother:

> Seeing her [Katy's adoptive mother] here, in Korea, reminded me just how far I was from home and how different the context of our lives had become. (260)

> It was an odd sensation to see my mother set against this Korean backdrop. For most of my life, I had been the person who stood out in a crowd as someone who didn't quite belong. But now here was my mother, with every one of her Western features illuminated in my brother's eyes — her white skin, deep round eyes, red hair. (265)

It is through this act of displacement and deidealization, of seeing her mother against a different background and context, that allows her to re-imagine her adoptive mother. Likewise, her brother and father are always doing things that she did not anticipate. Her biological family's failure to embody certain ideals fosters the capacity for projection and thus the hate, aggression, sympathy, and affection that attend that act of projection. Opened up in this way, her biological father is open to transformation, never remaining the static figure that her absent biological mother is.

Thus the stark contrast between the static image of her mother and grandmother and the father's changing background and image. The "single square picture" of the title is the picture of Katy Robinson with her mother and grandmother at the airport moments before she is taken to the United States. This moment remains imaginatively fixed. It opens the book ("When I was seven years old, my mother and grandmother took me to the airport and watched as I boarded a plane for America" [1]) and it frames the closing of the book ("I have played and replayed the scene when I last saw my mother and grandmother at Kimpo Airport and wondered how we could have parted so quietly" [293]). It crops up periodically throughout the book as the unchanging face of Robinson's mother in her fantasy: "Her dark hair falls to her shoulders and is slightly curled, as it was the last time that I saw her at Kimpo Airport. Her face too is nearly unchanged . . . just as she looks in the Polaroid picture" (132). The descriptions of this moment are characterized by their passivity and stasis, almost as if to hold this moment as a world that can be possessed. The narration of the moment reduplicates the action of the photograph as it separates the three figures apart from other aspects of reality: "As I stood framed by my mother and grandmother, it seemed as though we were the only three people in the world" (3).

The biological father, however, becomes open to frustrations and projections precisely because of the failures of idealization. After discovering that she was an illegitimate child, Robinson's anger turns from thoughts of her mother to her father: "Instead, my anger turned toward my father for putting my mother in such a situation and for being indifferent, for causing endless shame while bearing none himself" (191). As person meets projection, Robinson is able to redescribe her father in multiple ways: "And with each description and newly discovered fact, my father began to take on new dimensions. I had encapsulated him into a regretful old man estranged from his children. But where I saw an old man with a *kimchee* stain on his tie had once been a brilliant, handsome man with the world at his fingertips" (218). As a surface bearing her projections, her biological father becomes someone that she can address. The reality–fantasy opposition in which adoptees are framed in both psychological and legal discourse can thus be redescribed. The search story in Robinson's hands does not give one the *reality* of one's origins located in the biological so much as it opens up the world to one's projections.

In the ideological conflict between biological forms of family and the "new ideology of family" of which adoption is a part, the search story has played a crucial role. It has been used as we have seen to provide a coherent picture of the self based on the reconstruction of biological normativity. It has been used to reconstruct notions of cultural origin as a primary condition for recognizable personhood. But a closer look at its dynamics shows how it reproduces race and nation as unities not so much out of belief in their essential realities but rather as just one part of the process whereby the adoptee projects herself out into the world and creates secure boundaries for one's personhood. The trajectory of idealization, moreover, is accompanied by the countermovement of deidealization and projection, a movement that reworks one's relation to the "family" and allows adoptees to remake the conditions of their legibility in the world. This is one way of redescribing the narrative and psychic trajectories that characterize many of the search stories discussed so far —*A Single Square Picture; The Language of Blood; Daughter from Danang; First Person Plural.*

Adoption as a Crisis of Internal Unity

Adoptee memoirs have disproportionately focused on individuals on a search and reunion plot. When the form shifts from that of the individual journey to the imagining of the family "as a whole," we see another dimension to the construction of norms around familial unity. Keeping the family whole and unified enables a conceptualization of the family as a metaphor for the nation, but adoption stories that take up this problem highlight how family stories are ways of performing and instituting what a family is; they are ways of describing how familial attachments are constructed in the first place. The struggle to make family in transracial adoption stories reveals that while adoption might disrupt ideologies of consanguinity, it could also reinforce them, or reinstitute and instantiate various other idealizations in the service of family unity. It allows us to see clearly the mediations between familial and social norms as they produce values around and regulate the appearance of relationality. Family, race, and nation appear as empty place-holders, not filled with any content, each reinforcing the other against anxieties regarding their lack of unity.

The problem of the proper grounds of family when not biologically defined — whether choice, or love, some imitation of biological norms, or some political reparation — remains a sticking point in arguments over the desirability of adoption. But adoption stories rarely focus on the family as a "whole," most often taking up this issue through the individual perspective of an adoptive parent, a birth parent, or an adoptee. This is likely due to a limitation in narrative capacities to represent multiple perspectives at the same time as well as the politics of adoption in which the three parts of the adoption triangle are often seen to be at odds. For the remainder of the chapter, I focus on two notable exceptions to this history, *Sudden Family* by Debi and Steve Standiford, published in 1986, and Gish Jen's *The Love Wife* published in 2004. Precisely because they dramatize the problem of defining family when the internal unity of the family cannot be taken for granted, they both reflect and rethink the tendency to homologize family with racial and national formations. Both of these texts take up the unusual narrative form of incorporating the points of view of both adoptive parents and adopted children into the same text. Each chapter (or shorter section in the case of *The Love Wife*) is written in a first-person "I" from the viewpoint of one of the members of the family. The implicit promise behind this narrative experiment is to more accurately perform what a family is by presenting the family members in some kind of dialogue and revealing how their viewpoints often clash and diverge from each other's understandings, thus giving us a fuller portrait of the intimate, internal structure of the family. The books themselves are something like a set of family stories in Bruner's sense that perform and justify the construction of family in the telling itself. They highlight above all how storytelling is a way of becoming family, of negotiating its internal pressures and norms. As such, they provide a window into the processes of idealization and identification that undergird the reproduction of family.

Sudden Family was written slightly before the big boom in transnational adoption and therefore is not as settled in terms of what adoption actually does. Its very title signals the question of how or even if adoption makes a family in the sense of a secure form of belonging. Adoption agencies have moved between different rationales for fostering this sense of belonging — the clean break and assimilation model of the 1950s to the multicultural model of fostering cultural differences today. Each of these rationales implicitly models the family on the nation, projecting its strategies for making a family out onto society for reflection and ratification. *Sudden Family* departs from both of these because it represents an older rescue narrative rationale that has by now been deeply questioned. For part of the rationale for Debi and Steve Standiford's adoption is both a humanitarian mission to save refugee children and a formation framed around God's providence. But while these external justifications frame the formation of family in this story, the problem of the family's internal unity persists. This is perhaps because the boys are adopted at an older age and have their own histories and stories that resist the erasures implicit in both the assimilation and the multicultural models of transnational family formation. The drama of the story hinges both on their struggles to adapt as a family and on the family secret that the two children, Nhi and Hy, share: they lied about being orphans so that Americans could adopt them more easily. Their parents are not dead, as they initially told their adoptive parents, but actually alive and living in Vietnam, too poor to raise them. Debi and Steve Standiford find out that Nhi and Hy's aunt and uncle to whom they write and send pictures, are in fact the biological parents of their adopted children. The story follows their struggles in being a family and is punctuated by Nhi's attempted suicide, which threatens to break the family's fragile sense of itself apart.

The promise and the danger of storytelling as a mode of instantiating familial norms are shown in Debi Standiford's account of the processes that went into writing *Sudden Family* itself. In describing her dialogues with her children in preparation for the book, she writes: "As one who had become their mother later in their lives, I was grateful for an opportunity to fill in the missing years. I felt that I was getting to know them better and better, and my sense of maternal attachment grew daily."[29] The promise of incorporating their stories is explicitly linked to how the parents construct their affective relationships to their children. But the dangers of storytelling are also highlighted. After Debi learns that her adopted children had been lying to her, that the people to whom they were referring as "aunt" and "uncle" were in fact their parents, she writes: "Now that I knew the truth, I was having a hard time getting my work on the book done. *My story keeps interrupting my story,* I mused. *Which story am I writing? How many stories will I write and find out later that they were false? And do I even have a story anymore?*" (148).

Notice the snowball effect of Debi's thoughts: she moves from the technical problem of telling a story ("my story keeps interrupting my story" — thus precluding the inability to tell a story straight); then an inability to know *which* story she is writing — hers or somebody else's; then a doubt about the ability of stories to be true, that is, an epistemological problem about the relationship between stories and truth; then finally the feeling of alienation regarding the inability to "even have a story." Assumptions around stories — that they can be possessed; that they are singular; that you can easily distinguish yours from another's — form the basis and narrative justification for the family structure of the Standifords. When these assumptions about the singularity and self-possession of stories are disrupted by the emergence of a secret, Debi can neither hold her story together nor construct a sense of a cohesive family. Her sense of familial unity relies on these norms that reinstitute and idealize a construction of possession and knowledge of the other.

Family stories, in Bruner's model, are the ways in which family is held together. They are "canonical" because they are endlessly repeated in ways that continually reinstall and restabilize who we are in relation to our family. They reconstitute our primary relations to ourselves through a set of repeatable fictions. But the disruption of certain assumptions about family — the unknowing of what families are — are symptomatized in the instability of storytelling: "Which story am I writing?" "Can I even have a story"? The act of storytelling can thus both stabilize and unravel the fictions of familial attachment. It provides ways of knowing and indeed possessing others and their lives at the same time that they reveal the profound gaps between persons that make a sense of family unity difficult to grasp. The appropriation and incorporation of others' stories thus becomes a powerful strategy of constituting family unity.

For this reason, the political allegory of Cold War humanitarianism remains a powerful way of imagining the family and reframing Nhi and Hy's struggles. Debi does precisely this when she redescribes Nhi and Hy's lying to her about their situation in terms of a political allegory. She paints Communist rule as a society of lying and deceit and American society as governed by a "truth ethic":

> Nhi and Hy had also grown up in a society where deception was necessary to insure survival.... To escape the concentration camps, men lied about their former occupations. Teenaged boys hid in the forest to avoid being sent to fight in occupied Cambodia.... After years of war and communist rule, Nhi and Hy suddenly found themselves in a society operating on radically different principles. There were no secret police and no spies waiting to turn them in for speaking the wrong political doctrine.... The truth ethic was so powerful that a President was forced to resign. (150)

This governing political and national framework becomes the mode for understanding Nhi and Hy's transition into America and the difficulties of making them feel like they were part of the family. The easy political narrative creates unities on one scale (nation, world) in order to ground unities at a smaller scale (family, individual). It becomes a mode of knowing that allows Debi and Steve to reinstitute the unity of their family and move on from the tragic break of Nhi's attempted suicide and the falsity of Nhi's and Hy's biographies.

At the same time, though, *Sudden Family* shows the diverging and conflicting ways in which each family member projects their desires onto family formation. Nhi and Hy's stories reveal their past histories, their own strategy of lying in order to ensure that they would be adopted. Nhi talks about class differences and how handicapped children are treated in Vietnam, enlarging the perspective of the family beyond its boundaries. If larger political frameworks are elaborated in order to ensure the circumscribed unity of the family, the personal histories of adopted persons simultaneously stretch the family into the social in ways that challenge that internal unity.

"Making a Family Look Like Real"

As *Sudden Family* demonstrates, the negotiations over the internal unity of the family are always in dialectic with the external norms that structure its legibility. The question then becomes not whether a multicultural model is "better" than a "clean break" model of adoption, but how different conditions structure the intelligibility of the appearance of family. Here I turn to Gish Jen's *The Love Wife*, which gives us a family story that demonstrates the relationships between narrations of attachment — how we construct rationales and logics for how we relate to each other — and the reimagination of categories of race and nation. Jen states in an interview about *The Love Wife*, that family is meant to be read as a "metaphor for the nation." [30] In response to an interviewer's statement that "[her] children are adopted and they're bi-racial, so they're black and white and Jewish," Gish Jen responds "Which is very American." [31] Jen's penchant in her fiction is to note the foibles and inconsistencies attendant on the legacy of race in the problem of defining Americans. But in *The Love Wife,* the proposition that family is a metaphor for the nation — that its materialization of interracial relations might serve as an analogue for the nation's already multiracial character — tests the ways in which family finds its own justification in the first place.

The beginning of *The Love Wife* nicely introduces us to the way that Gish Jen is playing with the language of family and the psychic desires behind family. It is spoken by the character nicknamed "Blondie":

> The day Lan came, you could still say whose family this was — Carnegie's and mine. We had three children. Two beautiful Asian girls — or should I say Asian American — Wendy, age nine, and Lizzy, age fifteen, both adopted; and one bio boy, Bailey, age thirteen months. Carnegie's ancestry being Chinese, and mine European, Bailey was half half, as they say — or

is there another term by now? With less mismatch in it —
"half half" having always spoken to me more of socks than
of our surprise child, come to warm the lap of our middle
years. Our family was, in any case, an improvisation. *The new
American family,* our neighbor Mitchell once proclaimed.…
But for Carnegie and me, it was simply something we made.
Something we chose. His mother, Mama Wong, thought this
unnatural.[32]

In this quote, we see the particular disjuncture between linguistic and narrative representation and the psychic ideal of family:
even though the idea of a natural family is debunked, the
assumption that a family could be "ours" in some unmediated
way already refigures some kind of primary tie. This disjuncture reveals how adoptive families pose category crises for the
idea of family itself. Not because they oppose some ideal of
choice to the idea of blood, but because they show the assumptions behind attachment. If family relies on the security of
nominalism — that "Mom" should refer within the "family"
to a single person and can define a set of coherent relationships — the importance of the relationship between language
and what it is supposed to refer to is highlighted immediately:
What do we call this family and how do we make sense of
their claims on each other? What does Blondie mean when
she questions "whose family this was" — can "family" ever be
said to be possessed by a single person or a couple? In this
first page, Jen already introduces us to the terms that will be
bandied about throughout the novel: chose; made; new American family; unnatural. But they don't signify singular political
positions or imperatives. Rather they function variously, sometimes as clichés, sometimes as defence mechanisms, other times
as ways to cover over or displace the uncertainty of "family."

This passage already gives a sense of the family dynamics
that this novel is playing with. But a brief plot description
shows just how crucial the rethinking of family structures and

norms is. The humor of the book revolves around grappling with the realities of an interracial family that includes both adopted children and a "bio baby." But the plot revolves around the arrival of a Chinese woman named Lan, whom Carnegie's mother, Mama Wong, has sent to live with them. Lan magnifies Blondie's anxieties about adoption, forcing her to question anew her own place in the family, where she belongs, if she is the "best" mother for her adopted children, Lizzy and Wendy, if she should be transmitting some form of Chinese or Asian culture to her children. And Lan herself is a site for the difficulties of familial and racial relations — what is her relation to this family; what are her ties to these children or to Carnegie. The novel moves back and forth between their present familial difficulties of inclusion and exclusion centered on the character Lan, and various past family stories including Blondie's difficulties with Carnegie's mother, and the story of how they adopted Lizzy and Wendy. Strained by these familial difficulties, Carnegie and Blondie end up separating, dividing the household into basically two families — a "white" one comprised of Blondie and Bailey, and an "Asian" one comprised of Carnegie, Lan, Lizzy, and Wendy. But in this comic version of the transracial adoption plot, the novel ends by reconfiguring the family unit once again: Carnegie discovers that he was in fact adopted; that Lan is actually Mama Wong's biological daughter, and thus, Carnegie's older sister. Of the entire Wong family Lan, then, is the only biological Wong.

But what does biological then mean? As this plot description suggests, far from celebrating the "new" American family, or metaphorizing the multiracial nation in terms of family, it is the need to make family real and the inability to homologize family, race, and nation that dominate this novel. Jen's narrative acts out two competing processes in how a family reproduces itself through unities that it enacts. First, it represents the nontraditional, transracial family through the variety of family stories that they tell, retell, and negotiate, showing how family is not based on any single ground or genetic tie, but rather through shared relations. Second, it represents the fantasy of the genetic that continues to haunt this desire to de-essentialize family and to make it into the "mere" experience of relationality. This genetic fantasy operates by displacing the problem of biological origins onto likeness, which is then read as the causal grounds for familial identification and attachment.

The formal structure of the novel acts out the first of these processes — the representation of "family" through a series of family stories that continually marks the differences within family. The form combines drama with that of the novel by including multiple first-person narrators. In this way, it is similar to *Sudden Family*, in its promise to represent family dynamics as opposed to just a single relationship or representative of the family. But it is also more dialogic in that the perspectives are not separated as chapters. In *The Love Wife*, each member of the "family" is in dialogue with the other, building the story bit by bit, sometimes commenting on other parts of the story, sometimes commenting on what others say, oftentimes putting words in each other's mouths. The effect of this form is to represent the interactions and behavior of the family: it concentrates both on the canonical family stories that the family tells over and over, and on the techniques that families have for being together and keeping people together, what Bruner calls "behaving family."[33] This structure reveals not just the different individual relationships to family stories, but also how and when they overlap and the psychic dissonances that they often create.

For example, Carnegie and Blondie take Lizzy to China with them when they adopt for a second time, in hopes of giving her a positive sense of her origins and of the process of adoption. The trip becomes a story that is continually revised, displaced, and rewritten depending on each person's different psychic needs. For Lizzy, the trip is traumatic and instead of relating it in the way that her parents would like her to, Lizzy uses the story as a refrain to every bad thing that happens in her life. Carnegie recounts, "Nothing traumatic could be recounted without Lizzy putting in, *You think that's bad, you won't believe what happened in China*. At least the memory was sometimes comforting: the day she fell out of a tree and broke her arm, for example, she did tell the doctor, *It wasn't as scary as what happened to me in China*" (131). Blondie later works with Lizzy on a photo album of good memories from China, and Carnegie frames their moments together as a picture-perfect "mother–daughter moment," reusing the story to recreate family. But this moment of familial attachment is then juxtaposed with Lizzy rewriting the photo album yet again: "What you don't see in this story is how crowded it was, and how people pushed, and how hot it was, like an oven" (132). Jen juxtaposes these different desires behind storytelling in ways that complicate the idea that the problem of making family can be reduced to origin stories. Each of the members of the family have partial and divided relationships to these family stories, even as there remains the desire to reframe these moments into clear "mother–daughter" moments or transparent claims between parent and child. In this same chapter, Blondie, who is dismayed by Lizzy's rewriting of the photo album, repeats a family story of her own: "I had had the heart to take these children in, after all. Had I not loved them deeply and well, as if they were from the beginning my own?" (133).

In this example of the rewriting of a family story, we see how family is acted out through the partial and often divergent desires of family members. Each family member enacts certain norms regarding what the family is through their storytelling practices. Looking for something more "primary," Carnegie and Blondie seek to recreate origins. Lizzy displaces these desires with her own contingent feelings and shared experiences. The novel stages this negotiation of idealization and deidealization. But there is a simultaneous drive within the novel toward a fantasy of the genetic through resemblance and similitude. Carnegie Wong, for example, is characterized by his search and desire for his "family book," his genealogical history. This fantasy of origins gets relayed through the production of a material object and its promise of representing the "real." Not surprisingly, Carnegie fixates on the book's appearance. He frets at one point: "How many volumes would it be? What color? And what would the pages be like? Would they be rice paper? Would they be conventional pages bound into a conventional book? Or those horizontal scroll-like sheets I had heard about, folded in half and bound with silk thread?" (201). The infusion of stereotypical signs of Chineseness is no accident here in imagining the family book: the book is made to accommodate in fantasy its likeness to the imagined Chinese ancestry. Through this drama around the book, Jen shows how crucial the production of likeness as a claim to the real is for familial formations.

The problem of making family real intersects with the logic of racial belonging, which similarly relies on using resemblance to supplement the uncertain ground of some more primary tie imagined as biology or genetics. We can see this in Blondie's imaginative reconstruction of family. Blondie catches everyone in the dining room and proceeds to "make" family:

> Thanks to the short hall between the front door and the dining room, they did not see me right away. . . . But for this half moment, for a half moment more, I saw them — Carnegie at the head of the table, in a baseball cap; Lan at its foot, in my seat. . . . All were quiet and absorbed. How much more natural this scene than the one that included me. How natural, and how quiet it was — the quiet was almost the worst part. . . . Carnegie and Lizzy and Wendy had in front of them lidded cups, such

as I'd seen in China and Chinatown; Bailey had his sippy cup, which I saw now was also a lidded cup. Everyone was wearing slippers. Lan's were blue, and perfectly plain. The love wife. (257–58)

The domestic "scene" of the dining room has a particularly theatrical valence: it is the place where family gathers and reproduces its norms and representational strategies. Blondie's attention in this scene moves from the theatrical, to the fantasy of naturalness, and then to the fantasy of similitude — similar cups; similar slippers. It moves smaller and smaller to the production of similarities by focusing on the details of objects: the fact that all of the cups were lidded; the fact that everyone was wearing slippers. The reference to China and Chinatown is minor, almost an afterthought, but it helps the scene cohere around an imagination of originary belonging that conflates the nation-space with a history of urban, segregated settlement. The figuration of the claims of family hinges on this prior production of similarities *as* sameness.[34]

As we can see from these examples, similarities are converted into something more substantive that provides the logics for racial and familial belonging. To return to the notion of Lacan's "semblant," appearances and similarities built on Chineseness are completely divorced from bodies and genealogies and made instead to inhere in the arrangement of persons and the details of objects. These resemblances fill in for some supposedly originary, more primal connections founded on "race" and "family" that are not there. They are made to legitimate conventional representations, alignments, and norms of family. Blondie's satisfaction in constructing this scene covers over her anxiety over the "real" grounds for family. This is why Lan's appearance in the novel is so contested: she is the character onto which all of the anxieties concerning the unity of the adoptive family are projected. Her character tests the limits of this process whereby the appearances of racial similarity or biological resemblance are substituted for the legal forms and social norms of family. In the beginning of the novel, her arrival exerts an uncertain claim on the family (she is a relative of the Wongs; they owe it to Mama Wong to take her in; she can help out with the kids). She is both outside and inside the family and it is the problem of her positioning within and without the family that constitutes the family romance/drama of the novel. It is her arrival, of course, that poses the challenge to the family's definition of itself and claims upon each other, unearthing the language that had been used to constitute the familial imaginary along the familiar and normalizing oppositions of natural/unnatural, born/chosen, matched/unmatched.

Lan's own marginal relationship to the narrative is symptomatic of how her difference is to be registered. Jen explains in an interview:

> In some of the very early drafts, Lan was silent—I was so busy getting to know the other characters, and trying to understand what was emerging, form-wise and story-wise, that it did not immediately occur to me that I could "hear" Lan too. And it was hard for me to imagine, at first, how I was going to pull off a book with four first-person narrators. (As it happened, of course, I ended up with five.) As soon as Lingzhen asked ["Why doesn't Lan speak?"], though, I realized Lan couldn't not speak — that in fact her story was very much part of the whole story. I realized that I was interested in her—very interested — interested enough that I simply had to find a way to work her perspective in.[35]

After the interviewer notes that Lan's sections are all written in italics, Jen justifies it in terms of signaling linguistic difference: "because she is theoretically speaking in Chinese, her speech is set in italics. I wanted her to be able to speak for herself, without a language barrier, the same as the other characters."[36] Jen's comments replicate the odd position in which Lan is placed with respect to the "family stories" of *The Love Wife*. Lan is both marked by her difference linguistically (her "Chinese" speech is in italics) and unmarked in relation to the other characters (she speaks "without a language barrier, the same as the other characters"). The labor of making her appear in a certain way indexes the problem that Lan poses for the novel as a whole: her appearance may or may not be able to be recuperated into conventional representations of familial unity based on biology or choice.

For example, as soon as Lan appears, she comes to stand in for the possibilities and impossibilities of creating resemblances. The "Lan Arrives" chapter is practically a catalogue of measuring minor differences. Measuring Lan's appearance and characteristics to some imagined frame of Chinese-ness, Blondie compares Lan to both Lizzy and Wendy, wondering which girl she is more "like":

> She [Lan] appeared an inch or two taller than Lizzy. . . . And yet how similar they seemed. . . . Or no, maybe Lan looked more like Wendy — so I thought when Wendy walked up. . . . From the first moment I saw the three of them together, I thought they seemed, despite their differences, a set. Was that racist? Like kitchen canisters, I thought. S-M-L. (15–16)

Comparison — the measure of similarity and difference — punctuates this first chapter, where Lan stands in for an imagined Chinese-ness that helps to establish each of these characters in their relation to that imagined form of cultural difference.

Incorporated in this way, Lan's appearance reinforces familial norms based on racial sameness. But Lan becomes a real problem when resemblance becomes identification: a threat to the familial function of transmission. Wendy narrates: "Lan-lan teaches us Chinese, starting with *Ni you mei you Zhongguo pengyou?* — Do you have any Chinese friends? That's weird. But pretty soon she figures out what works. She gives us all Chinese names, to begin with, which we sort of had already, Dad says, I guess his mom gave us some" (203). Blondie becomes concerned with the content of what Lanlan is teaching, remarking on the Chinese words for "strangeness" — "Mom doesn't like that song because it calls the tigers strange, she says she doesn't like all the talk about strangeness" (203). Her worry revolves around the values being transmitted to her children. This is marked by the very first lesson — *Ni you mei you Zhongguo pengyou?* Is this a lesson in language or a lesson in what Lanlan sees as a proper social identity? Carnegie, on the other hand, is "just glad that whatever Lanlan's teaching, it's Chinese" (203). Wendy narrates: "it's like [Carnegie] wants everybody to be at least a little Chinese, and me and Lizzy have the black hair. He doesn't have to worry as much about us, we're not in danger of turning total Baileys. — I want Bailey to be Bailey Wong, he says. Not Bailey Bailey" (204). Carnegie applies a synecdochal logic onto ethnic identification; he makes the part stand for the whole. He counts Lizzy and Wendy's black hair as the sign of ethnic identification that stands for a "whole" — whether it be "Chinese-ness" or Asian-ness, but wants to make sure Bailey Wong — who resembles his mother's ethnic characteristics — does not become "total Bailey." Both Blondie and Carnegie are concerned when a similarity in appearance becomes an identification, thus threatening their own contingent claims on their children. Lan's character oscillates between these two possibilities, reinforcing the norms of sameness within constructions of the family for Carnegie and threatening the set of group identifications for Blondie.

Many of these examples (Blondie looking at the dining room table; Lan's first appearance) where the appearance of race substitutes for and exposes anxieties within the grounds of family unity have to do with the act of seeing. While race is often conceptualized in terms of visibility, here the problem of visibility has to do with the overlapping logics of race, family, and nation. Making these categories into homologies suggests that one category is used to see the other: thus in the dining room scene, racial sameness is used as a lens onto familial unity. The process of measuring the similarities among Lan, Wendy, and Lizzy are ways of regulating the relations between racial and familial belonging, normalizing the conjunction of these three characters in the same space. Thus one of the ways to make family "look like real" — to structure the appearance of the family as real — is to recreate the "real" through different scales of belonging such as race or nation. Mama Wong, for example, gestures with one hand on the inability to tie family to the "natural" ("Nothing is natural," she tells Carnegie), at the same time that she displaces the question of family onto racial and national belonging. The fantasied conversation that Carnegie has with his mother turns on this joke about the grounds of family, which repeatedly slip out from under Carnegie's understandings and his desire to "fix" a particular structure. Mama Wong continually upsets Carnegie's sensibility by resituating the grounds of their relationship through the question of being American or Chinese:

> "Ma," I say. "I got the book, and it turns out I'm not even your son."
>
> "Only an American boy would read something and think, 'Oh, that must be true.' As if true is that simple!"...
>
> She laughs and laughs. "No one is so easy to surprise as an American," she says. "Let me ask you, now, honest way. How can you be my son?"

"How can I not be?" I say, after a moment. "After all, you wrecked my life."

"Ah! Now you are like real Chinese!" (376)

For a family to "look real," it must, as Mama Wong says, use periods: "A child should say this is my mother, period. This is my father, period" (377). But this form of closure often relies on other forms of closure such as racial identification in which one is pronounced to be either American or Chinese.

However, the ending of the novel offers another response to this question, one that interrogates this structuring and normalizing of the intelligibility of family. It presents an image of the family that deidealizes its own unity. It frames a family that "knows" its own fragility and dissolubility, because it knows that there is nothing there behind the image. In the end, everyone is gathered together, rejoicing that Carnegie Wong is okay after his heart attack. Wendy narrates this final family scene:

> It's happy, so happy, and who knows? — just might stay happy. Look at us all hugging, after all, Lizzy and Bailey and Mom and Lanlan and me, and look now! How Lanlan grasps Mom's hand, and Mom grasps hers. That's happy! But then they let go, and look away, blinking. We made it! And yet we know now, too, what we know. *This world can disappear like any other.* It's amazing how dark a room can suddenly get. (379)

Here Wendy's narration steps out like a photographer and observes and frames this family scene. But it is a family scene haunted by a knowledge that cannot be disavowed — the knowledge that family is not the ground but the fiction of permanence. That "world" and "room" correspond to each other in the final two sentences reveals the different scales on which unities are formed. Different groupings of persons create different unities, and it is the incapacity of "family" to accommodate these different unities that creates the perceptual crisis of disappearance and darkness at the end of this novel.

As Laura Briggs notes, there is a "common sense" idea that "because [transracial and transnational family-making] does not look like a white, suburban, heterosexually produced nuclear family ideal, it is an intrinsically radical cultural practice." [37] But what do these families look like, and what are the conditions of their legibility and intelligibility? What norms get reenacted and reidealized through the process of appearing? In order to think about how transnational adoption might transform normative ideas of kinship, I have suggested that we must first consider how the causal logics of biology and filiation are readmitted in order to make family, in Mama Wong's words, "look like real." At the end of this novel, all of the familial positions seem to be overturned. Everyone is, seemingly, out of place: Lan is the "real" daughter of Mama Wong; Carnegie is not biologically a Wong — he now wonders if he is Mama Wong's son. But to reorder relationships in this way would be to make the biological connection between two people into a causal relationship. What Gish Jen's novel dramatizes are the appearances that are mobilized — the registers of biological discourse, racial similarity, national imperative — in order to create a sense of familial unity. By recognizing the fragility of permanence, the tenuousness of unity, and the interface between the "inside" and the "outside" of the family at the end of the novel, Jen opens up familial relationships such that they may be derealized, reframed into a different picture that meditates on how different groupings are made to appear.

For *The Love Wife*, the transgression advanced by the prospect of transracial adoptive families is this vision of the lack of an internal unity at the heart of family. Making family "look like real" all too often relies on the reconstruction of normative racial and national orders. Gish Jen's version of this problem reproduces these logics at the same time that it requires acknowledging the failure of these attempts to produce a justificatory ground for familial unity. I have argued throughout that the phenomenon of transracial and transnational adoption does not simply rethink ideologies of consanguinity so much as it reconceives conditions of personhood. The long history of engagements with the idea and practice of transracial and transnational adoption links up with the continual production of stories by and about transracial and transnational adoptees as they demand an acknowledgment of their uncertain status within prevailing assumptions about what constitutes proper and legitimate personhood. As we have seen, transracial adoption stories negotiate the formation of familial attachments that both replicate the ways in which the logics of familial, racial, and national belonging reinforce one another and provide ways in which the boundaries of personhood can be redrawn. They interrogate models of personhood that use the norms and practices of "birth" in order to situate the self. Further, they explore how the regulation of interracial relations is intimately related to our narratives of individuation. As adoption becomes visible and prevalent in new ways, the question becomes how it will test and shift our assumptions about the legibility of persons. What these adoption stories make clear is the ongoing struggle to articulate the various modes of relating to another that continue to remake who we are.

Acknowledgments

This book could not have been written without the generous support, fellowship, and inspiration of friends, colleagues, mentors, teachers, and family. I am grateful for the various institutional supports that made this project possible. I received ample research time through a fellowship with the Davis Humanities Institute and a Faculty Development Award through the University of California, Davis. The New-York Historical Society and the staff at Houghton Library were especially helpful and efficient in gaining access to hard-to-reach stories and manuscripts. I thank Crystal Anderson, Catherine Fung, and Vanessa Rapatz for their invaluable research assistance for this project. Two anonymous referees for the University of Minnesota Press provided detailed suggestions and insights that were instrumental during the revision process. I thank them for their careful reading. Thanks to Richard Morrison for his interest and belief in this book.

Claiming Others began under the advice and guidance of three dedicated teachers and scholars: Lawrence Buell, Homi Bhabha, and John Stauffer. For their careful readings, intellectual passions, and unflagging support and dialogue, I am deeply grateful. I also thank David Eng, Marjorie Garber, Barbara Johnson, Douglas Mao, Elisa New, Elaine Scarry, Marc Shell, and Werner Sollors for advice, critique, and models of scholarship at this early stage. I sincerely appreciate those scholars who provided ideas, challenges, and constructive criticism that shaped this project during various professional occasions: Elizabeth Dillon, Shirley Geok-Lin Lim, Susannah

Gottlieb, Wendy Graham, Jay Grossman, Jane Kane, Michael Joyce, Maria Karafilis, Rosemary Kegl, Barbara Mann, John Michael, Greta Niu, Donald Pease, Ross Posnock, Martin Puchner, Bruce Robbins, Frank Shuffelton, Richard So, Julia Stern, Jeffrey Tucker, Eleanor Ty, Bryan Washington, and many others.

My interests in adoption as a literary scholar have been crucially enriched by both other adoption scholars and a larger "adoption community." I am fortunate to be in dialogue with many of them through the Alliance for the Study of Adoption and Culture and various panel presentations at the International Conference on Adoption, the Asian American Studies conference, and the meetings of the American Studies Association and Modern Language Association. I learned a great deal from my exchanges with them and their generous responses to my work: Cynthia Callahan, Emily Cheng, Vincent Cheng, Patricia Chu, Jill Deans, Sara Dorow, Jennifer Kwon Dobbs, Ellen Herman, Emily Hipchen, Tobias Hubinette, Eleana Kim, Dana Leventhal, Kimberly Leighton, Deann Borshay Liem, Young Hee Lowrie, Hope Ning, Kim Park Nelson, Sarah Park, Elise Prebin, Nicky Schildkraut, Carol Singley, Claudia Sadowsky-Smith, Toby Alice Volkman, Jenny Hei Jun Wills, and Barbara Yngvesson. Margaret Homans and Marianne Novy both read the entire manuscript, and I greatly benefited from their suggestions as well as their scholarship.

I could not have found a more nurturing and exciting scholarly community than the University of California, Davis. Colleagues there have enriched my thinking: Seeta Chaganti, Joshua Clover, Lucy Corin, Greg Dobbins, Fran Dolan, Margie Ferguson, Beth Freeman, Wendy Ho, Richard Kim, Desiree Martin, John Marx, Susette Min, Tim Morton, Riche Richardson, Parama Roy, David Simpson, David Van Leer, Claire Waters, and Karl Zender. Hsuan Hsu, Michael Ziser, and Fran Dolan were kind enough to make suggestions on individual chapters, and Colin Milburn saw this project from start to finish. Members of the DHI Fellowship Group on Transnationalism offered critiques that helped me refashion the manuscript: Glenda Drew, Omnia El Shakry, Jaimey Fisher, Ari Kelman, Carolyn de la Pena, Henry Spiller, and Grace Wang. Thanks to Jon Rossini for alerting me to the play by David Henry Hwang.

Friends and family have been a much-needed presence and ballast for the duration of this project. Many thanks to Alisa Braithwaite, Nadine Knight, Monica Lewis, Gillian Prowse, Laura Thiemann Scales, and Amanda Teo. Thanks to my father, mother, brother, sister, and their families for showing me the way and supporting me on the journey. Thanks to Seneca and Chloe for everyday surprises and daily joys. I dedicate this book to Liane for her love, encouragement, and support, which have seen me through both the struggles and the pleasures of writing.

Notes

Introduction

1. W. Clarke Hall and Justin Clarke Hall, *The Law of Adoption and Guardianship of Infants* (London: Butterworth & Co., 1928), 3.

2. Jamil Zainaldin, "The Emergence of a Modern American Family Law: Child Custody, Adoption, and the Courts, 1796–1851," *Northwestern University Law Review* 73 (1979): 1042.

3. David Henry Hwang, *Trying to Find Chinatown: The Selected Plays*, 1st ed. (New York: Theatre Communications Group, 2000), 11. Cited parenthetically hereafter.

4. For a catalogue of modern citizenship policies, see Jacqueline Stevens, *Reproducing the State* (Princeton, N.J.: Princeton University Press, 1999), 131–37.

5. In his comprehensive meditation on the meaning of recognition, Paul Ricoeur writes: "One is, by the very fact of being born, assigned a fixed place in one's lineage. This, before any egological self-awareness, is what confers an identity on me in the eyes of civil institutions, the identity of being the son or daughter of. . . . " See *Course of Recognition* (Cambridge, Mass.: Harvard University Press, 2005), 193. Alasdair MacIntyre has similar, if more implicit, assumptions about genealogy tied to birth parents in his description of a life story: "I am what I may justifiably be taken by others to be in the course of living out a story that runs from my birth to my death; I am the *subject* of a history that is my own and no one else's, that has its own peculiar meaning. . . . I am born with a past. . . . The possession of an historical identity and the possession of a social identity coincide." See *After Virtue: A Study in Moral Theory* (Notre Dame, Ind.: University of Notre Dame Press, 1984), 217, 221. On the centrality of birth in social contract theories and political philosophies of

249

political membership, including Locke, Hume, Rousseau, and Hegel, see Stevens, *Reproducing the State.*

6. For this last argument about transracial adoption, see David Hollinger, *Postethnic America: Beyond Multiculturalism* (New York: Basic Books, 1995), 117.

7. Michel Foucault defines biopolitics as the management of life through the regulation of bodies and processes of human reproduction, including everything from administrative apparatuses around pedagogy, psychiatry, statistical analysis of populations, and child-rearing, etc. He names these biopolitical mechanisms as governing the "entry of life into history." See *History of Sexuality* (New York: Vintage, 1990), 1: 141.

8. *Relative Values: Reconfiguring Kinship Studies,* ed. Sarah Franklin and Susan McKinnon (Durham, N.C.: Duke University Press, 2002), 19. Franklin and Mackinnon's introduction discusses how mobile and fluid constructions of kinship get used alternately to consolidate boundaries between nations, races, and peoples, and to cross them. Particularly relevant is Pauline Turner Strong's essay on how Native American tribalism challenges hegemonic norms of Euramerican kinship, "To Forget Their Tongue, Their Name, and Their Whole Relation: Captivity, Extra-tribal Adoption, and the Indian Child Welfare Act," collected in this volume, 468–95. On how kinship consolidates racial and national genealogies through the conflation of race reproduction and species reproduction, see Alyse Weinbaum, *Wayward Reproductions: Genealogies of Race and Nation in Transatlantic Modern Thought* (Durham, N.C.: Duke University Press, 2004).

9. On linkages between domesticity and imperialism, see Laura Wexler, *Tender Violence* (Chapel Hill: University of North Carolina Press, 2000), and Amy Kaplan, *The Anarchy of Empire in the Making of U.S. Culture* (Cambridge, Mass.: Harvard University Press, 2002), chapter 1.

10. Ann Anagnost, "Scenes of Misrecognition: Maternal Citizenship in the Age of Transnational Adoption," *Positions: East Asia Cultures Critique* 8, no. 2 (2000): 390–421; David Eng, "Transnational Adoption and Queer Diasporas," *Social Text* 21, no. 3 (2003):

1–37; Barbara Yngvesson, "'Going Home': Adoption, Loss of Bearings, and the Mythology of Roots," and Eleana Kim, "Wedding Citizenship and Culture: Korean Adoptees and the Global Family of Korea," in *Cultures of Transnational Adoption,* ed. Toby Alice Volkman (Durham, N.C.: Duke University Press, 2005). These and others are dealt with in more detail as the argument progresses.

11. Shklar defines citizenship not just as a "matter of agency and empowerment, but also of social standing," denoting one's place in society, a minimum of social dignity and the entitlement to respect. See Judith Shklar, *American Citizenship: The Quest for Inclusion* (Cambridge, Mass.: Harvard University Press, 1991), 2.

12. See Anonymous, "How It Feels to Have Been an Adopted Child" (1920), Adoption History Project, http://darkwing.uoregon .edu/~adoption/index.html (accessed February 9, 2008); Carol S. Prentice, *An Adopted Child Looks at Adoption* (New York: Appleton-Century, 1940).

13. On the notion of orphaning and genealogy as central to American national narratives from the Declaration of Independence on through the nineteenth century, see Jay Fliegelman, *Prodigals and Pilgrims: The American Revolution against Patriarchal Authority, 1750–1800* (Cambridge: Cambridge University Press, 1982), and Russ Castronovo, *Fathering the Nation: American Genealogies of Slavery and Freedom* (Berkeley: University of California Press, 1995). On the ubiquity of family discourse as a way of staging abolitionist and proslavery discourse, see Karen Sánchez-Eppler, *Touching Liberty: Abolition, Feminism, and the Politics of the Body* (Berkeley: University of California Press, 1993). On the homology between family and nation produced through modernist and nativist poetics in the service of making race into a heritable and inalienable identity, see Walter Benn Michaels, *Our America: Nativism, Modernism, and Pluralism* (Durham, N.C.: Duke University Press, 1995). On the figure of the child within the intersecting rhetorics of racialization and nation-formation, see Caroline Levander *Cradle of Liberty: Race, the Child, and National Belonging from Thomas Jefferson to W. E. B. DuBois* (Durham, N.C.: Duke University Press, 2006).

14. Ann Stoler, *Carnal Knowledge and Imperial Power* (Berkeley: University of California Press, 2002); Doris Sommer, *Foundational*

Fictions: The National Romances of Latin America (Berkeley: University of California Press, 1993); David Theo Goldberg, *The Racial State* (Malden, Mass.: Blackwell, 2002).

15. Stoler, *Carnal Knowledge and Imperial Power,* 144.

16. On the nation as an imagined assemblage or narrative process for continuity, transmission, and attachment, see Benedict Anderson, *Imagined Communities: Reflections on the Origin and Spread of Nationalism* (London: New York, 1991); Homi K. Bhabha, ed., *Nation and Narration* (London: Routledge, 1990); Étienne Balibar and Immanuel Wallerstein, *Race, Nation, Class: Ambiguous Identities* (London: Verso, 1991), chapter 5.

17. Stevens, *Reproducing the State,* 107.

18. Stevens writes: "citizenship depends first on ideas about ancestral lineage, and then on conventions of marriage, territory, and possibly language," ibid., 134.

19. Ibid., 268.

20. Balibar and Wallerstein, *Race, Nation, Class,* 101.

21. Ibid., 100.

22. Racial formation theory sought to isolate race and make clear its effects apart from other phenomena such as class or nationalism. Most centrally, Howard Winant defined race as "a concept which signifies and symbolizes sociopolitical conflicts and interests in reference to different types of human bodies." See Winant, "Race and Race Theory," *Annual Review of Sociology* 26 (2000): 172 and Michael Omi and Howard Winant, *Racial Formation in the United States* (London: Routledge, 1994), especially 53–77. Scholars have extended this framework by analyzing its intersectionality with other categories such as gender, sexuality, class, etc. My approach builds on such analyses by specifying the myriad ways in which these concepts are articulated in relation to each other and in fact rely on each other. I utilize insights from phenomenological and psychoanalytic approaches toward race in order to get at the affective formations through which race is felt at the level of attachment, dependency, and relationality. For a foundational analysis of intersectionality, see Kimberle Crenshaw, "Mapping the Margins: Intersectionality, Identity Politics, and Violence against Women of Color," *Stanford Law Review* 43 (1991): 1241–99. For phenomenological approaches, see Frantz

Fanon, *Black Skin, White Masks* (New York: Grove Press, 1967); Sara Ahmed, *Queer Phenomenology: Orientations, Objects, Others* (Durham, N.C.: Duke University Press, 2006); Linda Martín Alcoff, *Visible Identities: Race, Gender, and the Self* (Oxford: Oxford University Press, 2005).

23. Stoler, *Carnal Knowledge*, 159.

24. Stevens writes: "Nations, ethnicities, and races provide and depend on such an intergenerational form quite explicitly.... The analysis of the overlapping sets of rules that constitute affiliations (of political society, family, nation, ethnicity, and gender) shows that it is invocations of birth (and death, for religion) that separate the identities shaped by these group forms from the subject positions that follow from statuses of health (allergies), personal quirks (bedside or pizza-topping preferences, for instance), as well as numerous other predilections and conditions." *Reproducing the State*, 14–15.

25. On the production of race in relation to biological kinship categories, see Donna Haraway, "Universal Donors in a Vampire Culture: It's All in the Family: Biological Kinship Categories in the Twentieth-Century United States," in *Uncommon Ground: Rethinking the Human Place in Nature*, ed. William Cronon (New York: W. W. Norton, 1996), 321–66.

26. Locke, in an effort to explain the child's peculiar place, writes that "children... are not born in this full state of Equality, though they are born to it." In Filmer's family, the child never grows up, and the Law of God commands the obedience of every child and institutes the absolute authority of the patriarch. In Locke's family, the child grows up, and in doing so, learns to exercise the freedom and equality to which he is born. Locke, *Two Treatises of Government* (London: Dent, 1924), chapter 6, section 55. For an excellent explication of the role of the child in Lockean consent theory, see Gillian Brown, *Consent of the Governed: The Lockean Legacy in Early American Culture* (Cambridge, Mass.: Harvard University Press, 2001).

27. Carole Pateman, Susan Moller Okin, and others make clear that the consequences of analyzing the state in the tradition of a Lockean split and analogy between family and nation is to neglect an analysis of social bonds as they constitute forms of personhood. These theorists not only draw out the dependence of norms of political

254 / *Notes to the Introduction*

participation on the regulation of specific social relationships but also demonstrate the centrality of a theory of affective bonds and relationality for theories of a just political order. See Carole Pateman, *The Sexual Contract* (Stanford, Calif.: Stanford University Press, 1988); Susan Moller Okin, *Justice, Gender, and the Family* (New York: Basic Books, 1989); Mary Shanley and Uma Narayan, eds., *Reconstructing Political Theory: Feminist Perspectives* (University Park: Pennsylvania State University Press, 1997); Mary Shanley and Carole Pateman, ed., *Feminist Interpretations and Political Theory* (Cambridge: Polity Press, 1991). On the relationship between state recognition and kinship practices, see Drucilla Cornell, *At the Heart of Freedom: Feminism, Sex, and Equality* (Princeton, N.J.: Princeton University Press, 1998); Judith Butler, *Antigone's Claim: Kinship between Life and Death* (New York: Columbia University Press, 2000); Martha Fineman, *The Neutered Mother, the Sexual Family, and Other Twentieth Century Tragedies* (New York: Routledge, 1995).

28. In psychology, Carol Gilligan critiques assumptions concerning moral development and individuation that delegitimize notions of personhood based on relationality, shared bonds, and cooperation among persons at the expense of understanding women's moral and emotional development. See *In a Different Voice: Psychological Theory and Women's Development* (Cambridge, Mass.: Harvard University Press, 1982). In anthropology, Marilyn Strathern demonstrates how notions of individuality based on property, rights, or autonomy are themselves conditioned by social relationships of a particular kind. See *After Nature: English Kinship in the Late Twentieth Century* (Cambridge: Cambridge University Press, 1992). Janet Carstens demonstrates that Western constructions of individuality rely on specific sources in philosophy, jurisprudence, and theology that neglect the central role that kinship and relationality plays in the expression of personhood. See *After Kinship* (Cambridge: Cambridge University Press, 2004).

29. Okin, *Justice, Gender, and the Family*, 9.

30. Discussing race as a "language of affiliation" in U.S. antebellum writing, Peter Coviello writes that "any understanding of race that excludes its affective and relational dimensions will of necessity remain damagingly partial, whatever its claims to historical acuity

and breadth" (5). See *Intimacy in America: Dreams of Affiliation in Antebellum Literature* (Minneapolis: University of Minnesota Press, 2005).

31. For excellent sociological analyses, see Sandra Patton, *Birthmarks: Transracial Adoption in Contemporary America* (New York: New York University Press, 2000), and Sara Dorow, *Transnational Adoption: A Cultural Economy of Race, Gender, and Kinship* (New York: New York University Press, 2006); for an approach inflected by race and legal theory, see Hawley Fogg-Davis, *The Ethics of Transracial Adoption* (Ithaca, N.Y.: Cornell University Press, 2002).

32. Nancy Armstrong, *How Novels Think: The Limits of Individualism from 1719–1900* (New York: Columbia University Press, 2006).

33. Marianne Novy similarly notes the privileging of orphans as a paradigm in literature and makes the suggestion that seeing them as adoptees "allows us to see them more contextually. We can compare their relationships with their surrogate parents." See Novy, *Reading Adoption: Family and Difference in Fiction and Drama* (Ann Arbor: University of Michigan Press, 2005), 89.

34. Otto Rank codifies and analyzes this traditional device through several different cultures and time periods, arguing for its significance as the prototype of myth and storytelling themselves. See Otto Rank, *The Myth of the Birth of the Hero and Other Writings* (New York: Vintage, 1959). Similarly, Northrop Frye identifies the discovery of "true parentage" as a central theme in romance, its structure consisting of the "individual loss or confusion or break in the continuity of identity." See Northrop Frye, *The Secular Scripture: A Study of the Structure of Romance* (Cambridge, Mass.: Harvard University Press, 1976), 101, 104.

35. Novy's *Reading Adoption* is a foundational work for correcting this blind spot. Reading works from Sophocles to Shakespeare to George Eliot, as well as twentieth-century authors, she demonstrates the continual engagement of these works with the problems of defining kinship, adoptive parenthood, and childhood. See also Carol Singley, "Building a Nation, Building a Family: Adoption in Nineteenth-Century American Children's Literature," in *Adoption*

in America, ed. E. Wayne Carp (Ann Arbor: University of Michigan Press, 2002); Margaret Homans, "Adoption Narratives, Trauma and Origins," *Narrative* 14, no. 1 (2006): 4–26, and "Origins, Searches and Identity: Narratives of Adoption in China," *Contemporary Women's Writing* 1, no. 1/2 (2007): 59–79; Jill Deans, "Performing the Search in Adoption Autobiography: Finding Christa and Reno Finds Her Mom," *Biography* 24, no. 1 (2001): 85–98; Eng, "Transnational Adoption and Queer Diasporas."

36. Singley argues that adoption stories in the nineteenth century reflect and reproduce U.S. national ideologies of choice and freedom. See "Building a Nation, Building a Family."

37. Dorow writes that because of the need for justification required more dramatically by transnational and transracial adoptive families, narrative becomes crucial to the problem of creating a sense of identity: "This permanent relationship of difference in the heart of normative family and nation demands of adoptive parents (as well as adopted persons and adoption practitioners) a regular and conscious *narrative* maintenance." See "Racialized Choices: Chinese Adoption and the 'White Noise' of Blackness," *Critical Sociology* 32, nos. 2–3 (2006): 359.

38. Emily Hipchen, *Coming Apart Together: Fragments from an Adoption* (New Jersey: Literate Chigger Press, 2005), 9–10.

39. Nancy Miller, *But Enough about Me: Why We Read Other People's Lives* (New York: Columbia University Press, 2002), 2–3.

40. Sigmund Freud, "Family Romances," *Standard Edition of the Complete Psychological Works of Sigmund Freud,* ed. James Strachey (London: Hogarth Press, 1959), 9: 237.

41. Ibid.

42. Ibid., 240.

43. As Ken Corbett reminds us, the question "'Where did I come from?'... often places children and parents alike in the manifold grip of wish, anxiety, and defense." See "Nontraditional Family Romances," *Psychoanalytic Quarterly* 70, no. 33 (2001): 599.

44. Klein suggests that infants incorporate and internalize aspects of the mother as an object (associating the breast with a psychic feeling of satisfaction or a feeling of frustration). The infants, according to Klein, form this internal object as a way of negotiating their

relationship to their mothers and external conditions more generally. Winnicott theorizes the transitional object as occupying the space between subject and object; it is both part of the external world and part of the subject's psychic reality. Both writers concentrate on that ongoing circuit between subject and object through which the subject's boundaries are formed. See Melanie Klein, *Envy and Gratitude and Other Works: 1946-1963* (New York: Simon and Schuster, 1975), especially 1–25 and 141–76; Donald Winnicott, *Playing and Reality* (London: Tavistock, 1971), especially 1–26, 86–95.

45. Jean Laplanche constructs an other-centered psychoanalysis, one that decenters the self in suggesting that the unconscious is a sedimentation of messages that arrive primarily from the outside, from externality. See Jean Laplanche, *Essays on Otherness* (London: Routledge, 1999). Leo Bersani also reads against the grain of a psychoanalysis that sees the relationship between subject and object (world) as fundamentally oppositional, and developing instead a vocabulary of relationality that does not take the individuated subject for granted and traces what he calls the "uncertain nature of the very tracing of boundaries" between subject and object, self and world. See "Sociality and Sexuality," *Critical Inquiry* 26 (2000): 641–56.

46. Analyses of adoption acknowledge the role of fantasy, idealization, and projection as central. See in particular David Eng and Shinhee Han, "Desegregating Love: Transnational Adoption, Racial Reparation, and Racial Transitional Objects," *Studies in Gender and Sexuality* (2006) 7, no. 2: 141–72.

47. See Hortense Spillers, "All the Things You Could Be by Now, if Sigmund Freud's Wife Was Your Mother," *Black, White, and in Color* (Chicago: University of Chicago Press, 2003), 376–428. David Eng, *Racial Castration* (Durham, N.C.: Duke University Press, 2001); Anne Cheng, *Melancholy of Race* (Oxford: Oxford University Press, 2001); Saidiya Hartman, *Scenes of Subjection* (Oxford: Oxford University Press, 1997); Claudia Tate, *Domestic Allegories of Political Desire* (Oxford: Oxford University Press, 1996); *The Psychoanalysis of Race,* ed. Christopher Lane (New York: Columbia University Press, 1998).

48. They argue that colonial Americans cared for orphaned and illegitimate children under a system similar to the English poor law

system — a system of apprenticeship that removed children from impoverished families and placed them with masters: "Under the legal doctrine of *parens patriae,* derived from the belief that the king is the father and protector of his people, the role of the state included the right to intervene, on behalf of the child, in the biological family." See E. Wayne Carp, *Family Matters: Secrecy and Disclosure in the History of Adoption* (Cambridge, Mass.: Harvard University Press, 1998), 5–6; Julie Berebitsky, *Like Our Very Own: Adoption and the Changing Culture of Motherhood, 1851–1950* (Lawrence: University Press of Kansas, 2001); Zainaldin, "The Emergence of a Modern American Family Law."

49. The 1851 Massachusetts statute had no common law precedent, thus making it something of an anomaly in United States legal jurisprudence. It was passed seventy-six years before England passed its Adoption Act in 1927. As Zainaldin notes, the Massachusetts adoption statute "contradicted the most fundamental principles of English domestic relations law, and overruled centuries of English precedent and legislation which prohibited the absolute, permanent, and voluntary transfer of parental power to third persons." Zainaldin, "The Emergence of a Modern American Family Law," 1042. Also see David J. Rothman and Sheila M. Rothman, *The Origins of Adoption* (New York: Garland, 1987).

50. On the unevenness of this history of secrecy, see Carp, *Family Matters.*

51. Here transracial adoption is seen as a way of accommodating these different social conditions and serving the "joint needs of these two groups [white couples and nonwhite children]." See Rita Simon and Howard Altstein, *Adoption, Race, and Identity: From Infancy through Adolescence* (New York: Praeger, 1992), 2.

52. This narrative was famously contested in 1972 by the National Association of Black Social Workers, which sought to protect the interests of black families and question their devaluation. Because of these competing arguments pitting a form of cultural nationalism against the claims of a cultural pluralism, black–white transracial adoptions have waxed and waned until the present day.

53. Barbara Melosh, *Strangers and Kin: The American Way of Adoption* (Cambridge, Mass.: Harvard University Press, 2002), 2.

54. Advancing a notion similar to Melosh's, Pertman pronounces: "It [the adoption revolution] is advancing the ethnic, racial, and cultural diversity that is a hallmark of twenty-first-century America" (7). Pertman, *Adoption Nation: How the Adoption Revolution is Transforming America* (New York: Basic Books, 2000).

55. Transnational adoptions increased from 7,093 in 1990 to 22,884 in 2004 and have continued steadily at over 20,000 a year since 2004. Statistics are taken from the U.S. Department of State http://travel.state.gov/family/adoption/stats/stats_451.html (accessed October 14, 2007).

56. Pertman, *Adoption Nation*, 5.

57. Barbara Rothman writes, "Adoptions challenge the natural order; adoptions across race lines do so all the more" (28). See *Weaving a Family: Untangling Race and Adoption* (Boston: Beacon Press, 2005). Janet Beizer writes in a similar vein, "I would argue that transracial family structures . . . are as potentially subversive of traditional American kinship patterns as are open adoptions. All of these patterns are iconoclastic in the sense that they make visible the irrelevance of consanguinity to family bonds and the reality of alternatives to conventional family structures" (248). See Janet Beizer, "One's Own Reflections on Motherhood, Owning, and Adoption," *Tulsa Studies in Women's Literature* 21, no. 2 (2002).

58. Hollee McGinnis, "Who Are You Also Known As?" *New York Times Blog: Relative Choices, Adoption and the American Family,* November 13, 2007, http://relativechoices.blogs.nytimes.com/2007/11/13/who-are-you-also-known-as/ (accessed January 13, 2008).

59. The grammar of "neither this nor that" or claiming both has a long history within African American and Asian American literary and social discourse. Werner Sollors does an excellent historical and thematic genealogy of the phrase "neither black nor white yet both," showing the pervasiveness of this trope for thinking about interracial relations and biracial or bicultural identity. See *Neither Black Nor White Yet Both: Thematic Explorations of Interracial Literature* (Cambridge, Mass.: Harvard University Press, 1999). Lisa Lowe critiques the trope of staging assimilation versus nativism, Asian versus American, in her essay "Heterogeneity, Hybridity, Multiplicity: Marking Asian American Differences." See *Immigrant Acts: On Asian*

American Cultural Politics (Durham, N.C.: Duke University Press, 1996).

60. "Julie" begins her response: "I was not adopted, but I too am conflicted by 'where' I belong and by 'who' I am. I was born in Brasil and I am fourth-generation Japanese–Brasilian, but I've spent most of my life living in the U.S. and grew up with American influences. I feel American, but I'm not." "Aubrey" similarly writes: "I am not adopted, but I do have a lot of the same identity crises (of a lesser magnitude) that some adoptees face: my mother is Korean, my father is caucasian." Adoptees take up the same vocabulary. "Tess" describes her condition as an adoptee: "As an international adoptee now into my 50s, I've straddled what I've always termed, the great divide — the neither here nor there." "Relative Choices," *New York Times* blog, November 13, 2007, http://relativechoices.blogs.nytimes.com/2007/11/13 (accessed January 13, 2008)

61. See Patton, *Birthmarks;* also Rickie Solinger, *Beggars and Choosers: How the Politics of Choice Shapes Adoption, Abortion, and Welfare in the United States* (New York: Hill and Wang, 2001), and Dorothy Roberts, *Shattered Bonds: The Color of Child Welfare* (New York: Basic Books, 2002).

62. Christina Klein, *Cold War Orientalism: Asia in the Middle-brow Imagination, 1945–1961* (Berkeley: University of California Press, 2003). Laura Briggs, "Mother, Child, Race, Nation: The Visual Iconography of Rescue and the Politics of Transnational and Transracial Adoption," *Gender and History* 155, no. 2 (2003): 179–200.

63. Eleana Kim, "Wedding Citizenship and Culture" and "Our Adoptee, Our Alien: Transnational Adoptees as Specters of Foreignness and Family in South Korea," *Anthropological Quarterly* 80, no. 2 (2007): 497–531.

64. Dorow, *Transnational Adoption*, 25. In addition to works cited above, see Yngvesson, "Refiguring Kinship in the Space of Adoption," *Anthropological Quarterly* 80, no. 2 (2007): 561–79.

65. Eng and Han, "Transnational Adoption and Queer Diasporas," "Desegregating Love." See also Eng, *The Feeling of Kinship: Queer Liberalism and the Racialization of Intimacy* (Durham, N.C.:

Duke University Press, 2010), in which he frames the question of transnational adoption in terms of the politics of colorblindness. He argues that transnational adoption is part of a larger racialization of intimacy that shows how the private structures of kinship have become a "privileged site for the management of ongoing problems of race, racism and property in U.S. society" (6).

66. Homans, "Adoption Narratives."

67. *Outsiders Within: Writings on Transracial Adoption,* ed. Jane Jeong Trenka, Julia Chinyere Oparah, and Sun Yung Shin (Boston: South End Press, 2006).

68. Beizer, "One's Own," 245.

1. Competing Logics of Possession

1. J. Hector St. John de Crevecoeur, *Letters from an American Farmer and Sketches of Eighteenth-Century America* (New York: Penguin, 1981), 213.

2. Ibid., 214.

3. Ibid., 214–15.

4. *Papers of Benjamin Franklin,* ed. Leonard Labaree (New Haven, Conn.: Yale University Press, 1959), 17: 381. See also Franklin's May 9, 1753, letter to Peter Collinson, where he notes that even those Indians "habituated to Our Customs" will return to their relations while white persons taken by Indians cannot be "reclaimed." See *The Writings of Benjamin Franklin,* vol. 2, *The History Carper,* www.historycarper.com/resources (accessed July 24, 2008).

5. Quoted in James Axtell, *The Invasion Within: The Contest of Cultures in Colonial North America* (New York: Oxford University Press, 1985), 322.

6. On the lives and fates of these adoptees and captives, many of whom became translators or mediators between Europeans and Indians, see Colin Calloway, *New Worlds for All: Indians, Europeans, and the Remaking of Early America* (Baltimore: Johns Hopkins University Press, 1997), chapter 8.

7. See Jane Merritt, *At the Crossroads: Indians and Empires on a Mid-Atlantic Frontier* (Chapel Hill: University of North Carolina Press, 2003).

8. For discussions of how comparisons of kinship practices between Euramericans and Indians related to political relations

between them, see Carole Shammas, *A History of Household Government in America* (Charlottesville: University of Virginia Press, 2002); Axtell *The Invasion Within;* Richard White, "What Chigabe Knew: Indians, Household Government, and the State," *William and Mary Quarterly* 52, no. 1 (1995): 151–56. White provides a useful corrective by noting that Euramericans also observed similarities, not just revulsion.

9. Merritt, *At the Crossroads*, 55.

10. Richard White, *The Middle Ground: Indians, Empires, and Republics in the Great Lakes Region, 1650–1815* (New York: Cambridge University Press, 1991), 18.

11. Quoted in Merritt, *At the Crossroads,* 55.

12. Ibid., chapter 2.

13. Richard White, "Although I Am Dead, I Am Not Entirely Dead: Constructing Self and Persons on the Middle Ground of Early America," in *Through a Glass Darkly: Reflections on Personal Identity in Early America,* ed. Ronald Hoffman, Mechal Sobel, and Fredrika J. Teute (Chapel Hill: University of North Carolina Press, 1997), 411.

14. White, *Middle Ground.* He describes the end of the "middle ground" in terms of the redescription of Tenskwatawa, an Indian negotiator and mediator, as a savage: "Tenskwatawa had become an exotic. He was no longer a figure familiar to whites, although whites had lived among Indians for nearly two centuries and were, in multiple senses of the word, their relatives. Instead, Tenskwatawa had reverted to a *sauvage*" (522–23). Merritt, *At the Crossroads.* She writes that in the early 1760s, "whites also became adept at formulating metaphysical differences, especially through racial descriptors" (266). This establishment of more formal divisions occurred on both sides, with Indians creating political alliances based more on "national and racial affiliations" and whites "defin[ing] themselves in relation to the savage" (266–67).

15. Not all, but many of the tribes that played prominent roles in relation to white settlers — Mohawks, Mohegans, Pequots, Narragansett — practiced this form of adoption as substitution.

16. Judith Modell elaborates the term "as if" kin in order to describe how adoptees were matched by appearance to families "as if" they were biological kin. The forms of adoption that I elaborate later anticipate this formation by keeping the legal forms of inheritance and emotional bonds granted to the adoptee as modeled on the

relationships to one's "own" child. See *Kinship with Strangers: Adoption and the Interpretation of Kinship in American Culture* (Berkeley: University of California Press, 1994).

17. Étienne Balibar, *Politics and the Other Scene* (London: Verso, 2002), 31.

18. *The Cherokee Nation vs. The State of Georgia*, 30 U.S. 1(1831).

19. Zainaldin, "The Emergence of a Modern American Family Law," 1043. See also Stephen Presser, "The Historical Background of the American Law of Adoption," *Journal of Family Law* 11, no. 443 (1971): 455–528.

20. These practices were a carryover from English practices of apprenticeship with a few changes. Colonists often placed indigent children in households in order to relieve welfare problems. They were also more likely than their English counterparts to apprentice children at younger ages. For an account of English practices of apprenticeship, see Paul Griffiths, *Youth and Authority: Formative Experiences in England, 1560–1640* (Oxford: Clarendon Press, 1996), and Ilana Krausman Ben-Amos, *Adolescence and Youth in Early Modern England* (New Haven, Conn.: Yale University Press, 1994). For apprenticeship in colonial states, see Shammas, *A History of Household Government in America*, 35–39, and John Demos, *A Little Commonwealth: Family Life in Plymouth Colony* (London: Oxford University Press, 1971).

21. Quoted in Demos, *A Little Commonwealth*, 109.

22. Quoted in Yasuhide Kawashima, "Adoption in Early America," *Law, Society, and Domestic Relations*, ed. Kermit L. Hall (New York: Garland Publishing, 1987), 342.

23. Quoted in Kawashima, "Adoption in Early America," 347.

24. Carp, *Family Matters*, 11–12.

25. Modell, *Kinship with Strangers*, 21. Legal action often formed and codified the conditions of families. In 1838, a justice of the Pennsylvania Supreme Court decided on the removal of a child from the father's household in order to place her in an orphanage: "may not the natural parents, when unequal to the task of education, or unworthy of it, be superseded by the *parens patriae*, or common guardian of the community? It is to be remembered that the public has a paramount interest in the virtue and knowledge of its members, and that, of strict right, the business of education belongs to it.... The right of parental control is a natural but not an inalienable one." Quoted in Lawrence Grossberg, *Governing the Hearth: Law and*

the Family in Nineteenth-Century America (Chapel Hill: University of North Carolina Press, 1985), 267.

26. Grossberg, *Governing the Hearth*, 6.

27. Catherine Maria Sedgwick, *Home, Scenes and Characters Illustrating Christian Truth* (Boston: J. Munroe, 1970), 89. Cited parenthetically hereafter.

28. Sabina Matter-Seibel places a similar emphasis on domestic virtues as the lens through which Child values Native Americans' national belonging. See "Native Americans, Women, and the Culture of Nationalism in Lydia Maria Child and Catherine Maria Sedgwick," *Early America Re-explored*, ed. Klaus H. Schmidt and Fritz Fleischmann (New York: Lang, 2000), 411–40. On Child's evolving sentimental politics and its limitations, see Laura Mielke, "Sentiment and Space in Lydia Maria Child's Native American Writings, 1824–1870," *Legacy* 21, no. 2 (2004): 172–92. Mielke argues that Child's sentimental vision "naturalizes segregation" and "denies Native American sovereignty" by incorporating them within civilizing, domestic settings (173). On Child's political model of feminine and domestic virtues, see Nina Baym, *American Women Writers and the Work of History, 1790–1860* (New Brunswick, N.J.: Rutgers University Press, 1995); Lucy Maddox, *Removals: Nineteenth-Century American Literature and the Politics of Indian Affairs* (New York: Oxford University Press, 1991).

29. Lydia Maria Child and Caroline Karcher, *A Lydia Maria Child Reader* (Durham, N.C.: Duke University Press, 1997), 82.

30. Child, "Willie Wharton," in *A Lydia Maria Child Reader*, 327.

31. Ibid.

32. Ibid., 333.

33. See also Mielke's reading of this ending, "Sentiment and Space."

34. Richard Drinnon, introduction to John Dunn Hunter, *Memoirs of a Captivity among the Indians of North America* (New York: Schocken Books, 1973), xv.

35. See Richard Drinnon, *White Savage: The Case of John Dunn Hunter* (New York: Schocken Books, 1972).

36. See Susan Scheckel, *The Insistence of the Indian: Race and Nationalism in Nineteenth-Century American Culture* (Princeton, N.J.: Princeton University Press, 1998), chapter 4.

37. On textual issues in defining Native American autobiography, see Arnold Krupat, *Native American Autobiography: An Anthology*

(Madison: University of Wisconsin Press, 1994). On analyses of editors' influences on Jemison's text, see June Namias, *White Captives: Gender and Ethnicity on the American Frontier* (Chapel Hill: University of North Carolina Press, 1993); Susan Walsh, "'With Them Was My Home': Native American Autobiography and *A Narrative of the Life of Mary Jemison,*" *American Literature* 64 (1992): 49–70.

38. Gordon Sayre, "Abridging between Two Worlds: John Tanner as American Indian Autobiographer," *American Literary History* 11, no. 3 (1999): 486.

39. James Seaver, *A Narrative of the Life of Mrs. Mary Jemison* (Norman: University of Oklahoma Press, 1995), 76–77. Cited parenthetically hereafter.

40. Hunter, *Memoirs of a Captivity*, 14. Cited parenthetically hereafter.

41. John Fierst, "Strange Eloquence: Another Look at The Captivity and Adventures of John Tanner," *Reading beyond Words: Contexts in Native History,* ed. Jennifer Brown and Elizabeth Vibert (Peterborough, Ont.: Broadview, 1996), 222.

42. John Tanner, *The Falcon: A Narrative of the Captivity and Adventures of John Tanner* (New York: Penguin Books, 1994), 35. Cited parenthetically hereafter.

43. Sayre, "Abridging between Two Worlds," 489. Sayre goes on to argue that this scene is the first act of a "quasi-oedipal family drama" in which Tanner both fears "being revenged on by a powerful father-figure and wishes to protect Netnokwa from the attentions of other men."

44. This argument follows Sayre's points that "Tanner's narrative argues that identity among Indians was not formed out of race or blood but through familial bonds and conflicts. If Tanner therefore failed to gain reacceptance as a white male because of a prejudice against racial degeneration, he failed to achieve his own desires because he could not hold together his biracial family." "Abridging between Two Worlds," 495.

45. This is in contrast with the account of Jemison's Indian husband, who gains legitimacy through deeds and the history of war.

46. On *Hope Leslie* within the context of historical romance and the revision of Puritan historiography, see Michael Davitt Bell, *Hawthorne and the Historical Romance of New England* (Princeton, N.J.: Princeton University Press, 1971); Philip Gould, *Covenant and Republic: Historical Romance and the Politics of Puritanism* (New York: Cambridge University Press, 1996). On the constitution of a nation's

political identity through family configurations, see Shirley Samuels, *Romances of the Republic: Women, the Family, and Violence in the Literature of the Early American Nation* (Oxford: Oxford University Press, 1996).

47. On the relationship between the problems of sympathy and various definitions of the family, see Cindy Weinstein, *Family, Kinship, and Sympathy in Nineteenth-Century American Literature* (New York: Cambridge University Press, 2004). She argues that far from presuming the stability of the bourgeois, nuclear family, in sentimental fictions "the idea of family is constantly trying to be 'fixed,' as if it were in need of definitional repair, as if idea and practice have become unhinged" (19–20).

48. On the use of racial kinship to achieve reconciliation, see Richard Slotkin, *Regeneration through Violence: The Mythology of the American Frontier, 1600–1860* (Middletown, Conn.: Wesleyan University Press, 1973). On enacting King Philip's War as a family drama, see James Wallace, "Race and Captivity in Cooper's *The Wept of Wish-ton Wish*," *American Literary History* 7, no. 2 (1995): 189–209.

49. George Dekker places *The Wept of Wish-ton Wish* within the context of the American historical romance and notes the frequency of adoptive relationships: "In American romances, where crossing from one culture to another frequently means crossing racial lines as well, such relationships are especially prominent and charged with emotion." See *The American Historical Romance* (New York: Cambridge University Press, 1987), 70. See also Christopher Castiglia, *Bound and Determined: Captivity, Culture-Crossing, and White Womanhood from Mary Rowlandson to Patty Hearst* (Chicago: University of Chicago Press, 1996); Mielke, *Moving Encounters: Sympathy and the Indian Question in Antebellum Literature* (Amherst: University of Massachusetts Press, 208); Wallace, "Race and Captivity."

50. On these works as revising the history of King Philip's War, see Sayre, "Melodramas of Rebellion: Metamora and the Literary Historiography of King Philip's War in the 1820s," *Arizona Quarterly* 60, no. 2 (2004), and Jill Lepore, *The Name of War: King Philip's War and the Origins of American Identity* (New York: Vintage, 1999).

51. On how the uses of domesticity lead to a narrow notion of family limited by "racial/cultural and religious identity," see Mielke, "Domesticity and Dispossession: Removal as a Family Act in Cooper's *The Wept of Wish-Ton Wish* and *The Pathfinder*," *American Transcendental Quarterly* 16, no. 1 (2002): 18.

52. James Fenimore Cooper, *The Wept of Wish-Ton Wish* (New York: D. Appleton and Company, 1873), 112. Cited parenthetically hereafter.

53. Catherine Sedgwick, *Hope Leslie, or, Early Times in the Massachusetts* (New York: Penguin Books, 1998), 20. Cited parenthetically hereafter.

54. Jacques Derrida develops the notion of the supplement as to both add to and replace. See "Plato's Pharmacy," *Dissemination* (Chicago: University of Chicago Press, 1981).

55. On Cooper's negotiation of border states, see Philip Fisher, *Hard Facts: Setting and Form in the American Novel* (New York: Oxford University Press, 1985); John P. McWilliams, *Political Justice in a Republic* (Berkeley: University of California Press, 1972); Geoffrey Rans, *Cooper's Leather-Stocking Novels: A Secular Reading* (Chapel Hill: University of North Carolina Press, 1991).

56. On Whittal Ring and Narra-mattah as symbolizing the intermingling and blending of the two races, or the threat of miscegenation, see Wallace, "Race and Captivity."

57. On parallels between *Hope Leslie* and *The Wept of Wish-Ton Wish*, see Ezra Tawil, *The Making of Racial Sentiment* (New York: Cambridge University Press, 2007). Tawil argues that the use of kinship in these novels constructs a racial logic not based on skin color or appearance but on sentiment. On *Hope Leslie*'s racial representations, see Maria Karafilis, "Catharine Maria Sedgwick's *Hope Leslie:* The Crisis between Ethical Political Action and the U.S. Literary Nationalism in the New Republic," *American Transcendental Quarterly* 12, no. 4 (1998): 327–44; Matter-Seibel, "Native Americans"; Dana Nelson, "Sympathy as Strategy in Sedgwick's *Hope Leslie*; Shirley Samuels, ed., *The Culture of Sentiment* (New York: Oxford University Press, 1992), 191–202.

58. On *Hope Leslie*'s feminist liberatory or egalitarian agendas and their limitations through racial politics, see Castiglia, *Bound and Determined;* Lucy Maddox, *Removals;* Nina Baym, *American Women Writers and the Work of History;* Judith Fetterley, "My Sister! My Sister! The Rhetoric of Catherine Maria Sedgwick's *Hope Leslie*," *American Literature* 70, no. 3 (1998): 491–516. For an alternative reading of Magawisca in terms of the racialization of principles of liberty, see Laura Doyle, *Freedom's Empire: Race and the Rise of the Novel in Atlantic Modernity, 1640–1940* (Durham, N.C.: Duke University Press, 2008), chapter 11.

59. Lepore, *In the Name of War*, xiii.

60. John Demos, *The Unredeemed Captive: A Family Story from Early America* (New York: Vintage Books, 1995).

2. Unmanageable Attachments

1. Lydia Maria Child, "Loo Loo," *Atlantic Monthly* 1858 (May–June): 809. Cited parenthetically hereafter.

2. For further discussion, see Tawil, *The Making of Racial Sentiment*.

3. On the interrelations between domestic discourses and projects of nationalization more generally, see Lora Romero, *Home Fronts: Domesticity and Its Critics in the Antebellum United States* (Durham, N.C: Duke University Press, 1997); Kaplan, *The Anarchy of Empire*; Samuels, *The Culture of Sentiment*.

4. Carolyn Karcher and Russ Castronovo tie the trope of adoption to a specific political ideology: a vision of assimilation in the former; a patriarchal act that reconstitutes a familial economy of plantation slavery in the latter. For Karcher, the act of adoption is ultimately reproductive of the inequalities under a paternalist vision, hierarchizing white/black culture. In analyzing the antebellum fiction of Caroline Lee Hentz, Castronovo calls adoption the "patriarchal act par excellence": "Adoption enables transcendence of economic factors and elision of racial associations" through invoking a "fatherly intervention" that "sustains American commercial and institutional life." See Carolyn Karcher, *The First Woman in the Republic: A Cultural Biography of Lydia Maria Child* (Durham, N.C.: Duke University Press, 1994), and Castronovo, "Incidents in the Life of a White Woman: Economies of Race and Gender in the Antebellum Nation," *American Literary History* 10, no. 2 (1998): 249, 251.

5. On the discourse of benevolence as a form of organizing social and familial relations in antebellum America, see Susan M. Ryan, *The Grammar of Good Intentions: Race and the Antebellum Culture of Benelovence* (Ithaca, N.Y.: Cornell University Press, 2003).

6. *The Collected Works of Abraham Lincoln,* ed. Roy P. Basler (New Brunswick, N.J.: Rutgers University Press, 1953), 5: 527, and 8: 333.

7. Frederick Douglass, *Autobiographies* (New York: Library of America, 1994), 918.

8. For readings of these intersections of abolitionism, proslavery, and domesticity, see Karen Sánchez-Eppler, *Touching Liberty;* Hartman, *Scenes of Subjection*; Fisher, *Hard Facts,* chapter 2; Gillian Brown,

Domestic Individualism: Imagining Self in Nineteenth-Century America (Berkeley: University of California Press, 1992), chapters 1 and 2.

9. Nancy Cott, *Public Vows: A History of Marriage and the Nation* (Cambridge, Mass.: Harvard University Press, 2000), 80.

10. Ibid.

11. Peggy Cooper Davis, *Neglected Stories: The Constitution and Family Values* (New York: Hill and Wang, 1997), 113.

12. Ibid., 108.

13. Ibid., 113–14.

14. Ibid., 112.

15. Edlie Wong highlights this paradoxical position of kinship ties through her analysis of freedom suits in which antislavery activists acted on behalf of children for their freedom in the North, sometimes against the wishes and claims of these children's relatives and even the children themselves: "The freedom proffered in such antislavery legal actions marked the necessary violence and loss attendant upon certain forms of social inclusion as Med and Anson [two slave children who gained freedom in the North through legal petition] were required to forgo their actual kin ties to be remade into free Northern children." See Edlie Wong, "Freedom with a Vengeance: Choosing Kin in Antislavery Literature and Law," *American Literature* 81, no. 1 (2009): 19. On how the family was used to shore up ideologies of free contract labor, see Amy Dru Stanley, *From Bondage to Contract* (New York: Cambridge University Press, 1998).

16. See Katherine Franke, "Becoming a Citizen: Reconstruction Era Regulation of African American Marriages," *Yale Journal of Law and the Humanities* 11 (1999): 251–309; and "Taking Care," *Chicago-Kent Law Review* 76 (2001): 1541–56; Hartman, *Scenes of Subjection*, part 2.

17. Bernie Jones, *Fathers of Conscience: Mixed-race Inheritance in the Antebellum South* (Athens: University of Georgia Press, 2009), xii, 2. For further analysis of the delegitimation of mixed-race families in the transmission of property and status, see Kevin Maillard, "The Color of Testamentary Freedom," *Southern Methodist University Law Review* (2009) http://papers.ssrn.com/sol3/ (accessed April 15, 2009). On the racialization of legitimacy in family law, see Eva Rubin, *The Supreme Court and the American Family: Ideology and Issues* (New York: Greenwood Press, 1986).

18. Franke, "Becoming a Citizen," 23.

19. Dylan Penningroth, *The Claims of Kinfolk: African American Property and Community in the Nineteenth-Century South* (Chapel Hill: University of North Carolina Press, 2003), 168.

20. Quoted in Grossberg, *Governing the Hearth*, 272–3.

21. Ibid., 213.

22. William Whitmore, *The Law of Adoption in the United States* (Albany, N.Y.: Joel Munsell, 1876), 65.

23. Ibid.

24. Jones, *Fathers of Conscience*, 65.

25. As Hortense Spillers notes, this is a particular issue for African Americans because "parenting is historically fraught with laws that at one time overdetermined the legal status of the child as property, but the question is to what extent the legal relations — a child who neither 'belonged' to the mother, nor to an African father — might have been translated into an affective one." "All the Things You Could Be by Now If Sigmund Freud's Wife Was Your Mother," 139.

26. Hartman, *Scenes of Subjection*, 87.

27. Ibid., 80. See also her discussion on p. 81.

28. In the psychoanalytic narrative of seduction, the ambiguity of agency manifests itself as whether the child has an inherent sense of sexuality or if infantile sexuality is only projected onto the child by the parents. Laplanche explains, "We must conceive of the child both as outside time . . . and as one already endowed with sexuality. . . . We must reconcile the passivity which is implied by merely receiving meaning from outside with the minimum of activity necessary for the experience even to be acknowledged." See "Fantasy and the Origins of Sexuality," in *Formations of Fantasy*, ed. Victor Burgin (London: Routledge, 1989), 11.

29. Noble's difficulties in bringing these two realms together contrasts with Stowe's ability to reconcile them in what Gillian Brown calls "sentimental possession." See Brown, *Domestic Individualism*.

30. Several critics cast skepticism not just on contract theory as a tool of liberation, but also the "formal equality" and forms of personhood that undergird liberalism's emancipatory ethic. For elaboration on how the rights of contract served the ends of racial subjection and humiliation rather than liberation, see Hartman, *Scenes of Subjection*. On the relationship between slavery and legal conceptions of property, see Stephen Best, *The Fugitive's Properties: Law and the Poetics of Possession* (Chicago: University of Chicago Press, 2004). Russ Castronovo critiques the "abstraction" of the liberal subject. See "Political Necrophilia," *boundary 2* 27, no. 2 (2000): 113–48.

31. On the nationalizing of the orphan, see the analyses of the figure of the orphan in Fliegelman, *Prodigals and Pilgrims,* and Castronovo, *Fathering the Nation.* For an argument that the child plays a prominent role in antebellum fiction and nonfiction in order to maintain racial distinctions after slavery was abolished, even as she was a centerpiece for abolishing slavery, see Levander, *Cradle of Liberty,* chapter 3. On children in relation to the development of class and national ideologies, see Sánchez-Eppler, *Dependent States: The Child's Part in Nineteenth-Century American Culture* (Chicago: University of Chicago Press, 2005). For the notion of "infantile citizenship" — that the child is iconic precisely because it constitutes a kind of prehistory of the status of the citizen, see Lauren Berlant, *The Queen of America Goes to Washington City: Essays on Sex and Citizenship* (Durham, N.C.: Duke University Press, 1997).

32. Quoted in Brown, *Domestic Individualism,* 33.

33. Fisher, *Hard Facts,* 101.

34. Isaac Kramnick, "Children's Literature and Bourgeois Ideology," in *Culture and Politics from Puritanism to the Enlightenment,* ed. Perez Zagorin (Berkeley: University of California Press, 1980), 217.

35. Child, "The Industrious Family," *Juvenile Miscellany* (July 1831): 217–30.

36. Child, "The Orphans," *Juvenile Miscellany* (July 1828): 314–26.

37. The merging of Child's antislavery work and the project of socialization embedded in children's literature was not a perfect match. Indeed, her children's magazine, *Juvenile Miscellany,* lost its readership and went under after Child published her *Appeal in Favor of That Class of Americans Called Africans* (1833). See Karcher, *The First Woman in the Republic.*

38. Child, "The St. Domingo Orphans," *Juvenile Miscellany* (September 1830): 81–94.

39. Child, "Jumbo and Zairee," *Lydia Maria Child Reader,* 153.

40. Ibid., 159.

41. Ibid., 153.

42. Nancy Bentley, "The Fourth Dimension: Kinlessness and African American Narrative," *Critical Inquiry* 35 (2009): 273.

43. Orlando Patterson, *Slavery and Social Death: A Comparative Study* (Cambridge, Mass.: Harvard University Press, 1985), 35.

44. See Herbert Gutman, *The Black Family in Slavery and Freedom, 1750–1925* (New York: Pantheon Books, 1976).

45. See Franke, "Becoming a Citizen"; Brenda Stevenson, *Life in Black and White: Family and Community in the Slave South* (New York: Oxford University Press, 1996); Anthony Kaye, *Joining Places: Slave Neighborhoods in the Old South* (Chapel Hill: University of North Carolina Press, 2007), chapter 2; Penningroth, *The Claims of Kinfolk.*

46. Douglass, *Autobiographies,* 60. For an extended reading of this line, see Henry Louis Gates, *Figures in Black: Words, Signs, and the "Racial" Self* (New York: Oxford University Press, 1987), chapter 3.

47. Castronovo notes that *My Bondage and My Freedom* always situates freedom materially and circumstantially in ways that critique the abstract construction of freedom that empties it of any content. Priscilla Wald reads the second autobiography as both based in and uncomfortable with the "patrilineal (and patriarchal) inheritance of freedom." Eric Sundquist reads the increased emphasis on kinship and the negotiation with father figures in *My Bondage and My Freedom* as a developing critique of abolitionist paternalism and an act of self-fathering rebellion. Jenny Franchot complicates this rhetoric of self-fathering by demonstrating that concomitant with this self-constitution is the "construction of the feminine" as a surrogate by which he can assert his mastery. See Castronovo, "Political Necrophilia"; Wald, *Constituting Americans: Cultural Anxiety and Narrative Form* (Durham, N.C.: Duke University Press, 1995), 75; Eric Sundquist, "Frederick Douglass: Literacy and Paternalism," in *Critical Essays on Frederick Douglass,* ed. William Andrews (Boston: G. K. Hall, 1991), 217; Franchot, "Douglass and the Construction of the Feminine," in *Frederick Douglass: New Literary and Historical Essays,* ed. Eric Sundquist (Cambridge: Cambridge University Press, 1990), 295.

48. For further discussion of the beating scenes as a process of identification and disidentification, see Gwen Bergner, "Myths of Masculinity: The Oedipus Complex and Douglass's 1845 *Narrative,*" in *The Psychoanalysis of Race,* ed. Christopher Lane, 241–61.

49. Brown argues that Stowe constructs a realm of "sentimental possession" that is divorced from the dictates of male (market) ownership and control. See *Domestic Individualism,* chapter 2.

50. Brown, *Domestic Individualism,* 55.

51. Harriet Beecher Stowe, *Uncle Tom's Cabin: Authoritative Text, Backgrounds, and Contexts* (New York: W. W. Norton, 1994), 105.

52. Ibid., 216.

53. Catherine Beecher and Harriet Beecher Stowe, *The American Woman's Home* (New Brunswick, N.J.: Rutgers University Press, 2002), 331.

54. For a reading of this relationship in terms of shifting disciplinary formations at the time, see Richard Brodhead, "Sparing the Rod: Discipline and Fiction in Antebellum America," *Representations* 21 (1998): 67–96.

55. See Karcher, *The First Woman in the Republic.*

56. Lydia Maria Child, "Dedication," *Fact and Fiction: A Collection of Stories* (New York: C. S. Francis and Co., 1854).

57. Karcher provides the definitive account of this relationship in *The First Woman in the Republic.*

58. Lydia Maria Child and John Greenleaf Whittier, *Letters of Lydia Maria Child* (New York: AMS Press, 1971), 206.

59. Ibid.

60. Quoted in Karcher, *The First Woman in the Republic,* 366–67.

61. Quoted in ibid., 367.

62. Ibid.

63. On how sentimentalism negotiates interracial sexuality, see Robyn Wiegman, "Intimate Publics: Race, Property, and Personhood," *American Literature* 74, no. 4 (2002): 876.

64. Lydia Maria Child, *Romance of the Republic* (Boston: Ticknor, 1867), 236. Cited parenthetically hereafter.

65. Shirley Samuels, *Romances of the Republic* (New York: Oxford University Press, 1996), 125–26.

66. Ibid., 127.

67. See Samuels, "Part of the post–Civil War attempt to resolve the trauma of families in a miscegenous republic, the novel tries to recover postbellum national identity in the wake of national disintegration." *Romances of the Republic,* 127.

68. For further analysis of convoluted familial bonds, see Mark Patterson, "Surrogacy and Slavery: The Problem of Consent in Baby M . . . Romance of the Republic, and Puddn'head Wilson," *American Literary History* 8, no. 3 (1996): 448–70.

69. On linkages between incest and miscegenation, see Werner Sollors, *Neither Black Nor White Yet Both,* 286–335, and Eva Saks, "Representing Miscegenation Law," *Raritan* 8 (Fall 1988): 39–69.

70. Lydia Maria Child, *Freedmen's Book, the American Negro, His History, and Literature* (New York: Arno Press, 1968), 93.

3. The Character of Race

1. Donald Glover in Charles Chesnutt's *The Quarry* (Princeton, N.J.: Princeton University Press, 1999), 91.

2. Joe Christmas in William Faulkner's *Light in August* (New York: Vintage, 1990), 254.

3. This notion of individuation that I use differs from normative accounts that emphasize individuation as a developmental process that realizes the core, inherent part of the self as a kind of end-product. Rather, I follow Gilbert Simondon's critique of this notion by suggesting that individuation is an ongoing process of individuating, of continually coming to be through interacting with social conditions and the environment. This suggests the continual tensions between dependence on external conditions and independence. See Simondon, "The Genesis of the Individual," *Incorporations,* ed. Jonathan and Sanford Kwinter Crary (New York: Zone Books, 1992), 297–319.

4. Judith Butler, *Undoing Gender* (New York: Routledge, 2004), 42.

5. For the account of norms and normalization, I have relied not only on Butler, but also on Michel Foucault, *History of Sexuality,* 1: 133–61, and *The Use of Pleasure,* trans. Robert Hurley (New York: Pantheon, 1985), 25–33; Georges Canguilhem, *The Normal and the Pathological* (New York: Zone Books, 1989), 151–81; Janet Halley, *Split Decisions: How and Why to Take a Break from Feminism* (Princeton, N.J.: Princeton University Press, 2006), 119–32.

6. Butler, *Undoing Gender,* 52.

7. On Joe Christmas as complicating the theme of passing, see Gena McKinley, *"Light in August:* A Novel of Passing?" in *Faulkner in Cultural Context,* ed. Donald Kartiganer and Ann Abadie (Oxford: University of Mississippi Press, 1997), 148–66; Sundquist, *Faulkner: A House Divided* (Baltimore: Johns Hopkins University Press, 1983); Donald Kartiganer, *The Fragile Thread: The Meaning of Form in Faulkner's Novels* (Amherst: University of Massachusetts Press, 1979); Thadious Davis, *Faulkner's "Negro": Art and the Southern Context* (Baton Rouge: Louisiana State University Press, 1983); Cynthia Callahan's study argues that Chesnutt creates "an anti-passing novel" through the figuration of adoption: "The Confounding Problem of Race: Passing and Adoption in Charles Chesnutt's *The Quarry,*" *MFS: Modern Fiction Studies* 48, no. 2 (2002): 318.

8. For insightful analysis of the critical potential of passing, see Amy Robinson, "Forms of Appearance of Value: Homer Plessy and the Politics of Privacy," *Performance and Cultural Politics,* ed. Elin Diamond (London: Routledge, 1996), 239–61. For an excellent collection of essays on the various practices of passing across history and literary representation, see *Passing and the Fictions of Identity,* ed. Elaine K. Ginsberg (Durham, N.C.: Duke University Press, 1996).

9. Kartiganer, Davis, and John run through several versions of the idea that Christmas can or must choose his identity. Kartiganer, *The Fragile Thread,* 10; Davis, *Faulkner's "Negro,"* 137; John Longley, *The Tragic Mask, A Study of Faulkner's Heroes* (Chapel Hill: University of North Carolina Press, 1963), 196.

10. See Philip Brian Harper, "Passing for What? Racial Masquerade and the Demands of Upward Mobility," *Callaloo* 21, no. 2 (1998): 382. For other discussions of the limited assumptions regarding passing, see Michele Elam, "Passing in the Post-race Era: Danzy Senna, Philip Roth, and Colson Whitehead," *African American Review* 41, no. 4 (2007): 749–69; Anne Cheng, "Passing, Natural Selection, and Love's Failure: Ethics of Survival from Chang-rae Lee to Jacques Lacan," *American Literary History* 17, no. 3 (2005): 553–74.

11. For psychoanalytic approaches, see Cheng, *Melancholy of Race;* Eng, *Racial Castration;* and Spillers, *Black, White, and in Color;* on race and affect, see Coviello, *Intimacy in America;* Jose Esteban Munoz, *Disidentifications: Queers of Color and the Performance of Politics* (Minneapolis: University of Minnesota Press, 1999).

12. Coviello, "Intimacy and Affliction: Dubois, Race, and Psychoanalysis," *Modern Language Quarterly* 64, no. 1 (2003): 26.

13. As Adam Phillips writes, "Relationships constitute so-called identities, not the other way around, and this makes selves always provisional and circumstantial, not creatures of either/or (to suffer is often to feel a self fixed in something)." See *Terrors and Experts* (Cambridge, Mass.: Harvard University Press, 1977), 84.

14. On "placing out," see Ellen Herman, *Kinship by Design* (Chicago: University of Chicago Press, 2008), 21–55.

15. Linda Gordon, *The Great Arizona Orphan Abduction* (Cambridge, Mass.: Harvard University Press, 1999), 11. On the orphan trains, also see Stephen O'Connor, *Orphan Trains: The Story of Charles Loring Brace and the Children He Saved and Failed* (Boston: Houghton Mifflin, 2001), and Charles Loring Brace, *The Dangerous Classes of New York* (New York: Wynkoop & Hallenbeck, 1872).

16. Gordon, *Great Arizona Orphan Abduction,* 12–13.

17. Ibid., 71.

18. Melosh argues for a sharper break between these two practices than I do, stating that "the developing profession of social work helped to displace the moralism of nineteenth-century evangelical reformers." *Strangers and Kin,* 19. As I demonstrate, the problem of individuation in relation to racial and religious markers demonstrates the uneasy coexistence of these two sensibilities.

19. Melosh, *Strangers and Kin,* 51.

20. Michel Foucault, *Society Must Be Defended,* trans. David Macey (New York: Penguin, 2004), 248, 253; Ann Stoler, *Race and the Education of Desire* (Durham, N.C.: Duke University Press, 1995), 83.

21. Quoted in Berebitsky, *Like Our Very Own,* 136.

22. Ibid., 148.

23. Michael Shapiro, ed., *A Study of Adoption Practice* (New York: Child Welfare League of America, 1955), 2: 9–10.

24. Theis quoted in Berebitsky, *Like Our Very Own,* 134.

25. Ibid.

26. Colette Guillaumin emphasizes the place of race within bourgeois projects of normalization. See *Racism, Sexism, Power, and Ideology* (New York: Routledge, 1995).

27. Rothman and Rothman, *The Origins of Adoption,* 84.

28. Ibid., 45–46.

29. Ibid., 46.

30. Melosh, *Strangers and Kin,* 103.

31. Herman, *Kinship by Design,* 57. See also Judith Modell and Naomi Dambacher, "Making a 'Real' Family: Matching and Cultural Biologism in American Adoption," *Adoption Quarterly* 1, no. 2 (1997): 3–33.

32. See Shapiro, ed., *A Study of Adoption Practice,* 1: 84.

33. Quoted in Berebitsky, *Like Our Very Own,* 142.

34. Quoted in Melosh, *Strangers and Kin,* 87.

35. Étienne Balibar, *Masses, Classes, Ideas* trans. James Swenson (London: Routledge, 1994), 200.

36. Berebitsky, *Like Our Very Own,* 31.

37. Ibid.

38. Hanna Segal, *Introduction to the Work of Melanie Klein* (New York: Basic Books, 1973), 126.

39. Helene Deutsch, *The Psychology of Women* (New York: Grune and Stratton, 1945), 399–400.

40. In subsequent references to how Joe Christmas imagines himself, I use the terms "nigger blood" and "black blood" because it most accurately depicts the convergence of Christmas's own imagination of himself in relation to others and other characters' projections onto him — Gavin Stevens, Brown, and the white community more largely use either "nigger blood" or "black blood." See Faulkner, *Light in August,* 449, 465. Cited parenthetically hereafter. The term itself signifies the racist logic used everywhere from the "one-drop rule" to eugenics discourse whereby "blackness" is figured as contamination and denigration. That Christmas uses this notion of blood to relate to the world and others' imaginings is evidence not simply that he echoes the racism of his time and place, but that he deploys this anxiety of contamination and boundary transgression in measuring how he relates to others.

41. For varying approaches to race in *Light in August,* see Judith Wittenberg, "Race in *Light in August:* Wordsymbols and Obverse Reflections," in *The Cambridge Companion to William Faulkner,* ed. Philip Weinstein and Warwick Wadlington (New York: Cambridge University Press, 1995), 146–67; Sundquist, *Faulkner: A House Divided;* Spillers, *Black, White, and in Color,* 301–19.

42. This inability to assign action to person, and thus separate Christmas from other characters, is one example of why the life story of Joe Christmas has been the subject of so much critical concern, all of it revolving around the relationship between the inability to project some form of organic unity to either Christmas or the text. A good example is Malcolm Cowley's remark in a letter to Faulkner, "It would be easy for you to *write* Joe Christmas into a separate novel... but the anthologist can't pick him out without leaving bits of his flesh hanging to Hightower and Lena." See Cowley, *The Faulkner-Cowley File* (New York: Viking Press, 1966), 28–29. For analysis of the relationship between narrative coherence and the coherence of Christmas's life, see Martin Kreiswirth, "Plots and Counterplots: The Structure of *Light in August,*" in *New Essays on Light in August,* ed. Michael Millgate (Cambridge: Cambridge University Press, 1987), 55–79.

43. John Matthews argues a similar point that the lack of self-sufficiency within the process of establishing identity "fills with particular sexual and racial content in societies like the South's." Matthews, "This Race Which Is Not One: 'the Inextricable Compositeness' of Faulkner's South," in *Look Away! The U.S. South in New World Studies,* ed. Jon Smith and Deborah Cohn (Durham, N.C.: Duke University Press, 2004), 212.

44. Heinz Ickstadt, "The Discourse of Race and the 'Passing' Text," *Amerikastudien/American Studies* 42 (1997): 533.

45. Laura Doyle, "The Body against Itself in Faulkner's Phenomenology of Race," *American Literature* 73, no. 2 (2001): 341–42.

46. André Green, *On Private Madness* (London: Hogarth Press, 1986), 88–89. Green provides a full theoretical reconstruction of the psychoanalytic concept of projection, emphasizing this back and forth movement that both creates the distinction between ego and object and denies it: "the projected can only be what has already been introjected. Only that which has been swallowed can be vomited" (85). Also see Laplanche, *Essays on Otherness,* chapter 4.

47. I borrow Althusser's phrasing, "It therefore appears that the subject acts in so far as he is acted by the following system." See Louis Althusser, *Lenin and Philosophy and Other Essays* trans. Ben Brewster (New York: Monthly Review Press, 1971), 158–59. This formulation posits the subject not as first having beliefs and then producing a series of actions. Rather, it is by the installation of the individual into a certain set of practices and rituals that constitute the subject's integrity and thus constitute his subjection in both senses of the word.

48. Philip Weinstein, *Faulkner's Subject: A Cosmos No One Owns* (New York: Cambridge University Press, 1992), 106–7.

49. See McKinley, *"Light in August:* A Novel of Passing?" 156.

50. S.v. "Own" in the *Oxford English Dictionary.*

51. On this back and forth of projection as a mode of creating and securing the external world of reality, thus establishing the reciprocal, shared space between individual and environment, see Donald Winnicott, "Primitive Emotional Development," *International Journal of Psychiatry* 26 (1945): 137–43. Instead of thinking of external reality as a limit and frustration to the individual's projections and desires, as in Freud's notion of the reality principle, Winnicott breaks down the distinction between the self's projections and external reality, suggesting the ways in which reality is discovered in order to confirm and support fantasy. Christmas's projections can be read as a navigation of this transitional space.

52. Genesis 22:7, 27:1, 18 (KJV).

53. Scott Romine, *The Narrative Forms of Southern Community* (Baton Rouge: Louisiana State University Press, 1999), 185.

54. On the labyrinthine imagery of allegory, see Angus Fletcher, *Allegory: Theory of a Symbolic Mode* (Ithaca, N.Y.: Cornell University Press, 1970), 182–83. On the chess match figuration, see

Sacvan Bercovitch, "Culture in a Faulknerian Context," in *Faulkner in Cultural Context*, 284–311.

55. Chesnutt, *The Quarry*, 9. Cited parenthetically hereafter.

56. Quoted in Dean McWilliams, "Introduction," *The Quarry*, x.

57. Ibid.

58. See McWilliams, "Introduction" and Callahan, "The Confounding Problem of Race."

4. The Right to Belong

1. Helen Doss, "Our International Family," *Reader's Digest*, August 1949, 59. Adoption History Project http://darkwing.uoregon.edu/~adoption (accessed September 15, 2007).

2. Christina Klein, *Cold War Orientalism*, 146.

3. "The 1957 Anisfield-Wolf Awards," *Saturday Review*, ed. Norman Cousins, June 28, 1958, 22. Quoted in Klein, *Cold War Orientalism*, 178. As Klein explains, Buck is characterizing Jessie Bennett Sams's book, *White Mother*, in the announcement of the Anisfield-Wolf Award in Race Relations.

4. Klein, *Cold War Orientalism*, 178.

5. "The 1957 Anisfield-Wolf Awards," 22.

6. Pearl S. Buck, "The Children Waiting: The Shocking Scandal of Adoption," *Woman's Home Companion* (September 1955): 33. Adoption History Project, http://darkwing.uoregon.edu/~adoption (accessed April 15, 2008)

7. As such, Buck collapses two familiar models of cosmopolitanism, one moving centrifugally outward starting with the family, the other moving centripetally inward from a notion of common humanity. On these two models of cosmopolitanism, see Martha Nussbaum, *For Love of Country: Debating the Limits of Patriotism* (Boston: Beacon Press, 1996), 141–43.

8. Pearl Buck, *My Several Worlds: A Personal Record* (New York: The John Day Company, 1954), 362.

9. See Klein, *Cold War Orientalism*.

10. Pearl Buck, "I Am the Better Woman for Having My Two Black Children," Today's Health (January 1972): 64. Adoption History Project, http://darkwing.uoregon.edu/~adoption (accessed May 7, 2008)

11. Buck speaks of the adoptive parents that she chooses: "They must want our babies for what they are, they must value the Asian heritage." *My Several Worlds*, 365.

12. See Duncan, "Regulating Inter-Country Adoption: An International Perspective," in *Frontiers of Family Law*, ed. A. Bainham and D. S. Pearl (London: John Wiley & Sons); Barbara Yngvesson, "Refiguring Kinship in the Space of Adoption," *Anthropological Quarterly* 80, no. 2 (2007): 564–65.

13. On the implications of this analytic division between transracial and transnational, see chapter 5.

14. See *Outsiders Within;* Dorow, *Transnational Adoption;* Eng, *The Feeling of Kinship,* chapters 3 and 4; Jodi Kim, "An 'Orphan' with Two Mothers: Transnational and Transracial Adoption, the Cold War, and Contemporary Asian American Cultural Politics," *American Quarterly* 61, no. 4 (December 2009): 855–80.

15. "Our Mission for Adoptee Rights," Bastard Nation: The Adoptee Rights Organization, www.bastards.org (accessed April 15, 2008).

16. See Vincent Cheng, *Inauthentic: The Anxiety over Culture and Identity* (New Brunswick, N.J.: Rutgers University Press, 2004), chapter 4.

17. On "return" not as "predicated on a single origin" but as "evok[ing] the coexistence of multiple, radically different, but analogous worlds in which selves materialize." See Yngvesson, "Backed by Papers: Undoing Persons, Histories, and Return," *American Ethnologist* 33, no. 2 (2006): 178.

18. Briggs, "Locating Adoption in Relation to State Processes: War, Economies, Trauma, Politics," paper presented at the University of Michigan, May 21, 2005.

19. Florence Clothier, "The Psychology of the Adopted Child," *Mental Hygiene* 27 (1943): 222.

20. Jacqueline Rose, *The Case of Peter Pan, or, the Impossibility of Children's Fiction* (London: Macmillan, 1984), 13.

21. Clothier, "The Psychology of the Adopted Child," 223.

22. Ibid., 229–30.

23. Ibid., 228.

24. H. J. Sants, "Genealogical Bewilderment in Children with Substitute Parents," *British Journal of Medical Psychology* 37 (1964): 139.

25. Viola Bernard, "The Application of Psychoanalysis to the Adoption Agency," in *Psychoanalysis and Social Work,* ed. Marcel Heiman (New York: International Universities Press, 1953), 207.

26. Ibid.

27. Sants, "Genealogical Bewilderment," 136.

28. Marshall Schecter, "Observations on Adopted Children," *Archives of General Psychiatry* 3 (1960): 31, 30.

29. Carp, *Family Matters,* 119.

30. Ibid., 114–20. Carp delineates the ways in which psychoanalytic assumptions played a large role in the sealing of adopted records — the policy whereby adoptees could not learn the identity of their birth parents or any further identifying information without a judicial order (and this was almost never granted).

31. Ibid., 12.

32. Ibid., 11.

33. On the development of psychiatric institutions and their effects on familial and social norms, see Foucault, *Psychiatric Power,* trans. Graham Burchell (New York: Palgrave, 2006), especially chapters 5, 6, and 9.

34. For this prehistory, see E. Wayne Carp, *Adoption Politics: Bastard Nation and Ballot Initiative 58* (Lawrence: University Press of Kansas, 2004), 5–25.

35. Ibid., 18.

36. Betty Jean Lifton, *Journey of the Adopted Self: A Quest for Wholeness* (New York: Basic Books, 1994), 60–61. Cited parenthetically hereafter.

37. For an excellent discussion of the expectation that adoptees should want to know the identity of their birth parents, see Kimberly Leighton, "Being Adopted and Being a Philosopher: Exploring Identity and the 'Desire to Know' Differently," in *Adoption Matters: Philosophical and Feminist Essays,* ed. Sally Haslanger and Charlotte Witt (Ithaca, N.Y.: Cornell University Press, 2005), 146–70.

38. Erica Haimes, "'Now I Know Who I Really Am': Identity Change and Redefinitions of the Self in Adoption," in *Self and Identity: Perspectives Across the Lifespan,* ed. Terry Honess and Krysia Yardley (London: Routledge, 1987), 366.

39. Ibid., 363.

40. Haimes explicitly draws on Alasdair MacIntyre, whose theories have provided something of a model for this relationship between narrative and personhood. See the discussion in the introduction.

41. "Our Mission for Adoptee Rights," *Bastard Nation: The Adoptee Rights Organization,* www.bastards.org/ (accessed October 17, 2008).

42. "A Transracially Adopted Child's Bill of Rights" *Pact: An Adoption Alliance,* www.pactadopt.org (accessed March 27, 2008).

43. Pertman, *Adoption Nation,* 70.

44. For this critique, see Homans, "Origins, Searches, and Identity," 61–62.

45. "Convention on the Rights of the Child," *UNICEF,* online www.unicef.org/crc/ (accessed November 17, 2007).

46. Ibid.

47. Ibid.

48. *The United Nations Convention on the Rights of the Child: A Guide to the "Travaux Preparatoires,"* ed. Sharon Detrick (Dordrecht: Martinus Nijhoff Publishers, 1992), 308.

49. "Preamble," Convention on the Rights of the Child.

50. See Detrick, *United Nations Convention on the Rights of the Child,* 299.

51. Sharon Stephens, *Children and the Politics of Culture* (Princeton, N.J.: Princeton University Press, 1995), 35. For other arguments that emphasize the protections for children created by the Hague Convention, see Ann Lacquer Estin, "Families across Borders: The Hague Children's Conventions and the Case for International Family Law in the United States," *Florida Law Review* 62, no. 47 (January 2010): 48–108; Christina Yang, "Redefining and Reclaiming Korean Adoptee Identity: Grassroots Internet Communities and The Hague Convention on Protection of Children and Co-operation in Respect of Intercountry Adoption," *Asian American Law Journal* 16, no. 13 (2009): 132–72.

52. On the relationship between a tradition of rights-thinking based on the freedom from others and the formation of rights within government protection and regulatory statutes, see Cass Sunstein, *After the Rights Revolution: Reconceiving the Regulatory State* (Cambridge, Mass.: Harvard University Press, 1990), 11–47. For a related argument developing a model for a more child-centered children's rights, see Ruth Zafran, "Children's Rights as Relational Rights: The Case of Relocation," *American University Journal of Gender, Social Policy, and the Law* 18, no. 163 (2010): 165–217.

53. Michael Ignatieff, *The Needs of Strangers* (New York: Picador, 1984), 13.

54. Karl Marx, "On the Jewish Question." *The Marx-Engels Reader,* ed. Robert Tucker (New York: W. W. Norton, 1972), 42.

55. See Yngvesson, "Going Home."

56. Jane Jeong Trenka, *The Language of Blood: A Memoir* (St. Paul: Borealis Books, 2003), 14. Cited parenthetically hereafter.

57. For further discussion of introjection and projection, see chapter 3.

58. For close readings of the ways in which generationality gets constructed through this text, see Eun Kyung Min, "The Daughter's Exchange in Jane Jeong Trenka's *The Language of Blood*," *Social Text* 26, no. 1 (2008): 115–33; Seo-Young Chu, "Science Fiction and Postmemory Han in Contemporary Korean American Literature," *MELUS* 33, no. 4 (2008): 97–121.

59. Kim Park Nelson, "'Loss Is More Than Sadness': Reading Dissent in Transracial Adoption Melodrama in *The Language of Blood* and *First Person Plural*," *Adoption and Culture* 1, no. 1 (2007): 122.

60. See the recent controversy over Tama Janowitz's article on the *New York Times* adoption blog, where she characterizes *Outsiders Within* as a "book in which many Midwestern Asian adoptees … complain bitterly about being treated as if they did not come from a different cultural background. … Because of this, they resent their adoptive parents." Sun Yung Shin, coeditor of *Outsiders Within* and author of *Skirt of Black,* offers a perceptive commentary. See "Tama Janowitz on NYT adoption blog," Sun Yung Shin author blog, www.sunyungshin.com/sun_yung_shin/ (accessed January 17, 2009).

61. Bharati Mukherjee, *Leave It to Me* (New York: A. A. Knopf, 1997), 9. Cited parenthetically hereafter.

62. Mukherjee, "Beyond Multiculturalism: Surviving the Nineties," *Journal of Modern Literature* 20, no. 1 (1996): 33.

63. Mukherjee, "Jasmine," in *The Middleman and Other Stories* (New York: Fawcett Crest, 1988), 135.

64. Inderpal Grewal, *Transnational America: Feminisms, Diasporas, Neoliberalisms* (Durham, N.C.: Duke University Press, 2005), 67. She writes: "The notion in *Jasmine* of what constitutes the 'ordinary' relies on a neoliberal idea of 'freedom' and 'choice,' the key terms through which a modern individual can be constituted, and on America's neoliberal ability to realize every individual's potential through the choices that it offers."

65. Grewal writes that *Jasmine* "ignores the histories of race, class, religion, nationality, sexuality, and gender that have enabled participation for migrants within particular transnational collectivities" (68). See Grewal, *Transnational America*. Kristin Carter-Sanborn critiques valorizations of Jasmine's agency and multiplicity by arguing that it is in fact predicated on the fantasy of dominant white American idealizations, of her making herself for the other. See "We Murder Who We Were: *Jasmine* and the Violence of Identity," *American Literature* 66, no. 3 (1994): 583. On Mukherjee's fiction as a

rewriting of Jewish American immigration narratives, see Jonathan Freedman, "Who's Jewish? Some Asian-American Writers and the Jewish-American Literary Canon," *Michigan Quarterly Review* 42, no. 1 (2003): 230–54.

66. On Mukherjee's *Jasmine* in terms of lateral mobility as opposed to upward mobility, see Bruce Robbins, *Feeling Global: Internationalism in Distress* (New York: New York University Press, 1999), chapter 5.

67. Grewal, *Transnational America*, 12. On flexible citizenship not bound by a single nation, see Aihwa Ong, *Flexible Citizenship: The Cultural Logics of Transnationality* (Durham, N.C.: Duke University Press, 1999); on the denationalization of citizenship, see Saskia Sassen, *Territory, Authority, Rights: From Medieval to Global Assemblages* (Princeton, N.J.: Princeton University Press, 2006), chapter 6.

5. Resisting Recognition

1. The term "comfort women" is the name given to those women, often from Korea, but also from Malaysia, Burma, and the Philippines, who were sexually abused by the Japanese army during their wartime occupation of parts of Asia during World War II.

2. Chang-rae Lee, *A Gesture Life* (New York: Riverhead Books, 1999), 73. Cited parenthetically hereafter.

3. Jacques Derrida and Elisabeth Roudinesco, "Disordered Families," *For What Tomorrow...A Dialogue,* trans. Jeff Fort (Stanford: Stanford University Press, 2004), 43. Derrida writes that the experience of legally identifying a father (in cases where fatherhood is in question) is "hastily called 'recognition'" when in fact its "modalities can be diverse, complex, convoluted" (43).

4. Melosh writes that adoption autobiography "was not established as a recognizable subgenre until the 1970s, when first adopted persons and then women who had relinquished children for adoption published their stories as testimony of their critique of adoption practices." See "Adoption Stories: Autobiographical Narratives and the Politics of Identity," in *Adoption in America,* 218, and Deans, "Performing the Search in Adoption Autobiography."

5. Derrida and Roudinesco, *For What Tomorrow...A Dialogue,* 43.

6. Cheng, "Passing, Natural Selection, and Love's Failure," 566.

7. Yngvesson, "Going Home."

8. Anagnost, "Scenes of Misrecognition," 390.

9. Ibid., 395.

10. Melosh, "Adoption Stories," 227.

11. Leighton, "Being Adopted and Being a Philosopher," 158.

12. Gail Dolgin and Vicente Franco, dir., *Daughter from Danang* (Berkeley, Calif.: Interfaze Educational Productions, 2002).

13. On *Daughter from Danang* as a film that reduces collective histories of adoption into individual melodramas, see Gregory Paul Choy and Catherine Ceniza Choy, "What Lies Beneath: Reframing *Daughter from Danang*," in *Outsiders Within*, 221–31.

14. Deann Borshay Liem, dir., *First Person Plural* (San Francisco: National Asian American Telecommunications Association, 2000).

15. Ibid.

16. Ibid.

17. Deann Borshay, "Remembering the Way Home: A Documentary Video Proposal," in *Seeds from a Silent Tree: An Anthology by Korean Adoptees*, ed. Tonya Bishoff and Jo Rankin (San Diego: Pandal Press, 1997), 120.

18. For a reading of *First Person Plural* in terms of melancholia and the psychic dilemma of two mothers, see Eng's illuminating discussion, "Transnational Adoption and Queer Diasporas."

19. Rita J. Simon and Rhonda Roorda, *In Their Own Voices: Transracial Adoptees Tell Their Stories* (New York: Columbia University Press, 2000), xiii. Cited parenthetically hereafter.

20. See Julie Stone Peters, "Law, Literature and the Vanishing Real: On the Future of an Interdisciplinary Illusion," *PMLA* 120, no. 2 (March 2005): 442–53.

21. Kwame Anthony Appiah, "Liberalism, Individuality, and Identity," *Critical Inquiry* 27, no. 2 (2001): 326–27. For further development of this point, see Kwame Anthony Appiah, *Ethics of Identity* (Princeton, N.J.: Princeton University Press, 2005), chapter 1.

22. Butler, *Giving an Account of Oneself* (New York: Fordham University Press, 2005), 39. Butler critiques this conflation of living and telling.

23. Appiah, *Ethics of Identity*, 23.

24. Butler critiques the assumption that narratives can transparently tell or recount our lives (38–39).

25. Charles Taylor, "The Politics of Recognition," in *Multiculturalism: Examining the Politics of Recognition*, ed. Amy Gutmann (Princeton, N.J.: Princeton University Press, 1994), 33–34.

26. My analysis is indebted to Homi Bhabha's critique of Taylor's notion of recognition as being based on a notion of reciprocity that presumes the horizon or "background" by which their dialogue

makes sense. Bhabha suggests that Taylor makes the negotiation of cultural difference into a synchronous process that already assumes a reciprocal relationship between two whole cultures. See "Minority Maneuvers and Unsettled Negotiations," *Critical Inquiry* 23, no. 3 (1997): 431–59.

27. This line of reasoning is indebted to Eng's essay "Transnational Adoption and Queer Diasporas," in which he asks: "Is the transnational adoptee an immigrant? Is she... an Asian American? Even more, is her adoptive family Asian American?... And how are international and group histories of gender, race, poverty, and nation managed or erased within the 'privatized' sphere of the domestic?" (1). See also his discussion of the racialization of intimacy in *The Feeling of Kinship,* 1–16.

28. On debates over transracial adoption, law, integration, and race-consciousness, see Elizabeth Bartholet, *Family Bonds: Adoption and the Politics of Parenting* (Boston: Beacon Press, 1993); Randall Kennedy, *Interracial Intimacies: Sex, Marriage, Identity, and Adoption* (New York: Pantheon, 2003); Fogg-Davis, *The Ethics of Transracial Adoption;* Patton, *Birthmarks;* Richard Banks, "The Color of Desire: Fulfilling Adoptive Parents' Racial Preferences through Discriminatory State Action," *Yale Law Journal* 107 (1998): 875–964.

29. Dorothy Roberts uses this framework to argue that attention to transnational adoption has meant less attention to both black children in need of homes and the system of foster care and welfare that devalues black families. The central issue is not, for Dorothy Roberts, adoption at all, but rather "why there are so many black children wallowing in foster-care in the first place." She writes further, "The debate over transracial adoption should not overshadow the predominant preference for white children. The vast majority of white adoptive parents are only willing to take a white child. Even when they adopt outside their race, whites generally prefer non-black children with Asian or Latin-American heritage." See *Killing The Black Body: Race, Reproduction, and the Meaning of Liberty* (New York: Vintage, 1997), 274, 273.

30. For further discussion of the interrelations between the two, see Dorow, "Racialized Choices," 360, and Eng, "Transnational Adoption and Queer Diasporas," 11. Dorow uses the term "transracial, transnational adoption" as part of a single complex in order to highlight how the racialization of transnational adoptees occurs through the shifting of racial meanings. Dorow's analysis of the adoptive choices of parents who adopted from China suggests that

"blackness becomes the constitutive outside to the white imaginary of Asian and Asian America." Eng writes that "the Asian transnational adoptee serves to triangulate the domestic landscape of black–white relations."

31. This can be seen in Dorow's interviews, where some adoptive parents divorce the question of race from their transnational adoption. One father states: "I mean, black is still, uh, not only a minority to me in this country, but a minority that doesn't, you know, fit in, as well as some other minorities. I mean, it goes back to why I wanted to do Chinese. For me, [race] doesn't come up. I've gotta admit that if I had a black child, I'd probably think of us as more biracial." Quoted in Dorow, *Transnational Adoption,* 371.

32. Bishoff and Rankin, *Seeds from a Silent Tree,* 1.

33. Choy and Choy, "Transformative Terrains: Korean Adoptees and the Social Constructions of an American Childhood," in *The American Child: A Cultural Studies Reader,* ed. Caroline Levander and Carol Singley (New Brunswick, N.J.: Rutgers University Press, 2003), 270.

34. Ibid.

35. *Seeds from a Silent Tree,* 143, emphasis added.

36. For further discussion of recognition and the dynamics of assimilation in *A Gesture Life,* see Cheng, "Passing, Natural Selection, and Love's Failure."

37. Dwight Garner, "Interview: Adopted Voice," *New York Times Book Review* September 5, 1999, 6.

38. Ibid.

39. Kay Schaffer and Sidonie Smith, *Human Rights and Narrated Lives: The Ethics of Recognition* (New York: Palgrave, 2004), 123–52.

40. "Transference" has been used in literature on social cognition to mean the way in which mental representations of (past) significant others are applied to encounters with new persons, thus distorting them through our applications. See Susan Andersen, Noah Glassman, Serena Chen, and Steve Cole, "Transference in Social Perception: The Role of Chronic Accessibility in Significant-Other Representations," *Journal of Personality and Social Psychology* 69, no. 1 (1995): 41–57.

41. Sigmund Freud, "Constructions in Analysis," *Standard Edition of the Complete Psychological Works of Sigmund Freud* (London: Hogarth Press, 1953), 23:258.

42. Ibid., 260–61.

43. Appiah, "Liberalism, Individuality, and Identity," 326.

44. Appiah, *Ethics of Identity*, 20.

45. Jacques Lacan, *The Four Fundamental Concepts of Psychoanalysis* (New York: W. W. Norton, 1998), 145.

46. This is what I take Lacan to mean when he says that the transference is "a making present of the *closure* of the unconscious" (my emphasis). Lacan elaborates: "If the transference is only repetition, it will always be repetition of the same missed encounter. If the transference is supposed through this repetition, to restore the continuity of a history, it will do so only by reviving a relation that is... syncopated. We see... that the transference... cannot be satisfied with being confused with the efficacity of repetition, with the restoration of what is concealed in the unconscious." Lacan, *Four Fundamental Concepts of Psychoanalysis*, 143.

47. Yngvesson characterizes adoption narratives as split between these two alternatives of the "story of the freestanding child" and the "story of the rooted child." Yngvesson, "Going Home," 8.

48. Laplanche's discussion of transference is central to my understanding. He begins his discussion of transference with a dialogue:

> ANALYST: You are taking me for someone else, I'm not the person you think.
>
> ANALYSAND: But the other in the originary relation was, precisely, not the person I thought. So I'm perfectly right to take you for someone else. Laplanche, *Essays on Otherness*, 214.

49. Yngvesson, "Refiguring Kinship," 570. Yngvesson notes that the Hague Convention on Intercountry Adoption established an uneasy balance between valorization of the birth country and the idea of a clean break, further hardening the logic of adopted children as commodities and resources transferred between nations.

6. Making Family "Look like Real"

1. Beizer, "One's Own," 245.

2. John Seabrook, "Tree of Me," *New Yorker*, March 26, 2001.

3. Mike Nizza, "Watson's Black D.N.A.: Ultimate Irony?" *New York Times*, December 10, 2007; Amy Harmon, "That Wild Streak? Maybe it Runs in the Family," *New York Times*, June 15, 2006.

4. Bartholet, *Family Bonds*, 181.

5. James David Velleman, "Family History," *Philosophical Papers* 34, no. 3 (2005): 359. Cited parenthetically hereafter. On a similar use of the adoptee search in the context of legal theory, see

Michael Freeman, "The New Birthright: Identity and the Child of the Reproduction Revolution," *International Journal of Children's Rights* 4 (1996): 273–97.

6. Velleman uses as evidence that one out of two adoptees search for their biological parents. But that of course leaves one out of every two adoptees who *do not* search, and is hardly conclusive evidence that this is a universal need.

7. Betty Jean Lifton, *Lost and Found: The Adoption Experience* (New York: Dial Press, 1979), 7.

8. Ibid., 41.

9. Ibid., 65.

10. Ibid., 34.

11. Velleman, "Family History," 375.

12. Charlotte Witt, "Family Resemblances: Adoption, Personal Identity, and Genetic Essentialism," in *Adoption Matters*, 141.

13. Ibid., 142.

14. I borrow here Russell Grigg's explanation of the term "semblant" in Lacan. Lacan's concept of semblance is quite operative here, since he rereads likeness not in relation to some more authentic reality, but rather as a mode of being in which appearance comes to stand in for something in order to make it real, in order to consolidate the reality of its appearance. The absence of this appearance creates anxiety, because what should be there — some certainty — is not there. Grigg, "The Concept of Semblant in Lacan's Teaching," *Lacan.com*, www.lacan.com/griggblog.html (accessed November 15, 2008).

15. R. D. Laing, *The Politics of the Family and Other Essays* (New York: Pantheon Books, 1971), 13.

16. Jerome Bruner, *Acts of Meaning* (Cambridge, Mass.: Harvard University Press, 1990), 126.

17. Ibid.

18. Beizer, "One's Own," 248.

19. In order to disrupt the hold that biological origins have in constructing personhood and disconnect biology from truth, Homans cogently argues that adoption stories outline forms for the embracing of fictional origins. I agree enthusiastically with her premise about adoption's potential to "put into practice 'another configuration of primary attachment'" but want to acknowledge the particular processes of normativity and the legal and social mechanisms in which fiction is incorporated such that fiction is often used, as in Velleman's argument, to strengthen biological normativity as opposed to contest it. See Homans, "Origins, Searches, and Identity," 63.

20. Butler, *Undoing Gender,* 48.

21. For a similar reading of this push and pull process that occurs when adult Korean adoptees "return" to their "homeland," see Eleana Kim, "Wedding Citizenship and Culture," and "Our Adoptee, Our Alien."

22. See Barbara Melosh's description of the primacy of the search story within adoption rights movements and literature, "Adoption Stories."

23. See Cheng, *Inauthentic.* As Cheng writes, there is a consensus in adoption policies that the "adopted baby's cultural roots and heritage . . . are a vital and functional key to the child's innate identity and need to be cultivated at great pains. [Adoptive] parents, no less than adoptees who expect to find their identity from their birth records, share in and participate in the need to believe in an essential and authentic identity handed down by one's cultural, racial, ethnic, or national 'heritage'" (66–67). Cheng charges these policies and practices for reifying cultural origin as a fetish object that supposedly holds the key to one's life meaning or arc.

24. See Barbara Yngvesson and Maureen Mahoney, "'As One Should, Ought and Wants to Be': Belonging and Authenticity in Identity Narratives," *Theory, Culture, and Society* 17, no. 6 (2000): 77-110; Yngvesson, "Going Home."

25. See David Eng's observation of a similar dual-movement embedded in the search story: "In transnational adoption's crossing of sexuality and diaspora, we are presented with both the desire to return to the "real" mother and the desire to return to the place of origins. These intersecting discourses of return underwrite a personal narrative of self-realization, completion, and closure that . . . is not only an impossible task to accomplish but also creates fragmentation and further displacement rather than wholeness." "Transnational Adoption and Queer Diasporas," 28–29.

26. Katy Robinson, *A Single Square Picture: A Korean Adoptee's Search for Her Roots* (New York: Berkley Books, 2002), 148–49. Cited parenthetically hereafter.

27. Eng, "Transnational Adoption and Queer Diasporas," 16. Eng further suggests that transnational adoptees' capacity to reinvest in new figures is curtailed. He writes: "To the extent lost ideals of Asianness (including homeland, family, language, property, identity, custom, status) are irrecoverable, immigration, assimilation, and racialization are placed within a melancholic framework — a state of suspension between 'over there' and 'over here.'" (16).

28. Green, *On Private Madness,* 87.

29. Debi Standiford, Steve Standiford, Nhi Phan, and Hy Phan, *Sudden Family* (Waco: Word Books, 1986), 140. Cited parenthetically hereafter.

30. Gish Jen, "The Love Wife: A New Phase in Gish Jen's Career," 2001, www.radcliffe.edu/research/arts/jen_01.php (accessed January 17, 2005).

31. "Writing about the Things That Are Dangerous," *Southwest Review* 78, no. 1 (January 1, 1993).

32. Gish Jen, *The Love Wife* (New York: Alfred A. Knopf, 2004), 3. Cited parenthetically hereafter.

33. Bruner, *Acts of Meaning,* 126.

34. For an opposing reading of the role of figuration, see Homans, "Origins, Searches, and Identity."

35. Jen, "The Love Wife: A New Phase in Gish Jen's Career."

36. Ibid.

37. Laura Briggs, "Making 'American' Families: Transnational Adoption and U.S. Latin American Policy," in *Haunted by Empire,* ed. Ann Stoler (Durham, N.C.: Duke University Press, 2006), 608.

Index

Marx, Karl, 147
Massachusetts adoption law (1851), vii, xiv, xxxiii, 10–11, 258n49, 263n20
matching, racial, xxxiii–xxxiv, xli, 92–99, 102–3, 111–14, 121, 169, 205
Matter-Seibel, Sabina, 264n28
Matthews, John, 277n43
McGinnis, Hollee, xxxvii–xxxviii
McKinnon, Susan, 250n8
McWilliams, Dean, 116
Melosh, Barbara, xxxiv–xxxv, 92, 94, 96, 170, 172, 259n54, 276n17, 284n4
memoirs, xxvii–xxviii, xxxvi, 126, 148–57, 170, 172, 189, 219, 225
Merritt, Jane, 5, 262n14
Michaels, Walter Benn, xvii
Mielke, Laura, 264n28
Miller, David, 190
Miller, Nancy, xxviii
Million Man March, xi
Min, Eun Kyung, 150–51
miscegenation, xi, 7, 38, 50, 81
Modell, Judith, 262–63n16
Moses, xxvi
motherhood, 12–13. *See also* parent-child bond; in antislavery fiction, 71–74, 83; and "birthmothers," 170; in *Daughter from Danang* (film), 173–74; in *First Person Plural* (Borshay Liem), 174–76; in frontier romances, 15, 32, 35–37; in *Language of Blood* (Trenka), 149, 151–52, 154; in *Leave It to Me* (Mukherjee), 162; in *Light in August* (Faulkner), 105; in *Love Wife, The* (Jen), 231–33, 235–42; in *Quarry, The* (Chesnutt), 117–18; in *Single Square Picture, A* (Robinson), 221–24;

motherhood (*continued*)
in slave narratives/autobiographies, 67–68; in *Sudden Family* (Standiford and Standiford), 228–30; and transracial/transnational adoption, 126, 132–33, 290n25
Mukherjee, Bharati, 131, 148, 157–67, 283nn64,65
My Bondage and My Freedom (Douglass), 47, 65–70, 272n47
My Several Worlds (Buck), 127

Narrative of the Life of Frederick Douglass (Douglass), 66–70
National Association of Black Social Workers, 184, 258n52
Native Americans, xxiii, xxxv, 250n8; adoption practices of, xiv, xxxix–xl, 5–8, 14–15, 17 (*see also* substitutability of persons); as domestic dependents, xv, xl, 8, 14–16, 26, 44, 264n28; in frontier romances, 14–17, 25–42, 44; and gift exchange, 6, 16–17, 30, 39, 41; political alliances of, 5–6, 262n14; redescribed as savage, 6, 8, 17–18, 26, 44, 262n14; removal of, xii, xv, xl, 9, 18, 26; and substitutability of persons, xxxix–xl, 5, 7, 19–24, 30, 34–37, 39, 42–44, 262n15, 265n43; and transracial/transnational adoption, 137, 186; and unredeemed captives, xl, 3–7, 16–18, 32–44, 261–62nn4,8
Nelson, Kim Park, 155
New Yorker, 209
New York Times, xxxvii–xxxviii, 259–60n59, 283n60
Nims, Elinor, 93–94
Novy, Marianne, 255–56nn33,35
"Now I Know Who I Really Am" (Haimes), 140–41, 281n40

Mark C. Jerng is assistant professor of English at University of California, Davis.